Yale Historical Publications

David Horne, Editor

Miscellany 76

Published under the

direction of the

Department of History

THE SOUTHERN SUDAN, 1883-1898

A STRUGGLE FOR CONTROL

BY ROBERT O. COLLINS

New Haven and London, Yale University Press, 1962

Set in Baskerville type and
printed in the United States of America by
Vail-Ballou Press, Inc., Binghamton, New York.

Library of Congress catalog card number: 62-8240

This is the forty-second volume published with
assistance from the Kingsley Trust Association
Publication Fund established by the Scroll and
Key Society of Yale College.

PREFACE

The purpose of this book is to describe the Mahdist invasions of the Southern Sudan, their success, and finally their defeat by the forces of the Congo Free State. The period of the Mahdīya, 1883 to 1898, has been obscured by its subordination to the larger questions of Egyptian and British Imperial History. Only in the past few years have scholars written of the Mahdīya against its Sudanese and Islamic background, and though sound and competent, these works have either neglected Mahdist activities in the Southern Sudan or treated them in a cursory manner. It it true that the Mahdist invasions of the Southern Sudan were only a small part of the history of the Mahdīya, but the importance of the invasions lies not so much in their influence on events in the Northern Sudan but rather their effect on the subsequent history of the Southern Sudan and the struggle for control of the Upper Nile by the European Powers.

The documents of the Mahdist State are found in the archives of the Sudan Government in Khartoum. In 1956 and 1957 I was granted access to these archives, and there, with the generous help and complete cooperation of the Sudan Government Archivist, Ibrāhīm Aḥmad, I searched among the records of the Mahdīya for manuscripts pertaining to the Southern Sudan. With these documents and the other sources listed in the bibliography, I have been able to reconstruct a continuous narrative of Mahdist activities in the Southern Sudan.

One of the principal problems is the spelling of personal and place names. In the Northern Sudan I have preferred to use the classical Arabic form to the European corruption. The one exception is the spelling of the capital of the Sudan, Khartoum for al-K͟harṭūm. In the Southern Sudan the problem is more complicated. On the one hand, I have used the classical Arabic form when the place name or personal name is clearly derived from an Arab source —for example, Daym az-Zubayr and Faḍl al-Mūlā. On the other hand, I have used the conventional form when the place name or personal name is derived from a local, non-Arab source—for example, Lado, Yambio, etc. In the transliteration of the Arabic I have followed an internationally recognized system which is already standard for much historical work.

I am deeply indebted to the Sudan Government and its officials, particularly to the Archivist, Ibrāhīm Aḥmad, whose assistance in finding and translating the documents of the Mahdīya has been invaluable; to the authorities of Khartoum University, and especially A. B. Theobald, G. N. Sanderson, and the late Professor Saad Ed Din Fawzi, from whom I received encouragement and assistance during my sojourn in Khartoum; to the Ford Foundation, whose grant made possible my research in the Sudan; and to Williams College, whose financial support facilitated the final preparation of the manuscript. Miss E. M. Nightingale, D. W. R. Bahlman, P. M. Holt, Richard Herzog, and Franz Rosenthal have all read the manuscript during its various stages of completion and have immeasurably improved it with their comments; I am deeply grateful for all their assistance and advice. Harry Rudin's useful suggestions during the years of preparing the manuscript have been invaluable, and his constant vigilance has prevented many careless errors. To him I owe a great, unpaid debt of gratitude.

R. O. C.

Williamstown, Massachusetts
November 1960

CONTENTS

INTRODUCTION

The Land and the People[1]

The land stretching southward from the second cataract of the Nile at twenty-two degrees north latitude to Lake Albert near the equator is known as the Sudan. In its full sense the term embraces the *Bilād as-Sūdān,* "land of the Blacks," of the medieval Muslim geographers, which extended across Africa from the Red Sea to the Atlantic, between Arab and African cultures. From that name the modern "Sudan" is derived. In the following pages it is used in the restricted sense of the Sudanese territories acquired by Egypt in the nineteenth century, which now constitute the Republic of the Sudan.

The Sudan is a vast country open in the north to the expansive wastes of the Libyan and Nubian deserts but confined in the central and southern provinces by the Red Sea and Abyssinia to the east, the Great Lakes of Central Africa to the south, and the massif of Jabal Marra to the west. The rivers and streams of the Sudan, all a part of the Nile River system, play a preponderant role in Sudanese life, while the amount of rainfall governs conditions in the enormous areas beyond the reach of the rivers.

The Nile, of course, is the dominant physical feature. It has two major sources. The first and most important is the Blue Nile, which emerges from Lake Tana and flows northward through the Abyssinian Highlands to the plains of the Sudan. It is the Blue

1. This introductory chapter is based largely on material found in F. R. Wingate, *Mahdiism and the Egyptian Sudan* (London, 1891); M. Shibeika, *British Policy in the Sudan, 1882–1902* (London, 1952); A. B. Theobald, *The Mahdīya* (London, 1955); and, particularly, P. M. Holt, *The Mahdist State in the Sudan* (Oxford, 1958).

Nile which accounts for 60 per cent of the total Nile waters and whose summer flood has given life to Egypt and the Sudan since man first settled in the Nile Valley. The second source is the White Nile, which flows out of Lake Victoria at Owens Falls to meander across the swamps of Lake Kioga before crashing through the narrow defile of Murchison Falls near Lake Albert. From Lake Albert, the White Nile, known locally as the Baḥr al-Jabal, River of the Mountains, flows northward over a series of waterfalls and rapids before its course is checked in the immense swamps of the Southern Sudan. Here the channel of the river is frequently choked by the *sadd,* floating islands of vegetation which obstruct and obscure the river, and its water is dissipated throughout the 12,000 square miles of swamp in which nearly one-half of its volume is lost by evaporation and transpiration. Emerging from the swamp at Lake No, the White Nile would at this point contribute only 10 per cent to the total Nile flood if not supplemented by an additional 20 per cent from the waters of the Sūbāt and the Baḥr al-G̱hazāl rivers. The Baḥr al-G̱hazāl, the Gazelle River, drains the huge basin between the Baḥr al-Jabal and the Congo-Nile watershed, but like the Baḥr al-Jabal it loses much of its volume in the swamps before meeting the White Nile at Lake No. The Sūbāt, on the other hand, rises in the Abyssinian Highlands and discharges unimpeded into the White Nile south of Fashoda. From there the White Nile flows steadily northward to unite with the waters of the Blue Nile at Khartoum. The combined waters of the two Niles continue northward from Khartoum for 1,500 miles to the Mediterranean Sea, supplemented only by the river 'Aṭbarā, which emerges from the Abyssinian Highlands to join the Nile just 200 miles north of Khartoum.

Rainfall has largely determined the way of life and the physical characteristics of the land beyond the Nile and its tributaries. In the extreme north along the present Egyptian-Sudanese frontier at Wādī Ḥalfā there is almost no rainfall, and only about one inch at Marawī over 200 miles to the south. The only cultivation possible is that which can be irrigated by the settled tribes huddled along the river banks, the most important of which are the Maḥass, lying north of the Third Cataract; the Danāqla, situated between the Third Cataract and Kurtī; the S̱hāīqīya, scattered upstream from the Danāqla with their capital at Marawī; and the Ja'liyīn, settled farther south between the 'Aṭbarā and the confluence of the Blue and White Niles at Khartoum. East and west of the Nile stretch, respectively, the wastes of the Nubian and the Libyan deserts, inhabited only by nomadic, camel-owning tribes. In the east live the 'Abābda, who control the caravan route from Kurūskū across the Nubian Desert to Abū Ḥamad on the great bend of the Nile. In the west are the Kabābīsh, who roam deep into Kurdufān and Dār Fūr and control the caravan routes from the western Sudan to Asyūṭ. South of the 'Abābda between the 'Aṭbarā and the Blue Nile the rainfall is sufficient to provide seasonal grass. The area is known as the Buṭāna and is dominated by the nomadic Shukrīya. Farther to the east are the Red Sea Hills, the home of the Bija, camel-owning Muslims who speak their own peculiar Hamitic language.

Southward from the latitude of Khartoum the rains are sufficient to permit cultivation and extensive cattle grazing. Between the Blue and White Niles is the area known as the *Jazīrat Sinnār,* Island of Sennar, which was the center of the great Funj Kingdom founded in the early sixteenth century and not destroyed until the coming of Muḥammad 'Alī in 1821. West of the White Nile to the slopes of Jabal Marra stretch the grasslands of Kurdufān and Dār Fūr, broken only by a series of hills south of al-Ubaiyaḍ known as the Nūba Mountains. The plains are inhabited by the nomadic Baqqāra or cattle-owning Arabs, chief among whom are the Rizayqāt and Ta'ā'isha tribes of southern Dār Fūr. In the mountains live the Nūbas, aboriginal pagans who, in their impregnable retreats, have successfully resisted attempts by the Arabs to interfere with their independence or with their traditional way of life. In a similar manner the Fūr and the Maṣālāṭ, whose non-Arabic origins, speech, and traditions have maintained a spirit of separatism in spite of their acceptance of Islam, have also resisted Arab encroachments from the rocky vastness of Jabal Marra in far western Dār Fūr.

The southern limit of the Baqqāra Arabs is the Baḥr al-'Arab, a tributary of the Baḥr al-Ghazāl flowing west to east and forming a natural barrier between the Arab Muslim North and the Negroid pagan South.[2] Between the Baḥr al-'Arab and the Great Lakes of

2. The term "Negroid," and not "Negro," is used in this work to designate the black-skinned peoples of the Southern Sudan, who are a mixture of Cau-

Central Africa is the land known as the Southern Sudan. During the Turkīya, the period of Egyptian rule, the Southern Sudan was divided for administrative purposes into the Baḥr al-G͟hazāl and the Equatoria, *K͟haṭṭ al-Istiwā'*, Provinces. Although the frontiers were undoubtedly drawn arbitrarily, the physical characteristics of the land and the tribal differences between the two provinces have more than justified such a division of this vast area.[3]

The Baḥr al-G͟hazāl is bounded on the north by the Baḥr al-'Arab, on the east by the White Nile, and on the south and west respectively by the sixth degree of north latitude and the Congo-Nile Divide. Everywhere in the Baḥr al-G͟hazāl the rainfall, which occurs within a well-defined season from April to October, exceeds thirty-five inches annually and in some areas is as high as forty-five inches. Physically, the Baḥr al-G͟hazāl is a low, grassy plain broken only by an occasional *jabal* (mountain) and sloping gently from the Congo-Nile Divide northeastward until it is inundated by the waters of the White Nile and transformed into the vast swamps of the Upper Nile. A network of rivers, all tributaries of the Baḥr al-G͟hazāl, drain this plain. Many dry up after the rains, but nearly all flood their banks during the wet season, making travel extremely difficult and military operations virtually impossible.

The province is dominated by three large, cattle-owning Nilotic tribes, the Shilluk, the Dinka, and the Nuer. The Shilluk are scattered along the banks of the Baḥr al-G͟hazāl and the White Nile as far north as Fashoda. At one time they had advanced northward along the banks of the river to within a hundred miles of the confluence of the Blue and White Niles, but they could not maintain their position before the advancing Arabs and so withdrew. The Dinka, on the other hand, are a larger but less cohesive group

casian and Negro types, to avoid confusing them with the purer Negro types of Africa. Although there is no agreement among anthropologists regarding nomenclature, anthropologically speaking the peoples of the Southern Sudan are divided by most authorities into Nilotes, Nilo-Hamites, Sudanic, and Azande. Similarly, the term "Arab" is here used in a historical rather than a racial sense, referring to those people who came to the Sudan from Arabia, their descendants, and the indigenous people they absorbed.

3. In 1936 the Sudan Government brought the Baḥr al-G͟hazāl and the Equatoria Provinces under one administration. So unsatisfactory was this experiment, however, that it was abandoned immediately following World War II.

than the Shilluks. Scattered from the river Sūbāt to the swamps of the Baḥr al-Jabal and beyond to the tributaries of the Baḥr al-Ghazāl, the Dinka are a loose confederation of tribes who, in spite of their essential disunity and constant intertribal strife, have remained remarkably impervious to the language, religion, and customs of alien invaders. Like the Shilluks, they are renowned warriors, but their military effectiveness has been continually hampered by tribal divisions. The Nuer have played a much less important role in the recorded history of the Sudan than either the Shilluk or the Dinka tribes. Although as warlike as their Nilotic neighbors, they have lived in such inaccessible areas of the great swamps that they have been left alone by conqueror and administrator alike. In the far western Baḥr al-Ghazāl near Ḥufrat an-Naḥās several small, Arabicized Negroid tribes are to be found, of which the Njangulgule and the Feroge are the most important. Although little is known of their past, their close relationship with the Arab tribes north of the Baḥr al-'Arab played an important part in the Mahdist invasions of the Baḥr al-Ghazāl.

At the present time Equatoria is that territory situated between the Baḥr al-Ghazāl on the north and the Republic of the Congo and the British Protectorate of Uganda on the south. In the past the Equatoria Province was considerably larger. During the Turkīya, Egyptian administrators actually controlled not only Lake Albert but also the Upper Uele Valley south of the Congo-Nile Divide, and it was not until the second decade of the twentieth century that the present boundaries were agreed upon by the Congo, Sudan, and Uganda authorities. Throughout the province rainfall is everywhere plentiful and in some places will exceed fifty inches annually. Physically, Equatoria is an undulating plain which rises sharply from north to south and terminates in high ridges, hills, and low mountains along the Congo-Nile watershed. Some of the mountains, the most famous of which is Jabal ar-Rajjāf, emerge conical-shaped from the surrounding plains, presenting the illusion of great height. Others are the culmination of long, parallel ridges separated by steep ravines from which the rivers and streams of the Baḥr al-Ghazāl rise. Near the Congo-Nile Divide the grasslands of the Baḥr al-Ghazāl are interspersed with gallery forests, named for the navelike effect of interlocking branches high above the ground. Gradually these forests thicken

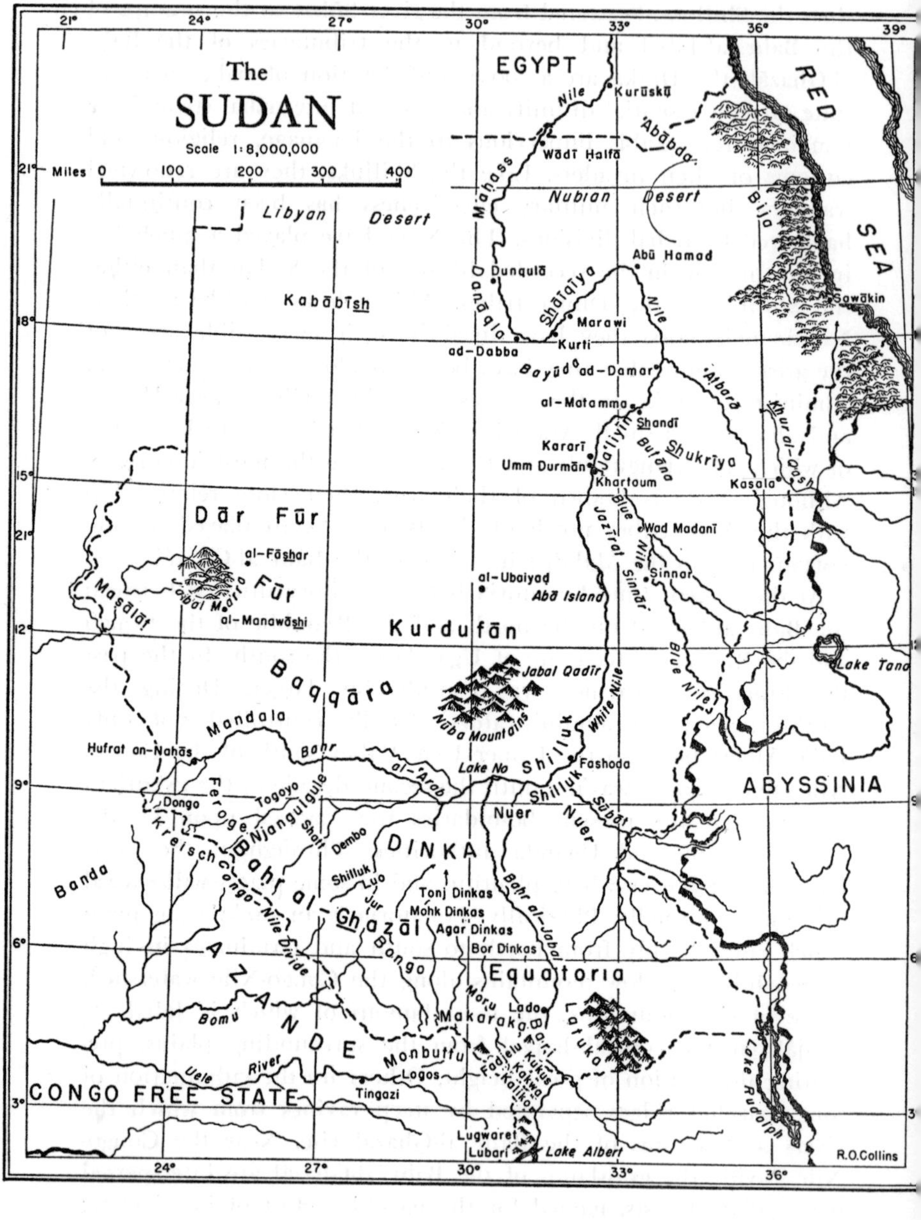
The SUDAN
Scale 1:8,000,000
Miles 0 100 200 300 400
EGYPT
RED SEA
Libyan Desert
Nubian Desert
Kabābīsh
Dār Fūr
Fūr
Kurdufān
Baqqāra
DINKA
AZANDE
Equatoria
ABYSSINIA
CONGO FREE STATE
Wādī Halfā
Kurūskū
Dunqulā
Abū Hamad
Sawākin
Marawi
Kurti
ad-Dabba
ad-Damar
al-Matamma
Shandī
Kararī
Umm Durmān
Khartoum
Kasala
Wad Madanī
Sinnar
al-Ubaiyad
Abā Island
al-Fāshar
al-Manawāshi
Jabal Qadīr
Nūba Mountains
Fashoda
Lake No
Hufrat an-Nahās
Mandala
Lake Tana
Lake Rudolph
Lake Albert
Lado
Logos
Tingazi
Lugwaret
Lubari
R.O.Collins

and soon elide to form the great tropical rain forest that stretches far into the Congo.

Equatoria is inhabited by a multiplicity of weak, relatively small tribes pressed between the powerful, warlike Nilotes to the north and the equally warlike Azande, or Niam-Niam, to the south and west. Northern Equatoria is dominated by the Dinka tribes, who graze their cattle herds on the grasslands stretching southward into Equatoria from the Baḥr al-G͟hazāl. Beyond, in the gallery forests and on the intervening plains, live the Nilo-Hamites, who closely resemble the Nilotes in stature but differ sharply in language, culture, and mode of living. The Nilo-Hamites are agriculturists whose sedentary habits and inability to resist attack have made them easy prey for alien invaders. Probably the most important Nilo-Hamitic tribes are the Latuka and the Moru, situated respectively east and west of the Baḥr al-Jabal, and the Bari settled along its banks. In the south and west along the Congo-Nile Divide are located the Azande tribes. The most Negroid of any Sudanese, the Azande are a loose confederation of powerful, warlike tribes who came from the west in the nineteenth century and marched over the Congo-Nile watershed to settle in southwestern Equatoria.

The Sudan to 1821

The Sudan, in spite of its inaccessibility, was well known to the ancient Egyptians. As early as 3000 B.C. the third pharaoh of the first Egyptian Dynasty captured Wādī Ḥalfā; and in the many centuries that followed, Egyptian settlements were established farther and farther up the Nile. These settlements prospered and grew into the strong province of Nubia. So powerful did Nubia become that in the eighth century B.C. the Egyptian viceroy asserted his independence, conquered all Egypt, and established the twenty-fifth Dynasty, which dominated the whole of the Nile Valley until its power was broken in Egypt by the Assyrians in 663 B.C. Having lost control of Egypt, and left to themselves, the Nubians gradually moved up the Nile and located their capital near S͟handī. In the sixth century A.D. Christian priests were sent from Egypt by Justinian to convert the Nubians to Christianity. They met with immediate though superficial success, and by the end of the century the whole of the Nile Valley from Aswān to Abyssinia was nominally Christian.

In the seventh century the Muslims conquered Egypt and in 641 dispatched an army under 'Abd Allāh ibn Sa'd ibn abū Sarḥ to invade Nubia. Although this first expedition achieved little, a second, in 651, reached Dunqulā and destroyed its Christian Church. The Arabs subsequently concluded a peace with the Nubians; and although it remained in force for nearly six centuries, it is from this date that Nubia was continuously infiltrated by Arabs moving both up the Nile and across the Red Sea. By the fifteenth century the Arabs had penetrated eastward into the Bija country, southward up the 'Aṭbarā to the grasslands of the Buṭāna, and westward to the plains of Kurdufān. At the beginning of the sixteenth century the ancient Nubian Kingdom was crumbling, Islam had almost extinguished Christianity, and Arabic had become the lingua franca.

In 1504 the Funj, in alliance with the Arabs, overthrew the Nubian Christian Kingdom and established a sultanate at Sinnār. It is not known who the Funj were or whence they came. Although pagans by origin, they had been muslimized, and it was probably on this basis that the participation of the Arabs in the downfall of the Nubians was obtained. On the other hand, the Arabs never seemed to have been strong enough to challenge the domination of the Funj and appear to have been content to pay tribute. The Funj soon controlled all of the Sudan northward to Dunqulā and westward to the White Nile, but beyond in Kurdufān and Dār Fūr they were never able to dominate the Fūr. The Fūr had established their hegemony over the tribes of Dār Fūr and Kurdufān at the end of the sixteenth century and founded a Fūr sultanate at al-Fās̲h̲ar. Although the Fūr sultans claimed to be of Arab extraction, they were obviously closer akin to the non-Arabic peoples farther west. In 1821, the Fūr sultanate lost Kurdufān to the invading army of Muḥammad 'Alī Pasha and, retiring to Dār Fūr, remained in hostile neutrality toward the Egyptian administration until 1874, when Dār Fūr was at last conquered, occupied, and administered by Egyptian authorities.

The Turkīya

Muḥammad 'Alī Pasha of Egypt, in his correspondence with his sons Ibrāhīm and Ismā'īl, has left little doubt as to his motives for the conquest of the Sudan. It was first to obtain Negroid slave-soldiers, known as *jihādīya,* for the Egyptian army, and second to acquire additional revenue for the Egyptian Treasury in the form of gold or trade goods. It was also quite probable that Muḥammad ʻAlī desired to eradicate the survivors of the Mamlūk massacre who had settled in Dunqulā. Consequently, an army composed largely of Albanians and Turks was assembled, transported to Wādī Ḥalfā, and there placed under the command of Muḥammad ʻAlī's son Ismāʻīl. The army marched up the Nile to Dunqulā, from which the Mamlūks fled, and then on to Abū Ḥamad. Here the S̱hāīqīya tribe offered stubborn resistance until overwhelmed in two pitched battles by the superior arms of the Egyptians. Ismāʻīl continued his march up the Nile. At S̱handī the remnants of the Mamlūks again fled and dispersed, to be swallowed up in the vastness of the Sudan and never heard from again. At Sinnār the Funj, torn by internal strife and intrigue, had no alternative but surrender. At Wad Madanī, the last of the Funj sultans, Bādī VI wad Ṭabl II, capitulated to Ismāʻīl.

While Ismāʻīl was marching victoriously to Sinnār, Muḥammad ʻAlī dispatched his son-in-law, Muḥammad Ḵẖusraw ad-Daramalī, the Bey Daftardār, with an army to establish Egyptian rule in Kurdufān. The Daftardār left the Nile at ad-Dabba near Dunqulā, marched south across the Bayūda, the desert enclosed by the great bend of the Nile, and after destroying the army of the Fūr governor of Kurdufān, occupied al-Ubaiyaḍ.

After the surrender of the Funj Kingdom, Ismāʻīl moved the capital from Sinnār to Wad Madanī, provided for a rudimentary administration, and then, exhausted by the climate and the hardships of life in the Sudan, obtained permission from his father to return to Cairo. Stopping at S̱handī on his return journey in 1822, Ismāʻīl rudely insulted the local *makk* (chief), Nimr Muḥammad Nimr, upon receiving an unfavorable reply to a demand for heavy taxes. Enraged at this affront, Makk Nimr had Ismāʻīl and all his party assassinated. This treacherous act could not be left unavenged. The Daftardār, fresh from his victories in Kurdufān, was ordered to punish the asssassins and quell the threatened Sudanese rising in the Nile Valley. For two years the Daftardār wreaked such devastation and destruction in the Sudan that the memory of his brutality had not been forgotten when the Mahdī rose in revolt.

He burnt al-Matamma, Shandī, Kabūshīya, and ad-Dāmar and massacred the inhabitants. He then marched up the Nile to Sinnār, killing and burning as he went, and turned eastward to devastate the Khūr al-Qāsh and the Bija tribes beyond in the desert. After this brutal display of authority, the Egyptian Administration in the Sudan was not seriously challenged for sixty years.

As the Egyptian Administration consolidated its position in the Sudan, large areas were added to the original conquest. Under the governor-general Aḥmad Pasha abū Widān, Kasala and Sawākin were acquired in 1840, and in the 1870's—during the reign of the Khedive Ismā'īl—Dār Fūr, the Baḥr al-Ghazāl, and Equatoria were occupied. To administer these new regions as well as the territories of the original conquest, an elaborate bureaucracy developed. At the head was the *ḥukumdār,* or governor-general, who was in charge of the whole Sudan and directly dependent on Cairo. Below the governor-general were the *mudīrs,* or governors, who were the administrative heads of the *mudīrīya,* or provinces, into which the Sudan was divided. The provinces, in turn, were subdivided into districts known as *ma'mūrīyāt* if administered by an Egyptian official, the *ma'mūr,* or *qism* if governed by a *nāẓir,* a local Sudanese official. The district was also divided into subdistricts, each called a *Khuṭṭ,* usually administered by an indigenous official known as the *ḥākim.*

Power in the Sudan was largely confined in the hands of the governor-general. This power was enhanced not only by the pyramidal structure of the administration but also by the remoteness of Khartoum from Cairo. In the first instance two attempts were made to decentralize the administration and so curb the powers of the governor-general. In 1843 Muḥammad 'Alī established in the various provinces separate administrations which were directly connected to Cairo, and in 1857 Muḥammad Sa'īd Pasha abolished the governorate-general at Khartoum and made each Sudanese province directly dependent on the viceregal Government at Cairo. Both attempts failed, and in each case centralized power was restored to Khartoum. In the second instance the Egyptian Government tried to overcome the political disadvantages of the distance to Khartoum by frequently replacing the governors-general. Between 1825 and 1885 only three of the twenty-five governors-general held office for more than five years. Although this policy successfully restricted the power of the governors-general, it furthered the jealousy and intrigue of political opportunists both in Cairo and in the Sudan and produced chronic instability at precisely that point where stability was most needed.

Unable to rely on the governor-general for any firm and constant direction of affairs, the Egyptian Government had to depend on the army to assert its control in the Sudan. The troops were principally jihādīya and S͟hāīqīya irregulars. The jihādīya, Negroid slaves confiscated from slave traders and conscripted into the Egyptian army, formed in the Sudan the major part of the Khedivial army, to which they showed considerable devotion and loyalty. The S͟hāīqīya, on the other hand, had largely replaced the Turkish and Albanian irregulars who had come with the army of Ismā'īl and were the only Sudanese tribe to become wholeheartedly an instrument of the administration. Egyptian rule in the Sudan was maintained by this army, whose loyalty and stability remained unquestioned until the victories of the Mahdī seemed to indicate that his was the cause of God and so divided the hearts and consciences of the government troops.

In addition to the army the Egyptian Government had hoped to keep the Sudan profitable, prostrate, and pacific by the management of its revenues. Although the fiscal policy of the administration succeeded in extorting sizable sums from the Sudanese, its very success aroused widespread resentment. Before the establishment of the Turkīya, the payment of taxes was not a widely recognized custom. After the surrender of the Funj, Ismā'īl imposed heavy taxes throughout the Sudan and instituted brutal methods of collection. With time the demands of the Government became heavier and the collection more cruel. To the Sudanese the taxes were not only hateful by tradition but more than abominable when the revenues were not repaid in social services but sent to Egypt or pocketed by the Egyptian officials who viewed their corruption as just compensation for their unpleasant exile in the Sudan. The discontent with this policy led many Sudanese to join the cause of the Mahdī, whose promises of equity and justice had a strong appeal to the oppressed tribesmen.

Although the Egyptians did not establish a wise and efficient administration in the Sudan, they did provide a greater measure of security and unity than had ever before been known. This security was to stimulate a widespread movement of Sudanese away from their tribes into areas in which intertribal animosities would have previously meant probable death. The S̲h̲āīqīya, as the irregular soldiers of the Government, were to be found throughout the length and breadth of the Sudan. Members of the Ja'liyīn and the Danāqla tribes traveled in Dār Fūr, Kurdufān, and the Southern Sudan as *jallāba,* merchants, frequently engaged in the slave trade. More often than not these northern emigrants settled in the districts in which they traded, where they often became powerful leaders. They were men of initiative and daring who had found insufficient scope for their schemes in the restricted life of the tribe and had moved on. It was these same men who gave wholehearted support to the Mahdī in the early days of his rebellion and who later played a large role in the Mahdist revolution.

In spite of the security and unity engendered by the centralized bureaucracy and the army, the administration did not succeed in winning the loyalty of the Sudanese. There was no attempt to eradicate the tribal system or tribal loyalties. Often a tribal chief would act as the agent of the Government, but his position as leader rested more on his individual prestige as a man than on his recognition by the Administration. The Sudanese deeply regretted the loss of their tribal independence to an unpopular, alien rule which at best was unremitting and exacting in its demands. They eagerly awaited any weakness on the part of the Government which might indicate a return to their old autonomy, and their adherence to the cause of al-Mahdī may be viewed as just such a ready release from their frustration.

Although the Sudanese were deeply loyal to the tribe, their loyalty to Islam was incomparably stronger and more vigorous than either tribal sentiment or allegiance to the Khedive. The Egyptian Administration was, of course, Muslim, but there was a great difference between the official Islam of the Egyptian Government and the personal religious faith of the Sudanese. During the days of the Funj Kingdom Islam in the Sudan had been revived and reformed by pious, ascetic men connected with a religious order known as a *ṭarīqa.* The *ṭuruq* (plural of ṭarīqa) are found throughout the Islamic world and are the institutional expression of *Ṣūfism* or Islamic mysticism. Ṣūfism, like most ascetic religious movements, is prone to extreme emotionalism in its practice and heresy in its ideas. Frequently, it has clashed with the exponents of the more orthodox theology of Islam. In the Sudanic areas which stretch across Africa, the ṭuruq in the eighteenth and nineteenth centuries were a part of the great religious revival of Islam based on a return to the pure and primitive faith of Islam made famous by the Wahhābīs in the Arabian peninsula and the Sanūsīya order in what is now Libya. The missionary work of a ṭarīqa, however, was carried on by individuals rather than the order as a whole, and often a missionary would gain such success that he would be regarded as a saint and found a suborder virtually independent from the parent ṭarīqa. The head, or local head, of a suborder was known as a *s̲h̲ayk̲h̲* and his office was hereditary. His followers were known as *darāwīs̲h̲*.[1]

The policy of the Egyptian Administration toward Sudanese Islam was threefold. In the first place the Egyptians brought with them orthodox Islam. They introduced a system of religious courts administering the *S̲h̲arī'a,* the Holy Law of Islam, in place of tribal law and custom; and they built mosques, staffing them with religious teachers trained in orthodox theology. This policy was never a great success. Orthodox Islam had little appeal compared with the emotional power of Sudanese Islam so dramatically displayed during the Mahdīya. Second, the Government used the leading religious *s̲h̲ayk̲h̲s,* like the tribal chiefs, as instruments of administration. Although this was a logical consequence of the conquest, the Egyptian Government tactlessly favored one particular sect, the *K̲h̲atmīya,* thereby arousing the enmity and jealousy of other religious groups. And finally, more a fact than a policy, there was the low morality of Egyptian officials, when judged by the puritanical standards of primitive Islam, which caused genuine feelings of religious revulsion and contempt among the Sudanese.

In the above description of the Egyptian Administration and the condition of the Sudan under it, many reasons can easily be found for Sudanese resentment against the alien Government and that Government's inability to cope with it. The memory of the Daftardār's massacres, heavy taxation, and the traditional religious differences and tribal jealousies, tactlessly encouraged by the administration, were all causes of discontent which were only ag-

1. *Darāwīs̲h̲* is the Arabic plural of *darwīs̲h̲* and is derived from the Persian *darvīs̲h̲* (English "dervish") meaning originally a mendicant.

gravated by the vacillating position of the governors-general, the corruptness of the bureaucracy, and the brutality of the army. Although these were most certainly all causes of dissatisfaction, they were neither specific enough nor sufficiently widespread to precipitate revolt. Only in the attempts of the Egyptian Government to suppress the slave trade can one find a more immediate cause for rebellion—a cause, however, which affected all classes of society in every part of the country.

The slave trade in the Sudan was as old as recorded history itself, but it was not until the Egyptian Government opened the Baḥr al-G͟hazāl and Equatoria provinces and brought relative security and unity to the Sudan that the trade assumed gigantic proportions. Under the protection of the Administration, a Ja'liyīn, Danāqla, or Syrian merchant could establish in the Southern Sudan a *daym* or camp fortified by a *zarība* (a palisade or thorn fence) for himself, his *wakīl* (agent), and his *bāzinqir* (slave-soldiers of traders, not to be confused with the jihādīya, the slave-soldiers of the Government). Originally the trade was in ivory, and the traders, often in alliance with a local chief, would make raids against neighboring tribes for grain and cattle to exchange for tusks. The prisoners taken in these forays became the slaves of the merchants, who soon developed a lucrative trade in them. The zarības of the traders then became staging areas for slaves on their way to the North either by way of the Nile or overland through Dār Fūr and Kurdufān. So profitable was the trade that great companies soon arose with armies of bāzinqir and many zarība scattered throughout the Baḥr al-G͟hazāl and Equatoria. The merchants of these companies were in a short time the virtual rulers of the districts in which they traded.

Although the earlier governors-general in Khartoum had made sporadic attempts against slavery and the slave trade, it was only under the Khedive Ismā'īl, in response to pressure from the British Government, that a concerted effort was made at suppression. In 1865 he established a police patrol on the Upper Nile at Fashoda and levied a heavy poll tax on the employees of the traders and an equally heavy property tax on their zarība. Although these measures had little effect in the Baḥr al-G͟hazāl, the trade in the Upper Nile, much to the indignation of the slave merchants, was considerably reduced.

Ismā'īl, perceiving the success of his police patrol, sent two expeditions—one to the Baḥr al-Ghazāl, the other up the Baḥr al-Jabal—to expand his dominions in the Southern Sudan as well as to suppress the slave trade. Both expeditions were unsuccessful. The Baḥr al-Ghazāl expedition under the command of Muḥammad al-Hilālī was a dismal failure. The expedition to the Baḥr al-Jabal was nearly as unsuccessful. The Khedive had appointed Sir Samuel Baker to command the expedition. Although an officer of great courage, his lack of tact and statesmanship aggravated the resentment of his Egyptian officers, whose ability had been questioned by the fact of Baker's appointment, and antagonized the southern tribes whose confidence was necessary to defeat the slave traders. Amidst intrigue, tribal warfare, and foraging raids, the expedition failed to suppress the slave trade and only managed to establish a few isolated, military posts.

Undaunted by these two failures, the Khedive made further efforts against the slave traders. In 1873 he appointed to the governorship of Equatoria Charles George Gordon, a British officer, who surrounded himself with a staff of nine European and American Christians, including the Italian Romolo Gessi, later governor of the Baḥr al-Ghazāl; the American Chaillé-Long; and the German, Eduard Schnitzer, who practiced Islam and is better known by his Muslim name Emin (Muḥammad al-Amīn) Pasha. As in the case of Baker, the appointment of Christians aroused the jealousy and animosity of the Egyptian officials and diminished the prestige of the Egyptian Government in the eyes of the Sudanese. In spite of these obstacles, however, Gordon was reasonably successful at suppressing the slave trade in Equatoria. He declared ivory a government monopoly, prevented the importation of arms and ammunition, and broke up the private armies of the slave traders. The traders were soon driven out of business but remained in the province to spread their dissatisfaction with the antislavery policy of the Khedive.

In the Baḥr al-Ghazāl the Khedive's policy was also successful. A Ja'lī merchant, az-Zubayr Raḥma Manṣūr, had gained complete control of the widespread chain of trading stations in the province, and his seemingly indisputable position was further strengthened by his defeat of the Rizayqāt Baqqāra in 1873. The Egyptian Administration, not having the means to defeat az-Zubayr, decided to make the best of a bad situation and officially recognized him as the governor of the Baḥr al-G͟hazāl. One of his first official duties as governor was to march his private army into Dār Fūr and, in cooperation with government troops advancing from the east, depose the Fūr Sultan Ibrāhīm Muḥammad Ḥusayn. On October 24, 1874, at the Battle of Manawās͟hī, az-Zubayr defeated the Fūr army, killed the sultan, and occupied al-Fās͟har. Dissension soon arose, however, between az-Zubayr and the commander of the government troops, Ismā'īl Pasha Ayyūb, and in July 1875 az-Zubayr traveled to Cairo to demonstrate his loyalty and to win Khedivial support for his cause. The Egyptian Government, always anxious to curb the power of az-Zubayr, seized this opportunity to place him under arrest. Dār Fūr was securely placed under an official of the Egyptian Government, who introduced energetic measures to impose a heavy tax on the people and to suppress the slave trade. Meanwhile, in the Baḥr al-G͟hazāl, Sulaymān, the son of az-Zubayr, assumed the leadership of the slavers and remained in open defiance against the Government.

Although the Khedive had scored a decisive military victory in Dār Fūr, the political advantage gained was more than offset by the subsequent alienation of the Egyptian officials, the only class on whom the Administration could still rely for support. The indecisive war in Abyssinia and the ruinous Wādī Ḥalfā railway project as well as the expedition to Dār Fūr hastened the collapse of the Egyptian Treasury. In a desperate attempt to avert financial disaster, Ismā'īl sought to increase the revenues from the Sudan by ordering the recovery of all sums due the Government. Until the sums in question were collected, all the salaries of the officials were to be suspended. As it was virtually impossible to carry out this order, the bureaucracy was embittered to the point of disloyalty—a bitterness that increased two years later when Gordon dismissed large numbers of Egyptian officials in favor of Europeans and Sudanese.

In spite of impending bankruptcy and the seething discontent among the officials and people alike, the Khedive steadfastly continued his antislavery policy. In August 1877 he concluded with Great Britain the Slave-Trade Convention, which was to prohibit the sale or purchase of slaves in the Sudan by 1889. To carry out the ambitious terms of the Convention the Khedive offered the governor-generalship of the whole Sudan to Gordon, whose work in Equatoria had shown him to be a man of vigor and integrity. At first Gordon adopted a pacific policy toward the slave traders and even established an uneasy peace with Sulaymān wad az-Zubayr, who was appointed governor of the Baḥr al-G͟hazāl. In the following year of 1878, however, Gordon began to enforce the policy of suppression and dealt more harshly with the slave traders. These traders consequently supported the rebellions which broke out in Dār Fūr, Kurdufān, and the Baḥr al-G͟hazāl. The rebellion in Kurdufān was the only one arising specifically from the discontent of the slave traders; those in Dār Fūr and the Baḥr al-G͟hazāl were initiated by the Fūr pretender on the one hand and the jealousy of Sulaymān toward a government rival on the other. But all the revolts were led and supported by the slavers and their bāzinqir. Gordon personally crushed the rebellion in Kurdufān while his lieutenant in the Baḥr al-G͟hazāl, Romolo Gessi, defeated the forces of Sulaymān, killing him and nine of his chiefs. In Dār Fūr the Italian governor-general, Messedaglia, suppressed the rebellion, which collapsed in July 1880 on the death of the Fūr pretender.

In June 1879 the Khedive Ismā'īl was deposed and Gordon left Khartoum the following month to be succeeded by Muḥammad Ra'ūf Pasha. A man of lesser character and ability than his predecessor, Ra'ūf Pasha was unable to deal with the complicated and dangerous dissatisfaction in the Sudan and was quite content to take no positive course of action. Furthermore, under the influence of his deputy, Giegler Pasha, a German who disliked Italians, he dismissed Gessi and Messedaglia, the only two men in the field capable of holding the slavers in check. With a weak governor-general at Khartoum, the ablest governors dismissed, the bureaucracy demoralized, and the people discontented, Muḥammad Aḥmad, on the island of Abā on June 29, 1881, declared himself to be the Mahdī.

The Rise of the Mahdī

The idea of the Mahdī is to be found in each of the two great divisions of the Muslim world. To the S͟hī'a the Mahdī is associated with the Hidden Imām or the infallible spiritual successor of

Muḥammad who is concealed awaiting the propitious moment to establish the era of righteousness. Since the Sudanese are not Shī'a but Sunnī Muslims, the manifestation of the Mahdī was not regarded by them as the appearance of the Hidden Imām nor did Muḥammad Aḥmad ever claim that title. Among the Sunnīs, however, the term al-Mahdī is associated with three interconnected themes all of which are a part of Islam in the Sudan. First, the Mahdī means "the guided one," a person with divine guidance. Second, the term is applied to the head of the Islamic community, whose function is to bring equity and justice to earth. Third, the appearance of a Mahdī is usually associated with the approaching end of the world. These three themes have all been combined in the past by the historical existence of Muslim leaders who have assumed the Mahdiship and with whom many parallels can be drawn between their careers and that of Muḥammad Aḥmad.

Muḥammad Aḥmad was born on August 12, 1844, on the island of Labab in Dunqulā. His father, 'Abd Allāh, was a boatbuilder, who moved up the Nile to Kararī, twelve miles north of Khartoum, when Muḥammad was still a child. At an early age Muḥammad displayed an aptitude for religious studies and consequently became a pupil of prominent religious teachers in the Jazīrat Sinnār and at Barbar. Feeling the call of the Sudanese religious life of asceticism and mystic experiences within the discipline of a Ṣūfī order, he joined the Sammānīya ṭarīqa. After seven years of learning, during which he gained a reputation for piety, Muḥammad Aḥmad was licensed as a Sammānīya shaykh and began to travel about the country on his religious mission. He soon made his headquarters on Abā Island, south of Khartoum, where his boat-building brothers had gone in search of wood, and here his asceticism and piety won him a large following among the local tribes. In 1879 Muḥammad Aḥmad journeyed throughout Kurdufān preaching his ever-constant theme of the renunciation of the vanities of this world as the only approach to God.

At this time in the Sudan there arose among the Northern Sudanese a belief that the coming of the Mahdī was imminent. This expectation was born from the frustration and discontent with Egyptian rule and nourished on the popular belief in the appearance of a Mahdī at the end of the thirteenth Muslim century, which was then drawing to a close. The followers of Muḥammad

Aḥmad began to look more and more upon him as the Mahdī, for they claimed that it was written in their holy books that the expected Mahdī should come from among their own ṭarīqa. Furthermore, tradition has it that when 'Abd Allāhi Muḥammad Tūrs̲h̲ain, the future K̲h̲alīfat al-Mahdī, came to Muḥammad Aḥmad to request admission into the Sammānīya order, 'Abd Allāhi swooned at the sight of his future master and, upon recovering, declared him to be the expected Mahdī. It is impossible to discern, of course, when Muḥammad Aḥmad conceived himself to be the Mahdī, but it is after this meeting with 'Abd Allāhi that he began to study the traditional Mahdist prophecies. These studies were accompanied by visions during which the Mahdiship was communicated to Muḥammad Aḥmad by the Prophet. In March 1881 he informed 'Abd Allāhi and his other close adherents of his election.

After disclosing to his disciples that he was the expected Mahdī, Muḥammad Aḥmad made a second journey to Kurdufān, during which he preached to the common people and religious leaders alike to abandon this world for the world to come and secretly informed them that he was the Mahdī. This declaration of Mahdism should not conceal the fundamental similarity between his mission and the reformist activities of the Ṣūfī orders in the Sudan, and indeed may be viewed as the culmination of his own efforts at reform. The people of Kurdufān quickly flocked to him to take the *bay'a,* an oath of allegiance, and to make his return journey to Abā Island a triumph. On June 29, 1881, Muḥammad Aḥmad openly declared himself and dispatched letters to various notables assuming the title of Muḥammad al-Mahdī and calling upon them to make the *hijra,* the flight for the Faith, from the infidels to the Mahdī.

The Government in Khartoum had not been totally unaware of the activities of the Mahdī, but the governor-general, Muḥammad Ra'ūf Pasha, viewed them as only another of the interminable religious squabbles which frequently occurred in the Sudan. Upon further inquiry, however, it was decided to arrest Muḥammad Aḥmad, and to execute this order two companies of troops led by Muḥammad Bey Abū as-Su'ūd were sent to Abā Island by steamer in August 1881. The expedition was seriously mismanaged, and the troops ambushed and put to rout by a few hundred followers of the Mahdī armed with sticks, swords, and spears. In the following evening the Mahdī and his followers crossed to the western bank of the Nile and began their *hijra* into Kurdufān. The *hijra* was no mere flight to safety, but a re-enactment of the sufferings of the early days of Islam from which the *Anṣār* could draw inspiration.[1]

By the time the Government had recovered from this astonishing defeat the Mahdī and his followers had established themselves in the fastness of Jabal Qadīr in the Nūba Mountains. It was then the height of the rainy season, and Ra'ūf Pasha prudently suspended military activities against the Mahdī. At Fashoda, however, the commander of the Egyptian garrison, Rāshid Bey Aymān, in spite of orders to the contrary, determined to march his force of 400 regulars and 1,000 Shilluk warriors against the Mahdī. Apprised of Rāshid's movements by an Anṣār woman, the Mahdī again prepared another ambush and on December 9, 1881, surprised and overwhelmed the government troops. Rāshid himself was killed and large quantities of arms and booty were collected by the Anṣār. This second victory, like the first, was hailed as a miracle. It increased the prestige of the Mahdī immensely and swelled the ranks of his followers.

This second defeat of the government forces precipitated the recall of Ra'ūf Pasha to Cairo. He was replaced by 'Abd al-Qādir Pasha, who remained, however, in Cairo for several months before traveling to the Sudan. In the meantime, the deputy governor-general, Giegler Pasha, assumed command at Khartoum. He was determined to crush the Mahdī and to this end ordered the concentration of all available forces at Fashoda on the White Nile. Under the command of Yūsuf Pasha Ḥasan as-Shallālī, this force of over 4,000 men advanced westward. Encamping near Jabal Qadīr, the troops neglected to construct a stout stockade or zarība of thorn-bushes, so that in the early dawn of May 30, 1882, the Anṣār were able to rush the sleeping camp unimpeded and to massacre the government troops to a man. This third and greatest victory yet achieved by the Anṣār seriously diminished the prestige of the Egyptian Administration and army in the eyes of the Sudanese

1. *Anṣār,* or "Helpers," was the name given to the supporters of the Prophet at Medina. The followers of the Mahdī were originally known as darāwīsh (sing., darwīsh), "dervishes," and this name is commonly used by European writers. The Mahdī, however, in a conscious effort to imitate the Prophet, proclaimed that the term Anṣār be substituted for darwīsh, which in colloquial Sudanese means "madman." The terms *Muhājirīn,* "Emigrants," and *fuqarā',* "paupers," were also used to designate the followers of the Mahdī.

and correspondingly raised that of the Mahdī. One after another the Baqqāra tribes of the western Sudan rose in revolt and joined the Mahdī. The slave traders, who had been particularly harassed by the administration, quickly came over to the Mahdī's standard, bringing leadership and their bāzinqir, who would just as soon fight for their paternalistic masters as be conscripted into the Egyptian army. Even the Fūr, who were little attracted to the Mahdī as such but saw in his revolt the chance to further their own cause of independence, gave him their support. With the whole of the western Sudan in open revolt, it was only a matter of time before the riverain peoples and the Bija tribes went over to the Mahdī.

With arms taken from the defeated forces of the Government and the whole countryside filled with his adherents, the Mahdī declared a *jihād,* a Holy War, against the Government and advanced toward the strategic town of al-Ubaiyaḍ. On September 1, 1882, the Mahdī encamped at Kābā, six miles southwest of al-Ubaiyaḍ, and within a week the town was cut off and besieged by the Anṣār.

Before leaving Jabal Qadīr for the siege of al-Ubaiyaḍ, the Mahdī had dispatched his agents throughout the Sudan to raise the tribes in the jihād against the Government. It was not long before agents appeared in the Baḥr al-G͟hazāl and induced the tribes to revolt against the Egyptian Administration of the province.

CHAPTER 1

THE FIRST MAHDIST INVASION OF THE SOUTHERN SUDAN

The Fall of the Baḥr al-Ghazāl

The Baḥr al-Ghazāl was the first of the Egyptian provinces in the Southern Sudan to be affected by the Mahdist revolt. Its proximity to Kurdufān and Dār Fūr, the heart of the Mahdist rebellion, made it a simple matter indeed for agents of the Mahdī to enter the province and, playing on the long-suffering and widespread discontent with the Government, incite the tribes to revolt. There were two important parties in the Baḥr al-Ghazāl to whom the Mahdists preached rebellion. The first was composed of the indigenous Negroid tribes of the province, who had long sought to regain the freedom they had lost upon the establishment of Egyptian Administration. Many of the tribes, in spite of their Negroid origins, felt themselves more closely akin to the Arab tribes north of the Baḥr al-'Arab, with whom they had long enjoyed friendly relations, and consequently they listened with enthusiasm to the message of the Mahdī to join the rebellion of the northern, Arab tribes against the Government. Others, like the Dinka, the Nuer, and the Shilluk, who felt no kinship with the Arabs, joined the revolt not from religious fervor or feelings of brotherhood with the Northern Sudanese but rather to rid themselves of an oppressive and unpopular Government. The second important faction to whom the Mahdists appealed were the many Northern Sudanese who resided in the Baḥr al-Ghazāl. Administrators, slave traders, merchants, and soldiers, these Northern Sudanese, led principally by members of the Danāqla tribe, had close family, tribal, and religious ties with the Mahdists. Long discontented with the policies of the Government, particularly the curtailment of the slave trade, they were easily won over to Mahdism. To them Mahdism meant a revival of the slave trade, and although that would mean suppression of the indigenous tribes of the Baḥr al-Ghazāl, this conflict of interests was overcome by mutual antipathy to the Government. Thus having lost the support of the Northern Sudanese and native peoples within the province, the Egyptian Government had to rely on the army to maintain its position. When in the spring of 1884 the army also joined the insurgents and went over to the Mahdists, the Egyptian Administration in the Baḥr al-Ghazāl collapsed and vanished from the province.

When the news of the revolt of Muḥammad Aḥmad al-Mahdī reached the Baḥr al-Ghazāl, the Negroid tribes bordering on Dār Fūr and Kurdufān became increasingly restless. They had long had intimate contact with the Arabs to the north; and such tribes as the Dembo, the Shatt, and the Shilluk Luo had become thoroughly Arabicized and were, in fact, ruled before the coming of the Egyptian Administration by a powerful Dunqulāwī merchant named Qināwī, whose manners, dress, and religion they readily imitated.[1] Other Arabicized tribes, like the Feroge, the Njangulgule, and the Togoyo, even claimed to be of Arab origin.[2] Therefore, it is not

1. S. Santandrea, "Minor Shilluk Sections in the Bahr el Ghazal," *Sudan Notes and Records, 21* (1938), II, 271, 275–76. Qināwī . . . (d. 1883), was a Dunqulāwī trader who had worked with Romolo Gessi Pasha in the Baḥr al-Ghazāl and was one of the merchants suspected of having engaged in the slave trade. He accompanied the army commanded by Hicks Pasha into Kurdufān and was killed at the massacre of Shaykān. See R. Hill, *A Biographical Dictionary of the Anglo-Egyptian Sudan* (Oxford, 1951), p. 312.

2. S. Santandrea, "A Preliminary Account of the Indri, Togoyo, Feroge,

surprising that the sympathies of these tribes lay with the Mahdī, particularly when he aimed at the overthrow of a government which they undoubtedly considered oppressive. It is true that the Njangulgule, led by their great chief Yanqu, had supported the Government in Romolo Gessi's campaigns against Sulaymān Bey wad Zubayr; but Yanqu's action at this time appears to have been motivated only by a personal desire to attack his enemies, the Feroge, who happened to be supporting Sulaymān. Later, after Yanqu had been robbed by an unscrupulous government official and since the departure of Gessi had been generally ill-treated, his superficial loyalty vanished.[3] When the influence of the Mahdī reached Yanqu through Madībbū, chief of the Rizayqāt Baqqāra, he was one of the first in the Baḥr al-Ghazāl to take up arms against the Government.[4]

Between the departure of Gessi and the arrival of his successor, Frank Miller Lupton, late in the year 1881, there was an interregnum during which the naẓīrs of the eight qisms or districts into which the Baḥr al-Ghazāl was divided enhanced, by unjust and oppressive means, their power and wealth at the expense of the tribes.[5] Not only did they ignore the slave raiding of Danāqla and

---

Mangaya, and Woro," *Sudan Notes and Records, 34* (1953), II, 239–40, 244–45.

3. C. Zaghi, *Gordon, Gessi e la Riconquista Del Sudan* (Florence, 1947), pp. 383–84.

4. Madībbū Bey 'Alī (d. 1886), chief of the Rizayqāt tribe of southern Dār Fūr. In 1878–79, he helped Romolo Gessi in the latter's campaigns against Sulaymān Bey wad Zubayr, but on the outbreak of the Mahdist rebellion he left his country to visit Muḥammad Aḥmad at Jabal Qadīr and in 1882 returned to Dār Fūr a firm supporter of the Mahdī. He was then instrumental in defeating the government troops in Dār Fūr and forcing the governor, R. C. Slatin Bey, to surrender the province. Later he quarreled with the Mahdist amīr Karam Allāh Muḥammad Kurqusāwī, who had been sent by the Khalīfa 'Abd Allāhi to occupy Shakkā where Madībbū ruled. Karam Allāh had Madībbū sent to al-Ubaiyaḍ, where he was killed by order of the amīr Ḥamdān abū 'Anja. See Hill, p. 222.

5. W. Junker, *Travels in Africa, 1882–1886* (London, 1892), pp. 178, 230. E. Marco, "Frank Miller Lupton," *Sudan Notes and Records, 28* (1947), I, 50–62. Frank Miller Lupton (1854–88), was a British administrator in the Egyptian Government service who was born at Ilford, Essex, and entered the merchant service in 1878. While at Sawākin in 1879, he journeyed to Khartoum, where he joined the staff of C. G. Gordon Pasha, governor-general of the Sudan. He was placed in charge of government steamers and in 1880 made deputy to Emin Bey, governor of the Equatoria Province. In 1881 he was appointed by

Ja'liyīn merchants, but even engaged in the trade themselves. Supported by government troops, the naẓīrs would obtain slaves as tribute or in return for protection. Furthermore, as absolute rulers of their qisms, they profited from the collection of taxes, which was often carried out by the army in a most brutal manner, and increased their wealth by selling everything from justice to mercy. As the administration of these Danāqla naẓīrs became increasingly more intolerable and the government forces in Dār Fūr and Kurdufān suffered one defeat after another at the hands of the Mahdists, the Arabicized Negroid tribes of the Baḥr al-Ghazāl became correspondingly more amenable to the doctrines of rebellion which the Mahdī was preaching in the North and less inclined to believe in the invincibility of the Egyptian army. The first to rise were the Togoyo of Liffi. Declaring open revolt against the Government at the end of 1881, they defeated a force of 450 government troops sent by Lupton Bey, the new governor, and commanded by Muḥammad an-Naṣrī. In a second battle in February 1882, however, an-Naṣrī with 1,000 troops managed to defeat the rebels and restore peace to the province.[6] But this victory for the government was only a temporary setback to the rebels. Soon many of the chiefs and shaykhs of the border tribes departed to offer their allegiance to the Mahdī. After an exhortation to join the jihād and drive the "Turks" from the Baḥr al-Ghazāl, they were sent back accompanied by selected Anṣār to instruct the tribesmen in the doctrines of Mahdism.[7] One such chief was Yanqu of the Njangulgule, who, on August 17, 1882,

---

Muḥammad Ra'ūf Pasha to succeed Romolo Gessi as governor of the Baḥr al-Ghazāl. For two years he resisted attempts by the Mahdists to capture the province but was finally forced to surrender in April 1884 to the Mahdist amīr Karam Allāh, who sent him captive to Umm Durmān, where he lingered in great misery and died in delirium on May 8, 1888. He was survived by his wife, Zaynūba, a former Abyssinian slave of F. Rosset Pasha, and two daughters. His widow later married Ḥasan Zakī, a medical officer in the Egyptian army. See Hill, p. 218.

6. Maḥmūd 'Abd Allāh al-Maḥallāwī, "Report on the Fall of the Baḥr al-Ghazāl, 1894," Cairint, III/14/240. Maḥmūd al-Maḥallāwī relates that the people of Liffi were Janghes (Dinkas). This is highly improbable, for Liffi has long been the headquarters of the Togoyo, who at this time were a tribe of considerable size and strength.

7. "The Statement of Maḥmūd 'Abd Allāh al-Maḥallāwī Respecting the Fall of the Mudīrīya of the Baḥr al-Ghazāl, June 26, 1890," Cairint, III/14/235. Wingate, *Mahdiism and the Egyptian Sudan*, p. 28. Macro, p. 52.

declared his hostility against the Government and attacked Telgauna. He killed six soldiers and a noncommissioned officer and took prisoner their families as well as those families of other officials who were absent.[8]

The Baḥr al-Ghazāl, like the rest of the Sudan, was ripe for revolt. Not only had the loss of their independence turned the tribes against the administration, but the antislavery policy of the Government had also alienated the influential traders and merchants. Lupton Bey, the governor of the Baḥr al-Ghazāl, had hardly been in the province long enough to correct the abuses of his Danāqla officials or to turn back the mounting resentment of the tribes. He could rely on only a few officials to be loyal to himself and the Government, and although his energetic military efforts to defend the province appear to belie his lack of control, Lupton remained a "mere figure-head." [9] The real power lay in the hands of the subordinate officials and the powerful merchants, whose sympathies were with the Arab settlers and slave traders. They were quite content to support the Government if the latter was threatened by a revolt of the Negroid tribes, for any Negroid success would endanger their own position as well as that of the Government; but if an Arab force, particularly if composed of Mahdists, invaded the Baḥr al-Ghazāl, the Northerners would most certainly desert the Government.

Learning of Yanqu's raid on Telgauna, Lupton immediately assembled four detachments of regular troops, 600 jihādīya, and a rocket apparatus and marched from the provincial headquarters at Daym az-Zubayr for Telgauna by way of Liffi. On arriving at Liffi, he was informed that Chief Yanqu had fled north of the Baḥr al-'Arab to the home of Madībbū, whose tribe, the Rizayqāt, was besieging Shakkā. Lupton therefore ordered Maḥmūd 'Abd Allāh al-Maḥallāwī, the antislavery inspector for the Baḥr al-Ghazāl, to pursue Yanqu with 1,000 men.[10] After a difficult march al-

8. al-Maḥallāwī, "Statement . . . 1890," and "Report . . . 1894."

9. Emin Pasha to Junker, April 14, 1883, Georg Schweitzer, *Emin Pasha, I* (London, 1898), 143.

10. Maḥmūd 'Abd Allāh al-Maḥallāwī (d. 189?), an Egyptian slave trader and afterward antislavery inspector, was a Ja'farī from the governorate of Isnā in Upper Egypt. He was brought up in Khartoum by his father, a merchant engaged in trade between Egypt and the Sudan. In 1859, while at Kasala, he was conscripted into the army, but to avoid military service he escaped to the

Maḥallāwī reached Telgauna, which Yanqu had left eighteen days before, only to find the route beyond made impassable by floods. He had no choice but to return to Liffi and await the dry season before proceeding against Yanqu and his Njangulgule warriors. Lupton, accompanied by 400 troops, returned to Daym az-Zubayr.[11]

During the dry season of 1882 Yanqu returned to Telgauna in December with reinforcements of Rizayqāts and the men of Chief Adwin.[12] At this time, however, al-Maḥallāwī was stationed at Liffi with only a small force, for he had sent the naẓīr of Liffi and 700 men to gather supplies. In danger of being overwhelmed by the combined forces of Yanqu, Adwin, and Madībbū, al-Maḥallāwī constructed a strong zarība (which his few troops could defend more easily), recalled the foraging party to Liffi, and sent off a request to Lupton for more troops. Lupton, who was touring the province in a vain attempt to recruit 7,000 Negroid tribesmen for use in the North as jihādīya by the Khartoum Government, could not be immediately contacted, but the wakīl of Daym az-Zubayr responded to al-Maḥallāwī's urgent request and dispatched a detachment of 200 men.[13] They arrived at Liffi a few days later, followed shortly by the foraging party. After inquiring whether al-Maḥallāwī required further reinforcements and receiving an affirmative reply, Lupton sent to Liffi from outlying stations 900 additional troops.[14] By mid-January 1883 al-Maḥallāwī, with over 1,800 men under his

---

camp of 'Umāra wad Nimr, the Ja'lī desperado living on the Abyssinian border, and accompanied 'Umāra on some of his raids. In 1863, he profited from the amnesty accorded to the Nimrāb to go to Egypt. He later returned to the Sudan, where he engaged in slave raiding in the Nūba Hills and was made chief of the elephant and ostrich hunters in the district by the governor of Fashoda. After a period of trade in al-Qaḍārif, he joined his brother Muḥammad Bey 'Abd Allāh al-Maḥallāwī in Dār Fūr in 1877. Here he was appointed the mu'āwin of the subgovernorate of Shakkā and was later made an antislavery inspector by Romolo Gessi. On the fall of the Baḥr al-Ghazāl in 1884, he was taken captive by the Mahdists. In 1890 he escaped to Sawākin and returned to Egypt, where he lived in retirement. See Hill, p. 223.

11. al-Maḥallāwī, "Statement . . . 1890," and "Report . . . 1894."

12. Maḥmūd al-Maḥallāwī called Chief Adwin a Janghe (Dinka), but his village, according to al-Maḥallāwī, is near the Biri River, which is outside the Dinka country. He was probably either a Banda or a Kreisch.

13. Lupton to Junker, November 8, 1882, R. Buchta, *Der Sudan unter ägyptischer Herrschaft* (Leipzig, 1888), p. 146; Junker, p. 168.

14. Lupton to Junker, December 6, 1882, Buchta, p. 147.

command, felt himself strong enough to advance against the supposedly superior military strength of Yanqu. But unknown to al-Maḥallāwī, Yanqu's force had dispersed. The Rizayqāt and the men of Chief Adwin had been forced by lack of supplies to retire to their own homes, while Yanqu himself was north of Telgauna gathering grain. Telgauna was deserted and virtually defenseless, and although Yanqu hurriedly returned to its protection, he was too late. Upon approaching Telgauna, the Njangulgule were overwhelmed and routed with heavy losses by the government troops who had occupied the village. Yanqu himself fled to Madībbū with the remainder of his followers, while al-Maḥallāwī occupied Yanqu's foraging camp north of Telgauna.[15] But the spirit of the rebellion in the western Baḥr al-G͟hazāl was by by no means broken, for al-Maḥallāwī soon learned that the Shatt, who were closely associated with and influenced by the Njangulgule, had followed Yanqu's lead and openly revolted.[16] They had allied with sections of the Dembo, the Bongo, and the Shilluk Luo and had established their war camp east of Telgauna. Maḥmūd al-Maḥallāwī naturally decided to march immediately against them, and at the end of January he sent in advance of his main column a detachment of regulars and some 200 jihādīya. Not waiting for the arrival of the main column, the advanced force surprised and attacked the Shatt and put them to flight, killing a great number and capturing nearly 4,000 prisoners. Unfortunately, al-Maḥallāwī was no longer able to lead the government troops. Taken seriously ill, he left for Daym az-Zubayr, handing the command to Rifā'ī Ag͟hā az-Zubayr.[17]

In spite of these two serious defeats, the tribes of the western Baḥr al-G͟hazāl were not yet prepared to submit to the Government. Several days after the departure of al-Mahallāwī, Rifā'ī Ag͟hā was informed by the naẓīr of Liffi that Yanqu had again returned from the home of Madībbū with large reinforcements of Rizayqāts. Hoping to catch the rebels unawares, Rifā'ī Ag͟hā hurriedly left his camp and marched to Liffi, where, on February 10, 1883, he successfully intercepted Yanqu outside the station. After a desperate battle the government troops were victorious, and Yanqu—having lost thirty men, ten horses, and some arms—fled for the third time to the

15. al-Maḥallāwī, "Statement . . . 1890." Wingate, pp. 100–01.
16. Santandrea, "A Preliminary Account . . . Wore," p. 245.
17. al-Maḥallāwī, "Report . . . 1894." Wingate, p. 101. Macro, p. 52.

safety of the Rizayqāt country.[18] For the moment at least the Egyptian Administration in the western Baḥr al-Ghazāl was secure. Of all the chiefs in the area only Adwin remained in open hostility against the Government, and his inferior forces could easily be forced to submit by the government troops under Rifā'ī Aghā. Consequently, three days after the defeat of Yanqu, Lupton ordered Rifā'ī and his men to march to the Biri River, construct a strong zarība, and from there carry out a punitive expedition against Adwin.[19]

While Rifā'ī Aghā az-Zubayr and Maḥmūd al-Maḥallāwī were occupied against Yanqu and his allies north and west of Daym az-Zubayr, the Dinkas to the east began a series of sporadic and scattered raids which soon developed into a full-scale rebellion against the Government. The Dinka, like the other tribes of the Baḥr al-Ghazāl, had good cause to revolt. During the campaigns against Sulaymān, son of az-Zubayr the great slave trader, the western Dinka tribes had suffered considerably, while in the east their unheeded demands for redress from taxes and the abuse of government officials only hardened their determination to exterminate their oppressors. Certainly conditions in the Baḥr al-Ghazāl affected the Dinkas as well as the Njangulgule and the Shatt, but the Dinka, unlike the Arabicized tribes to the west, were not spurred on to rebellion by the politicoreligious doctrines of the Mahdī. The Nilotes of the Baḥr al-Ghazāl have been and still are more impervious to outside influences, whether they be cultural, political, or religious, than the other tribes of the province. Convinced of the superiority of their way of life, they are proud, aloof, and certain of the efficacy of their old beliefs and traditional ideas. Today they are still the most introverted of all the peoples of the Sudan, wishing nothing more than to be left alone and, when this is not possible, resisting with determined opposition and only yielding slowly to the overwhelming pressure which the Egyptian and later the Sudan Government brought to bear upon them. Consequently any revolt on the part of the Dinka was probably divorced from Mahdist influence and arose almost solely from grievances against the Danāqla merchants and officials and the constant desire to eliminate the burdens of government from their domain. Later, it is true, the Dinka appeared

18. al-Maḥallāwī, "Statement of . . . 1890."
19. al-Maḥallāwī, "Report . . . 1894."

to have allied themselves with the Mahdists against the Government, but such an alliance was only of the most temporary and opportunistic nature and clashes between the two were not infrequent.

In mid-February 1883 Lupton was informed that a party of Dinkas who a year earlier had suffered a severe defeat at the hands of the Government and had since been plotting revenge had ambushed a column of fifty jihādīya guarding 400 slaves carrying ivory to the steamer at Mashra' ar-Riqq, the river port of the Baḥr al-Ghazāl.[20] They massacred all of the jihādīya, took their arms, the slaves, and the ivory, and closed the strategic road to Mashra'. Lupton immediately assembled a punitive expedition, but the news shortly arrived that Sā'tī Bey abū'l-Qāsim, who had led a strong patrol along the Jur Ghattas-Mashra' road in December 1882, had marched against the rebellious Dinkas and defeated them on February 23.[21] He recovered the arms and the ivory that the Dinkas had seized and captured many head of cattle and sheep.[22]

This Dinka rising was only the first of many to follow. In March 1883 the Dinka launched a ferocious attack against the station of Dembo, which fortunately had just been reinforced by 500 regulars under the command of Maḥmūd al-Maḥallāwī, who had returned to service after recovering from his illness. The Dinka lost a considerable number of men attempting to break through the zarība but withdrew at sunset to their camp on the Dembo River with the intention of continuing the engagement on the following day. The garrison, however, in spite of severe losses, moved out of the station at two o'clock in the morning under al-Maḥallāwī's direction, advanced silently, and fell upon the Dinka in the dark.[23] The Dinka, caught unawares, fled, many of them to their death in the waters

20. Ibid. Wingate (p. 28) put the number of jihādīya at seventy-five.

21. Sā'tī Bey abū'l-Qāsim (d. 1884), qā'immaqām (lieutenant-colonel) in the Egyptian army, served in the Baḥr al-Ghazāl in 1878 and in 1879 was with Gessi Pasha in his various campaigns in southern Dār Fūr. He took part in the defense of Khartoum in 1884, during which he burnt Kalakla, assaulted a Mahdist force at Maḥū Bey's (now Gordon's) Tree, and attacked al-Qiṭaina where he was killed along with three of his officers. His death was a great loss to Gordon.

22. al-Maḥallāwī, "Statement . . . 1890," and "Report . . . 1894." Wingate, p. 28.

23. Lupton to Junker, April 11, 1883, Buchta, pp. 147–48. Junker, p. 251.

of the Dembo River. Maḥmūd al-Maḥallāwī and his regulars returned to Daym az-Zubayr to rest and refit.[24]

In spite of the victories of the government troops, these sporadic outbreaks of rebellious Dinkas had grown into a general Dinka revolt by the spring of 1883. The Dinkas attacked again in the Dembo District, ravaged the country of their old enemies the Bongo and the Jur, and closed the roads to Mashra' ar-Riqq and Equatoria.[25] Lupton called upon Rifā'ī Aghā az-Zubayr, who had been leading a successful, punitive expedition against Chief Adwin, to move with 1,250 men against the Dinkas.[26] During the rest of April, May, and June 1883 Rifā'ī Aghā marched and countermarched throughout the Dinka country. He fought four hard battles and many minor engagements against Dinkas frequently well-armed with rifles and in each engagement he was victorious.[27] But Rifā'ī Aghā was not alone in the field. Sā'tī Bey, operating from Jur Ghattas with about 1,000 men, had several successful encounters with the Dinkas, in which he captured over 2,000 prisoners.[28] Yet all these efforts seemed to have little effect, for by the end of June 1883 the Dinka war showed no sign of abating.

While Lupton and his lieutenants were occupied suppressing the revolts of the Dinka and the Arabicized, Negroid tribes of the western Baḥr al-Ghazāl, the Danāqla merchants, traders, and administrators were busy plotting to overthrow the Government and to hand the province over to the Mahdists.[29] Such intrigues were not surprising. The Danāqla were sympathetic to the Mahdī if for no other reason than that he himself was a Dunqulāwī. More particularly, the merchants and traders thought that the cause of the Mahdī, if successful, would bring back the prosperous slave trade, which government interference had curtailed. Similarly the Danāqla administrators were equally resentful at the intervention of Euro-

24. al-Maḥallāwī, "Report . . . 1894."

25. Lupton to Junker, April 11, 1883, Buchta, pp. 147–48. Junker, p. 251. al-Maḥallāwī, "Report . . . 1894."

26. Lupton to Junker, April 3, 17, 1883, Buchta, pp. 147–48. Junker, p. 251.

27. Lupton to Junker, May 5, June 1, 1883, Buchta, p. 148. Junker, pp. 284–85.

28. Lupton to Junker, May 5, April 17, 1883, Buchta, pp. 147–48. Junker, p. 284.

29. For a graphic description of the venality of the Danāqla and their corrupt operations see Schweinfurth, Ratzel, Felkin, and Hartlaub, eds., *Emin Pasha in Central Africa* (London, 1888), pp. 311, 331–32, 409.

pean officials in their corrupt and lucrative practices and were anxious, since their positions if not their lives were at stake, not to support a lost cause. Among the many Danāqla in the province was a certain *fakī* (religious teacher), S͟hayk͟h Ibn 'Uf an-Naṣrī, brother of Muḥammad an-Naṣrī, relative of Sā'tī Bey, and a follower of the Mahdī.[30] He devised a plan whereby all the Danāqla of the western districts of the Baḥr al-G͟hazāl were to gather on June 20, 1883, at Daym Idrīs, seize the 800 tribesmen waiting there to be conveyed to Khartoum, and lead them to the Mahdī. Like most plots in the Sudan, however, this one was soon discovered, and the faithful al-Maḥallāwī proceeded to Daym Idrīs, disarmed the forty Danāqla there, and waited quietly for S͟hayk͟h an-Naṣrī, who was coming in to lead the revolt.[31] Arriving late that night an-Naṣrī was informed by his fellow conspirators that al-Maḥallāwī was already there to seize him the following morning. Thereupon the s͟hayk͟h fled from Daym Idrīs to a small village near Daym az-Zubayr. Here he summoned his brother Muḥammad an-Naṣrī and a leading Dunqulāwī merchant, Karam Allāh Muḥammad Kurqusāwī, to come to him. They soon arrived, and the three of them decided to leave immediately to joint the Mahdī. They made their way north, avoiding capture, and joined the Mahdī before al-Ubaiyaḍ. Here they took part in the Battle of S͟haykān, where Hicks Pasha and 8,000 Egyptian troops sent against the Mahdists were annihilated. Both Ibn 'Uf an-Naṣrī and his brother Muḥammad were killed in the battle. Karam Allāh Muḥammad Kurqusāwī was wounded.[32] After the battle, Karam Allāh was appointed by the Mahdī as the *amīr* of the Baḥr al-G͟hazāl and given 1,500 Anṣār with whom to conquer the province.[33]

30. Junker wrote in April 1883 that Muḥammad an-Naṣrī was a "sneaking Arab," who, Junker correctly thought, "was already a secret adherent of the Mahdī." Junker, pp. 248, 251; Emin Pasha considered "Satti Effendi [Sā'tī Bey abū'l-Qāsim] a faithless scoundrel even for a Dongolawi, who betrayed the Bahr el Ghazal province and then got safely off to Khartoum." Letter of Emin Pasha dated August 14, 1884, and quoted in *Emin Pasha in Central Africa,* p. 467. In reality this judgment could not be further from the truth. Sā'tī Bey not only served Lupton faithfully and well but, after his arrival at Khartoum, was one of Gordon's most able lieutenants; see above, p. 30 n.

31. al-Maḥallāwī, "Report . . . 1894"; Daym Idrīs was better known as Ganda, but the former name is preferred in order to avoid possible confusion with the station of Ganda located in Equatoria.

32. Lupton to Junker, July 13, 1883, Buchta, pp. 148–49. Junker, p. 285.

33. Karam Allāh Muḥammad Kurqusāwī (d. 1903), was a Dunqulāwī born on

Meanwhile, in the western Baḥr al-Ghazāl, Maḥmūd al-Maḥallāwī was again on the move to subdue the Njangulgule and their allies, who once more had rebelled against the Government. Led by Chief aṭ-Ṭayyib, brother of Yanqu, the Njangulgule had attacked a small village, killing the inhabitants and taking much loot. Under orders from Lupton, al-Maḥallāwī relentlessly pursued aṭ-Ṭayyib, caught up with him in a forest near Telgauna on June 23, 1883, and attacked him, scattering his men, killing fifty, and wounding the chief himself. Maḥmūd al-Maḥallāwī then returned to Liffi to wait for the end of the rainy season before carrying out further military operations.[34] Since the government troops in the western Baḥr al-Ghazāl were confined to their posts during the rains, the tribes seized this opportunity to renew their rebellious activities. Both the Dembo and the Shilluk Luo, who had never really submitted, raided and plundered throughout the district, and Yanqu, who had again returned from the Rizayqāt country, skillfully eluded the strong government patrols sent to capture him and continued to roam the countryside, exciting the people to rebellion.[35]

But the greatest threat to the Government did not come from the plots of the Danāqla or from the sporadic attacks of the Arabicized, Negroid tribes, but rather from the powerful tribal confederation known as the Dinka. What had begun as an isolated incident in February 1883 was by the spring and summer a general war. Rifā'ī Aghā and Sa'tī Bey continually defeated the Dinka but never succeeded in subduing them. The roads to Mashra' ar-Riqq and to

---

the island of Kurkus near Shandī. In his youth he was employed in the service of slave-raiding organizations in the Baḥr al-Ghazāl. He subsequently occupied the province, capturing the governor and the government garrisons. He was later in charge of a Mahdist force sent to suppress a rebellion of the Rizayqāt in southern Dār Fūr and discharged his mission with great slaughter. He fought in many of the Mahdist campaigns and was wounded at Farka in 1896. When the Khalīfa was defeated in 1898, he took refuge with Sultan 'Alī Dīnār of Dār Fūr, who later suspecting him of intrigue had him killed near al-Fāshar. See Hill, p. 197.

34. al-Maḥallāwī, "Report . . . 1894."

35. Lupton to Junker, August 14, 1883, Buchta, p. 150. Junker, pp. 285–86. Although Santandrea intimates that the Shilluk Luo supported the Government (Santandrea, "Minor Shilluk Sections," pp. 279–80), Lupton wrote on August 14, 1883, that Wad al-Makk (undoubtedly the Wadelmak, otherwise known as Yamo Kon, of Father Santandrea's article) was one of the few chiefs still holding out against the Government.

Equatoria were closed once more by the Dinka, and Sā'tī Bey was again sent out, this time from Daym az-Zubayr with 900 men, to open them. In June the naẓīr of Jur Ghattas defeated the Dinkas but lost seventy men.[36] In the middle of July the Agar Dinkas, enraged by the rapacious raids made against them by the ma'mūr, destroyed Rumbek, and only six soldiers escaped to bring the bad tidings.[37] The Nuers, not to be outdone, attacked Lang, a station southeast of Jur Ghattas, with several thousand men and were driven off only after three days of fighting and a loss of 500 men to the Government.[38]

Lupton's position in the summer of 1883 was becoming more and more precarious. He had lost many of his regular troops, and the jihādīya was becoming more unreliable. Ammunition was short and Mahdist agents from the north were everywhere in the Baḥr al-Ghazāl stirring up further trouble.[39] The Dinkas had destroyed much of the grain crop before it was harvested, and in spite of 1,000 loads of grain from the Zande Sultan Zemio, Lupton feared that his men, if besieged, would be persuaded by hunger to go over to the Mahdī. But most serious of all, there appeared little hope of any assistance from Khartoum. Lupton, in despair, wrote on August 17, 1883: "I am afraid that unless the Mahdī is killed or his power broken before the rainy season is over, we shall be heavily attacked when the rivers are low enough to allow troops to wade through them."[40]

In spite of Lupton's gloomy prediction, however, the situation in the Baḥr al-Ghazāl began to improve by September 1883. A combined force of Dinka and Nuer was severely defeated, and the garrison at Mashra' ar-Riqq repulsed a savage attack by the Dinka, with considerable loss to the latter.[41] Yanqu was still at large but causing little trouble. The Mahdī was preoccupied in Kurdufān,

36. Lupton to Junker, July 13, 1883, Buchta, pp. 148–49.

37. Lupton to Junker, July 19, 1883, Buchta, p. 149. Junker, p. 285. "Report of Emin Pasha, 1885," Cairint III/14/236. Schweitzer, pp. 147–48.

38. Lupton to Junker, August 10, 1883, Buchta, p. 149. Junker, p. 285.

39. Lupton had sent ammunition to Emin in the care of Maḥmūd al-Maḥallāwī. See al-Maḥallāwī, "Report . . . 1894." For an example of the propaganda being circulated in the Baḥr al-Ghazāl by Mahdists agents see Junker, pp. 379–81.

40. Lupton to Junker, August 17, 1883, Buchta, pp. 150–51. Junker, p. 286.

41. Lupton to Junker, September 1, 13, 1883, Buchta, pp. 151–52. Junker, pp. 288–89.

and in September news reached Daym az-Zubayr that a steamer had arrived at Mashra' with a load of arms and ammunition.[42] Sā'tī Bey, who had gone to Jur Ghattas after clearing the Mashra' road, returned to collect these supplies. The steamer had also brought a Dutchman, Jan Maria Schuver, who left Mashra' for Jur Ghattas two days after the steamer's arrival. Everyone had warned him that the road was not safe, and it was only after Schuver had produced a paper from the governor-general "saying that the Government had given him permission to go where he liked" that the naẓīr of Mashra' gave him an interpreter (known as a *tarjumān* or, popularly, a dragoman) and five jihādīya as guards, and let him go.[43] He started on the following day but was instantly killed at the village of a local Dinka chief. Sā'tī Bey, on hearing this, marched to the village and burned it, but he was unable to apprehend the murderers and so, pursuant to orders from Lupton, returned with the steamer to Khartoum to collect more arms and ammunition.[44] In spite of this unpleasant incident, Lupton was confident that his continuous military success was at last being felt by the Dinka. Some of the chiefs had already come in to submit when on September 13 he wrote, "I believe there is no danger that they will attack us again." [45]

Unfortunately such a statement was premature, for at the beginning of October news reached Daym az-Zubayr that Rifā'ī Aghā and 400 men had been killed by the Shilluk Luo and their allies. Rifā'ī had left Daym az-Zubayr in the beginning of September with 600 men to march against Chief Adwin and the intractable Wad al-Makk of the Shilluk Luo.[46] Wad al-Makk refused to submit to Rifā'ī, surprised his troops, and broke through his zarība.[47] A mere 200 men were able to escape and beat a retreat to Daym az-Zubayr. Not only

42. Lupton to Junker, September 23, 1883, Buchta, p. 152. The steamer had actually arrived on August 15, but communications were so disrupted by Dinka raiding parties that Lupton did not learn of its arrival until September.

43. Lupton to Malcom Lupton, November 6, 1883, "Mr. Frank Lupton's (Lupton Bey) Geographical Observations in the Bahr el Ghazal Region," *Proceedings of the Royal Geographical Society*, new ser. *4* (1884), 249–50.

44. Lupton to Junker, September 23, 1883, Buchta, p. 152.

45. Lupton to Junker, September 13, 1883, Buchta, p. 152.

46. Lupton to Junker, September 1, 1883, Buchta, p. 151. al-Maḥallāwī, "Statement of . . . 1890."

47. Lupton to Junker, October 13, 1883, Buchta, p. 152. Junker, p. 293.

was this a serious loss of troops, but Rifā'ī himself was killed. He was one of the most able commanders in the province, and his death was keenly felt by Lupton in the trying days ahead.[48]

Lupton, exasperated at the failure to extinguish the revolt in the Baḥr al-Ghazāl, decided to launch in the coming dry season a full-scale offensive under his personal command to crush, once and for all, the major threat to the provincial administration—the Dinka opposition. Recruiting additional troops from the friendly Bongo tribe to replace his heavy losses, Lupton even sent to Zemio for reinforcements of 1,000 Zande warriors, all the bāzinqir Zemio could spare, and, of course, ample supplies of grain and other foodstuffs.[49] Lupton wrote to Junker, the German explorer, on October 9, 1883, that "I see no way of putting down the revolt unless the Niam-Niam [Azande] princes come to our aid." [50] There was little doubt that the Zande sultan would not comply with Lupton's request, and in November a contingent of Azande warriors left Zemio's for Daym az-Zubayr.[51] The promise of booty was sufficient to bring the Azande warriors northward, but the farsighted Zemio knew well that it was to his best interest to maintain, if possible, the present administration in the Baḥr al-Ghazāl. If the Egyptian Administration were to crumble, the way would be clear for Arab encroachment into Zandeland. It was for this same reason that Zemio welcomed the Congolese when they came up the valley of the Bomu and became the most loyal of all their native allies.

While waiting for the dry season, Lupton began to assemble his troops at Daym az-Zubayr. He himself had marched to Mashra'

48. Lupton to Malcom Lupton, November 6, 1883, "Mr. Frank Lupton's Geographical Observations . . ." pp. 249–50.

49. Zemio, son of Tikima, was one of the great Zanda princes near the headwaters of the Bomu River. From the very first he supported the Egyptian Administration in the Baḥr al-Ghazāl and sent men and supplies to both Gessi Pasha and Lupton Bey. After the Mahdist left the Baḥr al-Ghazāl, he established his hegemony over the tribes situated along the Congo-Nile Divide and his raiding parties penetrated deep into the province. When the Van Kerckhoven expedition arrived in the Uele Valley in 1891, he immediately placed himself and his warriors at the services of the Congo Free State and remained a loyal servant of the state until his death in 1912.

50. Junker, pp. 293–94. Lupton wrote on November 5, 1883, "at least one-third of the Government defenders of the Province have gone, never to return." Lupton to Malcom Lupton, November 5, 1883: "Mr. Frank Lupton's Geographical Observations," p. 252.

51. Junker, p. 298.

ar-Riqq in October to try to apprehend the murderers of Schuver; and although he was unsuccessful, his force managed to defeat the Tonj and the Agar Dinkas with a loss to the Dinka of 400 men and 350 head of cattle.[52] This success against the Dinkas began to restore Lupton's confidence, and on November 6 he wrote from Jur Ghattas: "we shall, I have no doubt, beat the Janghe [Dinka] this year." [53] This optimism undoubtedly grew when, during his return march to Daym az-Zubayr, Lupton routed the Jurs and the Mohk Dinka, who lost 1,000 men, while news reached him that another government force of 600 men armed with Remington repeating rifles had marched against the Shilluk Luo and, although fiercely attacked, defeated Wad al-Makk, who lost forty-six killed.[54] Furthermore, Lupton's enemies, the Dinka and the Rizayqāt, were at war. It appears that thirty Danāqla and Rizayqāt had gone to a Dinka chief to buy slaves, had quarreled, and were killed by the Nilotes. Consequently, Madībbū, in spite of the Mahdī's prohibition against alienating the Dinka in any way, assembled several hundred men and marched south to attack them. In the ensuing fight the Rizayqāt suffered heavy losses; but they had not withdrawn, and Lupton expected the fighting to break out again at any moment.[55] In November Lupton had returned to Daym az-Zubayr, where he had assembled 1,000 men under his command and was expecting another 500 within ten days' time. The dry season was now at hand, making it possible for large-scaled military operations, and Lupton decided that he would move against the Dinka in January 1884 with nearly 2,000 men.[56]

In the meantime it appears that, in spite of the conflict between the Rizayqāt and the Dinka, Mahdist influence had begun to assert itself on the latter. In battle the Dinkas often used the Mahdist war cry and frequently carried into battle a green, Mahdist flag sent to them by the Mahdī. Nevertheless, it is extremely doubtful if this influence was ever anything but superficial.[57]

After the first of the year, 1884, Lupton advanced again into the

52. Lupton to Junker, November 11, 1883, Junker, p. 318; Lupton to Malcom Lupton, November 6, 1883: "Mr. Frank Lupton's Geographical Observations."

53. Lupton to Malcom Lupton, November 6, 1883: ibid.

54. Lupton to Junker, November 26, 1883, Buchta, p. 154. Junker, pp. 318–19.

55. Ibid.

56. Lupton to Junker, December 31, 1883, Buchta, p. 154.

57. Lupton to Malcom Lupton, November 6, 1883: "Mr. Frank Lupton's Geographical Observations."

Dinka country east of Daym az-Zubayr. He found himself opposed by a coalition of Dinka tribes gathered under the leadership of their chiefs. The governor sent to these chiefs a message demanding that they submit to the Government and return the arms which had been captured by them in their victorious engagements against his troops. The chiefs replied that they would not submit and that Lupton should prepare himself to meet the same fate as Rifā'ī Aghā. Thereupon, Lupton ordered a strong double zarība to be constructed and waited for the Dinka assault. At dawn on the following day, January 13, wave after wave of Dinka warriors moved toward, engulfed, and tried to break into the zarība. Maḥmūd al-Maḥallāwī estimated the number at 50,000. All day they charged at the zarība trying to penetrate the walls of thorn only to be mowed down by withering fire from the Remington rifles. Finally at night the Dinka broke off the fighting and withdrew to their camp thoroughly chastened and subdued by the heavy losses received during the day. The government troops, however, had so exhausted their supply of ammunition that hardly a sufficient amount remained to continue fighting. Lupton therefore had no choice but to retreat under cover of darkness and return to Daym az-Zubayr, for to have pursued the retreating Dinka with such a meager supply of ammunition would have meant disaster.[58] But the northern Dinka had nevertheless been subdued, and in this and the news of the capture and execution by government troops of the formidable Njangulgule chief, Yanqu, Lupton could rejoice.[59]

Lupton retreated from his zarība in the Dinka country to Daym az-Zubayr by way of the government post of Dembo. Upon reaching this station he was met by the ma'mūr, who had seized two members of the Mandala tribe carrying, to the Danāqla of the Baḥr al-Ghazāl, letters telling of the annihilation of the army of Hicks Pasha at the Battle of Shaykān and exhorting them to join the Mahdī in his jihād against the Government.[60] Although the Egyptian punitive

58. al-Maḥallāwī, "Statement of . . . 1890," and "Report . . . 1894."

59. Lupton to Emin, Beginning, 1884, Buchta, pp. 154–55. Junker, p. 365.

60. al-Maḥallāwī, "Report . . . 1894." Junker, p. 365. Colonel W. Hicks, who had resigned from the Indian army in 1880, was appointed a major-general in the Egyptian army in 1883 and given command of a field force intended to operate against the Mahdists. In September 1883 he marched at the head of a large Egyptian army into Kurdufān to relieve al-Ubaiyaḍ, which was besieged by the Mahdists. Demoralized, badly disciplined, and suffering from lack of

expeditions against the Mahdists in 1881 and 1882 had singularly failed, the Government had decided to try again to crush the Mahdist rebellion. To ensure success a large army of nearly 8,000 men had been assembled at Khartoum in the spring and summer of 1883 and placed under the command of Colonel William Hicks, a retired officer of the Indian army. From the start the expedition appeared doomed to disaster. The troops were ill-trained and badly led, the relations between Hicks and the senior Egyptian officer were strained, and the route of march, through hostile and waterless country, was poorly chosen. The march itself was a scene of indescribable confusion, which the harassing tactics of the Mahdists and the lack of water only made worse. On November 5, 1883, the exhausted, thirsty, and thoroughly demoralized army approached S̱haykān. They were surrounded and fiercely attacked by the Mahdists, who easily broke through the squares formed by the Egyptian troops. Once inside the squares, the battle quickly turned into a massacre. Hicks and all of his staff fell fighting, but the troops put up only token resistance. All but 250 men perished before the fury of the Mahdist assault.

S̱haykān was by any standard an overwhelming victory for the Mahdists, and its significance was not lost upon Britain, Egypt, or the Muslim world in general. The Mahdī's prestige reached new heights, and it is reported that after S̱haykān he received Muslim delegations from the Ḥijāz and as far away as India and Morocco. Certainly the Mahdist victory at S̱haykān doomed the Egyptian Administration in Dār Fūr and the Baḥr al-G̱hazāl. In Dār Fūr the governor, Rudolf Slatin Bey, an Austrian and a Christian, could no longer retain control of the province. Cut off from the central Government at Khartoum, his authority undermined from within by disloyal subordinates, and unable to subdue the recalcitrant and powerful Rizayqāt tribe, Slatin had no recourse but surrender. On December 23 he submitted to Muḥammad Ḵhālid, representative of the Mahdī, former Egyptian subgovernor of Dāra, and until his defection Slatin's lieutenant.

The fall of the Baḥr al-G̱hazāl was just as easy even though a little more prolonged. No longer threatened by an Egyptian army, the Mahdī was free not only to march on Khartoum but also to send an

water, the army was attacked at S̱haykān and annihilated. Hicks and all his staff were killed, although they fought with the utmost bravery.

expedition to stamp out all vestiges of Egyptian rule in the southern provinces. Consequently, he had appointed Karam Allāh Muḥammad Kurqusāwī to the position of amīr of the Baḥr al-Ghazāl and had sent him southward from al-Ubaiyaḍ with 1,500 men. But such was the effect of the Mahdist victory at Shaykān on the people of the Sudan that thousands of tribesmen along Karam Allāh's line of march rallied to his standard; and by the time the Mahdist amīr crossed the Bahr al-'Arab into the Baḥr al-Ghazāl, his force had swollen to over 5,000 men.[61]

The news of Hicks Pasha's defeat and the subsequent advance of Karam Allāh spread terror throughout the province. Not only were the government forces hopelessly outnumbered, but, disheartened by the continual lack of supplies and their exhausting campaigns against the Dinka, they were more amenable to the subversive influence of Mahdist doctrines. The Mahdist victory at Shaykān appeared to the Northern Sudanese merchants, soldiers, and officials in the Baḥr al-Ghazāl to be conclusive proof of the virtue of the Mahdī's cause and the divine nature of his mission. Hitherto the government officials had, for the most part, loyally fought to maintain the administration against the attempts by the tribes of the Baḥr al-Ghazāl to overthrow it. Although the tribes had eagerly listened to the exhortations of Mahdist agents to join the jihād, they had, unlike the Arab tribes to the north, made war on the Egyptian Government to win their independence rather than to promote the spread of Mahdism. To the Northern Sudanese in the Baḥr al-Ghazāl it was preferable to maintain Egyptian governmental rule in the province than to hand it over to the pagan, Negroid tribes. When, however, a former influential merchant of the province returned at the head of an army consisting of friends, relations, and fellow tribesmen of the Northern Sudanese in the Baḥr al-Ghazāl and preached adherence to a cause tested in battle and appealing not only to self-interest but to the deepest religious feelings, the Northern Sudanese enthusiastically welcomed the Mahdists and prepared to surrender the province to Karam Allāh.[62]

Therefore, when it became known that Karam Allāh was advancing into the Baḥr al-Ghazāl, capitulation appeared to the officers and men to be inevitable—but not so to Lupton. He ordered

61. al-Maḥallāwī, "Statement . . . 1890."

62. al-Maḥallāwī, "Report . . . 1894." Wingate, p. 134. Macro, pp. 54–55.

the commanders to withdraw their troops to Daym az-Zubayr, which was being put into a state of defense. All the houses around the fort were destroyed, the walls strengthened, and supplies collected. But such efforts were of little use, for the troops began to defect to the Mahdists. Upon the approach of Karam Allāh, the naẓīr of Liffi went over to him with all his troops, and he was shortly followed by the naẓīr of Bucho and his men. Most of the tribes, including those of the Dinka confederation, had joined Karam Allāh. With a force now numbering nearly 10,000, Karam Allāh encamped six hours' march from Daym az-Zubayr, from where he sent letters to Lupton ordering him to surrender the province. Lupton, who felt that he could depend on the troops at Daym az-Zubayr, still had visions of holding the station. He therefore sent two men to the Mahdist camp under the pretext of learning by what authority Karam Allāh had been appointed the amīr of the Baḥr al-Ghazāl but in reality to ascertain the strength of the Mahdists.[63] Lupton, full of fight, wrote to Emin, the governor of Equatoria, on April 12, 1884: "I will fight to the last. I have put the guns in a strong fort and if they succeed in capturing the Mudīrīya [the province] I will hope, from my fort, to turn them out again. They come to you at once if I lose the day, so look out." [64]

Lupton still had under his command 1,200 regular troops, four guns, and four rockets; determined to resist, he called a council of the leading officials. Although the Northern Sudanese and the Negroid tribes had ceased to support the Government, if the army remained loyal to the administration Lupton felt he could organize a successful resistance. Much to his disappointment, if not surprise, the men refused to fight and the officials made known their intention of surrendering to the Mahdists. Lupton, deserted by the army and alone in his desire to carry on the fight, had no choice but to dispatch on April 20, 1884, his letter of capitulation to Karam Allāh.[65] On April 26, he wrote his last letter to Emin, in which he opened with the gloomy greeting: "It's all up with me here. Everyone has joined the Mahdī, and his army takes charge of the mudīrīya the

63. Ibid.

64. Lupton to Emin, April 12, 1884, Cairint, I/5/30. Wingate, p. 136. Macro, p. 54.

65. Lupton to Emin, April 20, 1884, Cairint, I/5/30. al-Maḥallāwī, "Report . . . 1894." Wingate, p. 136. Macro, p. 54.

day after tomorrow"; and closed with the prophetic line: "Look out you; some 8,000 to 10,000 men are coming to you well-armed." [66] Two days later, on April 28, Lupton surrendered the province to the amīr Karam Allāh. He had done everything in his power, even becoming ostensibly a Muslim, to defend the Baḥr al-Ghazāl from the Mahdists. He had fought bravely, loyally, and well, and his conduct, in spite of his unfamiliarity with the province in which he found himself, was admirable. A few days after the surrender he was sent under guard to Umm Durmān, and there languished in miserable circumstances until he died in delirium on May 8, 1888.

The Mahdist Invasion of Equatoria

After the official surrender of Daym az-Zubayr on April 28, 1884, Karam Allāh quickly established Mahdist control over the whole of the Baḥr al-Ghazāl. All the arms, ammunition, ivory, and supplies of the Government were confiscated and either distributed to the Anṣār or sent to the Mahdī. The officials of the Egyptian Administration joined the ranks of the Anṣār, and the soldiers who did not escape were "either reclaimed by some of the Danāqla as their former slaves, or were publicly sold." [1] The Negroid tribes, who had hoped for the return of their independence now that the Egyptian Administration had disappeared, were required to pay tribute, preferably in slaves, or be plundered. In June, Karam Allāh wrote to the Mahdī that 1,360 slaves had already been sent to Shakkā and complained that "as the slaves taken as booty are exceedingly numerous in this part, and are continually arriving at the camp of the mudīr, we are much pressed in despatching them and in looking after them." [2]

66. Lupton to Emin, April 26, 1884, Cairint, I/5/30. Macro, p. 55. Wingate, p. 136. Wingate erroneously records the date of Lupton's last letter as April 28, not April 26. Furthermore, it appears that Lupton had at one time considered withdrawing to Lado via the home of the Zande Sultan, Zemio. "The Mambattu and Neighbouring Countries: Events which Took Place from the Departure of the Egyptians to the Arrival of the Agents of the Free State," Intelligence Report, Egypt, No. 8, November 1892, Appendix C.

1. Emin Bey to Dr. Schweinfurth, August 14, 1884, *Emin Pasha in Central Africa,* p. 465.

2. Karam Allāh to the Mahdī, Shaʿbān 22, 1301 (June 17, 1884). Wingate, p. 140.

Once Karam Allāh had secured the Baḥr al-Ghazāl, he led a strong expedition southwestward from Daym az-Zubayr over the Congo-Nile watershed to attack the Zande Sultan, Zemio.[3] It was Zemio who sent to Lupton troops and supplies with which to fight the Mahdists and whose Azande warriors constituted the greatest threat to the Mahdists in the Baḥr al-Ghazāl. Karam Allāh not only wished to punish Zemio for his support of the Government but desired to eliminate the Azande threat to his flank. When the news of the Mahdist advance was brought to the zarība of Zemio by some sixty government soldiers seeking refuge from the Mahdists, the Azande princes were panic-stricken. Some fled across the Bomu to the south, but others, commanded by Zemio and his uncle, Sasa, determined not to abandon their territory without a fight.[4] The Azande army met the Mahdists near the zarība of Zemio, located at approximately 5° 25′ north latitude and 25° 20′ east longitude.[5] The Azande were forced to retire, but in the retreat southward they laid their land waste. The Mahdists, unable to obtain supplies from the devastated countryside and under continual harassment from Azande war parties, abandoned their hard-won victory and withdrew across the Congo-Nile watershed into the Baḥr al-Ghazāl.[6] Zemio constructed a new zarība on the Bomu River near the present-day town which bears his name.[7]

After the fall of the Baḥr al-Ghazāl, Karam Allāh dispatched letters to the governor, Emin Bey, and the people of Equatoria demanding the surrender of the province and exhorting them to join the Mahdists. Equatoria had hitherto lain beyond the influence of the Mahdī but had been beset with the same internal problem found throughout the Southern Sudan—the inability to control effectively the government officials and, in particular, the Danāqla and Ja'liyīn emigrants. This lack of control led the officials in the southern provinces to appropriate government funds for personal

3. "Events which led to the Fall of the Baḥr al-Ghazāl," a statement by Abū al-Khayrāt Bahārī, Cairint, III/14/235. R. C. Slatin, *Fire and Sword in the Sudan, 1879–1895* (London, 1896), pp. 411–12.

4. "Events which led to the Fall of the Baḥr al-Ghazāl."

5. The position of Zemio's zarība was well known. See Junker, p. 170; and G. Casati, *Ten Years in Equatoria*, 2 vols. (London, 1891), map entitled "Kibali-Makua-Welle-Obangi," found in the cover pocket of Vol. 1.

6. "Events which led to the Fall of the Baḥr al-Ghazāl," Cairint, III/14/235.

7. See The International Map Series, Africa, 1/1,000,000, No. NB-35.

gain, to make frequent raids on the local tribes for cattle and slaves, and to engage in the slave trade in spite of the official antislavery policy of the Government. Occasionally, this lack of control would lead to open insubordination, as in the case of Bakhīt Bey Batrākī, who in 1882 had marched on Lado and had been suppressed only with great difficulty; but more frequently it drove the victims of the corruption, the Negroid tribes, into open revolt.[8] Emin Bey, the governor of Equatoria, did not possess the strong, resolute character needed to hold his subordinates in check and managed to maintain his administration only by his cleverness and extensive knowledge of his province and its people.[9]

The first disturbance in Equatoria Province attributed to Mahdist influence was the revolt of the Agar Dinka. Encouraged by the successful rebellion of the Dinka tribes in the Baḥr al-Ghazāl and incensed at the raids made upon them by the ma'mūr of Rumbek for slaves and cattle, the Agar Dinka surprised the garrison at Rumbek

8. E. Schnitzer, *Die Tagebücher von Dr. Emin Pascha,* ed. Dr. Franz Stuhlman, 2 (Hamburg, 1919), 400, entry of December 13, 1882.

9. Emin Pasha (1840–92), was born Edward Carl Oscar Theodor Schnitzer at Oppeln in Silesia. A German Jew of Christian Protestant parents, he studied medicine in Germany and later practiced in Albania and Anatolia as a medical officer in the Ottoman service. He became a Muslim, adopting Turkish dress, customs, and the Arabic name Muḥammad al-Amīn. He crossed to Egypt and traveled up the Nile to Khartoum, where he arrived penniless in 1875. In Khartoum he was aided by members of the European community in setting up a private practice, but in 1876, he accepted the invitation of Colonel C. G. Gordon to become the province medical officer in Equatoria and so left Khartoum for the South. Gordon liked him and appointed him chief medical officer of the province, but from the first employed him in other administrative work, including a diplomatic mission to Uganda and Unyoro. In 1878, he was appointed governor of Equatoria, a post he held until 1889. He explored the Latuka and Unyoro country and made valuable contributions to the natural history of the region. When Khartoum fell in January 1885 and the Egyptian army withdrew to the North, he found himself isolated and hemmed in on his northern border by a Mahdist force under 'Umar Ṣāliḥ. To crown his troubles, a mutiny broke out among his own troops, and it was only with the greatest fortitude that he maintained a semblance of administration until 1889, when, apparently against his will, he was rescued by the explorer H. M. Stanley, with whom he and a remnant of his troops and civilian staff retired to Zanzibar. In 1887 he had been promoted to Liwā' and Pasha. He later joined the German service in East Africa and was murdered by Arab slave traders near the Stanley Falls. He was not only a competent scientist but an accomplished musician. See Hill, p. 333.

on July 27, 1883, massacred seventy men and officers, and destroyed the station. On receiving this news, Emin Bey ordered the ma'mūr of Makaraka, Ibrāhīm Aghā, to recapture Rumbek and quell the rebellion. Collecting reinforcements at Amadi, Ibrāhīm Aghā marched northward, relieved the station of Shambe, which had been besieged, and occupied Rumbek. By the end of the year the district was again under the Government's control and the tribes pacified.[10]

The rest of the province, however, remained quiet, and the position of the administration at the beginning of 1884 appeared to be thoroughly secure. Emin was planning a new expedition to the Congo and despite disquieting news from the Baḥr al-Ghazāl, there was nothing which directly threatened Equatoria. Then, on March 27, news abruptly arrived from Lupton of the annihilation of Hicks Pasha's army at Shaykān and the surrender of Dār Fūr by the governor, Rudolf Slatin Bey.[11] Emin kept these bad tidings from becoming generally known, and the only defensive measures taken were the concentration of the garrisons of the southern stations of Fauvera and Fadibek at Wadelai and Dufile respectively and the strengthening of the station of Bor. April passed without incident; and although Emin had the powerful Bari chief, Loron, secretly assassinated for plotting an attack on Lado, the province headquarters, there was nothing which appeared to jeopardize the administration.[12]

On May 27 a letter arrived at Lado from the amīr Karam Allāh Kurqusāwī informing Emin of the Mahdist occupation of the Baḥr al-Ghazāl, a fact confirmed by Lupton in a postscript, and demanding that Emin and his officers come to the Baḥr al-Ghazāl and surrender Equatoria Province. Enclosed with the letter to Emin were other Arabic letters treating of the same matter but addressed to particular officials, and a copy of a proclamation from the Mahdī

10. "Report of Emin Pasha, 1885," Cairint, III/14/236. *Tagebücher, 2,* 490–91, August 4, 5, 1883. Wingate, pp. 103–04. "Statement Respecting the Equatorial Provinces, 1890," Cairint, III/14/237.

11. Junker, p. 365; "Report of Emin Pasha, 1885," Cairint, III/14/236; Wingate, p. 142; *Tagebücher, 3,* 12, March 27, 1884. There appears to be some discrepancy concerning the date on which this news was received. Junker writes that it arrived on March 26; Emin in his diary gives the date as March 27, and in his official report of 1885 as March 28.

12. Junker, p. 378. Casati, *1,* 285. *Tagebücher, 3,* 15, May 19, 1884.

to the people of the province.[13] The news quickly shattered the sense of security that had pervaded the province and created consternation among the government officials. At a conference hastily convened on the same day by Emin, the panic-stricken officials unanimously resolved to surrender. A delegation led by Emin was immediately chosen to go to the Baḥr al-Ghazāl to hand over the province, and preparations for its departure were begun. Meanwhile, news of the Mahdist demands had spread throughout Equatoria, and the officials at the various stations only awaited the appearance of a Mahdist force before capitulating. When, after a few days, the Mahdists did not appear, the initial fright of the officials and people disappeared, enabling them to consider the situation more dispassionately. Not only were the Mahdists still in the Baḥr al-Ghazāl, but there were in Equatoria about 2,000 regular officers and men armed with Remington rifles and long in the Khedivial service. Many of the stations were well fortified and adequately supplied; and although the defection of the many Danāqla in the province was almost certain, there was no valid reason to surrender the province without resistance. Emin himself changed his mind and decided to remain in Lado, but in order to gain time it was determined to send a deputation to Karam Allāh. On June 3 a delegation of four men guarded by ten troops and an officer left Lado for the Baḥr al-Ghazāl.[14]

The Danāqla did not wait long to declare themselves for the Mahdī. On June 13 news arrived at Lado that Ibrāhīm Aghā, the Dunqulāwī ma'mūr of Makaraka, "who had hitherto always proved trustworthy," had assembled all of his fellow Danāqla in the district and declared himself for the Mahdī.[15] Surprisingly unable to entice any of the regular troops to join him, he and the Danāqla therefore

13. For the English translations of the letter to Emin Bey and the proclamation of the Mahdī, see Junker, pp. 382–88.

14. "Report of Emin Pasha, 1885," Cairint, III/14/236. "Statement Respecting the Equatorial Provinces, 1890," Cairint, III/14/237. "Statement of 'Uthmān al-Ḥājj Ḥamad, Qādī of Equatoria," Cairint, III/14/239. "Report on Equatoria, 1890," Cairint, I/11/56. Emin Pasha to Dr. Schweinfurth, August 14, 1884, *Emin Pasha in Central Africa,* pp. 462–65. Junker, pp. 391–95. Wingate, pp. 142–44. *Tagebücher, 3,* 16, May 27, 1884.

15. Emin Bey to Dr. Schweinfurth, August 14, 1884, *Emin Pasha in Central Africa,* p. 465.

left Makaraka, pillaged the station of Wandi, and marched toward the station of Kurduma, plundering the countryside through which they passed. Stopping at Kurduma in order to prepare for the journey to the Baḥr al-G̱hazāl, the Danāqla quarreled among themselves. A few left for the Baḥr al-G̱hazāl with Ibrāhīm Ag̱hā, but most remained to occupy the government stations in western Equatoria.[16]

Meanwhile, in the Baḥr al-G̱hazāl, as Karam Allāh was preparing a strong expedition to invade Equatoria and join the Danāqla insurgents, the jihādīya stationed at Wau, Kuk̲hūk 'Alī, Abū Gurūn, and the other zarības located along the Wau-Rumbek road mutinied, seized the arms and ammunition, and massacred the Mahdists. These Negroid slave-soldiers had always shown a deep-rooted animosity for the Arabs, a hostility enhanced by the harsh treatment meted out to them by Karam Allāh. They destroyed the small station of Tonj, surrounded Jur Ghattas, and severed communications with Daym az-Zubayr. Karam Allāh immediately marched against the rebellious jihādīya, but it was several months before the mutiny was quelled, the zarības recaptured, and the province returned to order; and it was not until January 1885, nearly six months later, that he could turn again to the invasion of Equatoria.[17]

Undeterred by Karam Allāh's failure to invade Equatoria in 1884, the Danāqla in the province were more than holding their own. They had captured all the government stations west of Kabayendi, and in the north the Danāqla had seized the station of Sajjadīn with the intention of attacking Amadi.[18] Emin, no longer the symbol of unquestioned Khedivial authority, was bewildered, hesitant, and quite incapable of dealing with the situation. Never a man of action, he did nothing to thwart the Danāqla—a policy contemptuously described by Junker as one of "masterly inactivity"—and sent only

16. "Report of Emin Pasha, 1885," Cairint, III/14/236. "Statement Respecting the Equatorial Provinces, 1890," Cairint, III/14/237. "Report on Equatoria, 1890," Cairint, I/11/56. Junker, pp. 43–44. Wingate, p. 145. *Tagebücher, 3*, 18–19, June 13, 1884.

17. Emin Bey to Dr. Schweinfurth, August 20, 1884, *Emin Pasha in Central Africa*, pp. 469–70. *Tagebücher, 3*, 41–42, August 17, 1884. Ibrāhīm Ag̱hā was killed near Tonj during the mutiny of the jihādīya.

18. "Report of Emin Pasha, 1885," Cairint, III/14/236. *Tagebücher, 3*, 27, July 12, 1885. Junker, pp. 424–25.

the troops from the abandoned stations of Fadibek and Fauvera to strengthen the garrisons of Amadi and Makaraka.[19]

On October 10, 1884, more letters arrived at Lado from Karam Allāh. These were similar to the ones received the preceding May but warned Emin that the Anṣār were now coming to Equatoria for certain.[20] Evidently the jihādīya mutiny had been sufficiently suppressed to permit Karam Allāh to dispatch reinforcements to the Danāqla in Equatoria. Sixteen hundred Mahdists armed with Remington rifles were sent under the command of ʻAbd Allāhi as-Samat, who was to take charge of all the Danāqla in Equatoria.[21] After placing these Danāqla under his command, ʻAbd Allāhi seized the station of Takfara, near Amadi, and from there sent a letter to Emin demanding that he surrender the province. Emin, of course, ignored the summons. On November 11 the Mahdists attacked Amadi, which was garrisoned by 1,100 regular troops, but were compelled to retire. On the following day the attack was resumed, but again the Mahdists were driven off after suffering heavy losses. A third assault on the 17th was equally unsuccessful, and the Mahdists retired to await reinforcements. Although no additional men arrived from the Baḥr al-G͟hazāl, ʻAbd Allāhi secured the support of the Agar Dinkas, who had rebelled against the Government in July 1883, and with them launched a fourth attack against Amadi on December 2. Not only was this attack, like the others, repulsed, but the garrison sallied out from Amadi and inflicted heavy losses on the Mahdists and their Dinka allies. Unable to capture the station by assault, ʻAbd Allāhi had no choice but to besiege Amadi until the arrival of reinforcements from the Baḥr al-G͟hazāl.[22]

The besiegers did not have long to wait. In January 1885 news reached Lado that 400 Mahdists had arrived before Amadi. Although these additional troops allowed the Anṣār to invest the station more closely, they were insufficient to capture Amadi by assault. In fact the Mahdist force barely sufficed to throw back the sortie made by

19. Junker, p. 424.

20. Ibid., p. 433.

21. "Report of Emin Pasha, 1885," Cairint, III/14/236. *Tagebücher, 3,* 54–55, October 10, 1884. Junker, p. 440. Wingate, p. 146.

22. "Report of Emin Pasha, 1885," Cairint, III/14/236. Emin Bey to Dr. Schweinfurth, January 2, 1885, *Emin Pasha in Central Africa,* pp. 474–75. Wingate, pp. 146–47. Junker, pp. 439–42. *Tagebücher, 3,* 60–63, November 17–23, December 1–15.

the garrison on February 2, in which the besiegers lost many men, including their commander 'Abd Allāhi, and much ammunition. It was not until the arrival shortly thereafter of Karam Allāh himself and 2,000 Anṣār that the Mahdists seemed assured of victory. Closely besieging the station and keeping the garrison under constant attack, the Anṣār succeeded in cutting off the water supply and repelling all attempts by the Makaraka garrisons to relieve Amadi. Without food and water but refusing to surrender, the government troops made a desperate sortie; 260 men succeeded in making their way through the Mahdist lines and safely reaching Wandi, where they were joined by the garrisons coming from the government stations in the Monbuttu country.[23]

After the fall of Amadi Karam Allāh quickly pushed to within a few hours' march from Lado, while another Mahdist force took Kamari near Wandi. The capture of Kamari forced the remnants of the Amadi garrison and the regulars from Monbuttu to retire from Wandi. During the retreat the government troops paused to rest at the little station of Rimo. Here they were overtaken by the Anṣār and a fierce battle ensued, in which the Mahdists were repulsed with heavy losses in men, arms, and ammunition. The government troops retired in orderly fashion to Bedden on the Baḥr al-Jabal.[24]

On April 18 Emin received another letter from Karam Allāh informing him of the fall of Khartoum and the death of General Gordon. Following the Battle of S̲h̲aykān, the Mahdists had slowly marched against Khartoum and besieged the city. In March 1884 the telegraph line to Barbar was cut, but it was not until September, when the vanguard of the Mahdist forces arrived before Khartoum, that the siege was pressed. Throughout the autumn the cordon of the Mahdists was tightened, and in spite of all the efforts of General Gordon, who had been sent to Khartoum by the British Government to effect (so Gordon thought) the withdrawal of the Egyptian garrisons in the Sudan, conditions in the town became

23. "Report on Equatoria, 1890," Cairint, I/11/56. "Report of Emin Pasha, 1885," Cairint, III/14/236. Junker, pp. 487–91. Emin Bey to Dr. Schweinfurth, December 1, 1885, *Emin Pasha in Central Africa,* pp. 477–80. Wingate, pp. 258–60. *Tagebücher, 3,* 65–66, 71–72, 82, January 6, February 14, March 29, 1885, respectively.

24. "Report of Emin Pasha, 1885" Cairint, III/14/236. Junker, p. 493. *Tagebücher, 3,* 88–89, April 13–19, 1885.

increasingly worse. Although the Mahdists appeared content to starve the garrison into submission, the advance of a British relief force under Sir Charles Wilson so alarmed the Mahdī that he was determined to take the town before the arrival of the relief expedition. Encouraged by reports of extreme privation in Khartoum and the inability of the troops to defend it, the Mahdī gave the order to attack on January 25, 1885. Within a couple of hours the defenses had been breached, all resistance overcome, and the town securely delivered into the hands of the Mahdists. Gordon was killed, and Egyptian Administration in the Northern Sudan ceased to exist.

No longer having hope of relief from Khartoum and being pressed by the Mahdists, who were only a few hours' march from Lado, Emin and his officers decided to concentrate all troops in the river stations and withdraw the administration to the southern stations of Wadelai and Dufile, where supplies were plentiful. Emin soon left Lado for the south in order to supervise personally the evacuation. At Muggi, however, news reached him that the Mahdists were in full retreat back to the Baḥr al-Ghazāl. His ammunition and supplies nearly exhausted and his retreat soon to be cut off during the rainy season by flood-swollen rivers, Karam Allāh had received word of another mutiny of the jihādīya in the Baḥr al-Ghazāl. He immediately set out for the north, leaving behind only a small force that was to follow as soon as they had arranged for the transportation of the arms and luggage. By the end of June 1885 the Mahdists had disappeared from Equatoria, leaving behind an Egyptian Administration governing only its stations along the 180 miles of river from Lake Albert to Lado, and the native tribes, which in the interior at least were free.[25]

Although the Northern Sudanese and many of the native tribes in Equatoria had joined the Mahdists, just as their counterparts in the Baḥr al-Ghazāl had done, the Egyptian armed forces in Equatoria remained faithful to the Government and fought fiercely and loyally to support it. Certainly it was the admirable defense of Amadi which had forestalled the Mahdist advance, and it was their determination to carry on the defense of the province after

25. "Report of Emin Pasha, 1885," Cairint, III/14/236. Casati, *1*, 310–13. Junker, pp. 515–16. *Tagebücher, 3*, 99–100, 101, 105–06, 111–12, May 17, 24, June 8–14, July 3, 1885, respectively.

the fall of Amadi that prevented the precipitous collapse of Emin Bey's Government at Lado. Actually the steadfastness of the Equatorial battalions in contrast to those in the Baḥr al-Ghazāl was not so unusual as one might suppose. Not only had the Equatorial troops not been subjected to Mahdist propaganda, but unlike the Baḥr al-Ghazāl battalions many of the officers and nearly all the men were Southern Sudanese. These Southern Sudanese troops and particularly their Negroid officers had a profound loyalty to the Khedive of Egypt, whom they looked upon with mystical awe, and there were countless incidents in Equatoria where their actions were based solely on a blind devotion to the Khedive. Furthermore, unlike many of the officers and men in the Baḥr al-Ghazāl, the Equatorials, for the most part, had no tribal or family ties with the Mahdists. Many were nominally Muslims, but they did not have the deep-seated religious feeling which played such an important part in the acceptance of Mahdism by the Northern Sudanese. In many cases Equatoria was their original home; in others it was a home readily adopted. To the officers and men of the Equatorial battalions to repulse the Mahdists was to defend the province, not only for the Khedive but for themselves. In spite of the defection of the Northern Sudanese merchants, soldiers, and administrators in Equatoria and in spite of the hostility of the Negroid tribes toward the Government, so long as Emin Bey retained the confidence of the army, Egyptian rule in Equatoria was secure.

The Mahdist Withdrawal from the Baḥr al-Ghazāl

On June 22, 1885, the Mahdī died at Umm Durmān after a short illness. It was rumored that he had been poisoned, but Slatin relates, probably correctly, that he died of typhus.[1] Following the Mahdī's death a council of notables gathered to choose a successor and after some hesitation elected 'Abd Allāhi Muḥammad Tūrshain, the Khalīfat al-Mahdī.

During the years since the manifestation of the Mahdī on Abā Island in 1881, the Mahdīya had evolved from a religious movement into a militant Islamic state. At the head of the state was the Mahdī, occupying, by virtue of the divine nature of his mission,

1. Slatin, p. 369.

a position of supreme and unquestioned authority. Although he delegated many of the routine matters of state, he remained in control of the Mahdīya and embodied all supreme legislative, financial, and judicial functions in his divinely inspired person. It was during this period that the Khalīfa 'Abd Allāhi gradually assumed a position of authority second only to that of the Mahdī himself, and as the Mahdist state dramatically expanded through a series of military successes, the duties and consequently the power of the Khalīfa correspondingly expanded also. At the time of the Mahdī's death the Khalīfa 'Abd Allāhi had clearly established his pre-eminence over all possible rivals.

'Abd Allāhi was one of four sons of a holy man of the Ta'ā'isha Baqqāra of Dār Fūr. He was born at Turdat in the southwestern part of that province in 1846. On learning of Muḥammad Aḥmad al-Mahdī, he had journeyed eastward to join him at Abā Island on the White Nile. Here he served the Mahdī in a humble capacity and soon became his most trusted adviser. In 1881 the Mahdī appointed him one of his four caliphs, naming him after Abū Bakr aṣ-Ṣiddīq and handing him a black flag. He retired to Kurdufān with the Mahdī and there organized a series of victories over the government forces which secured the success of the Mahdist movement. He later fought in the Jazīra and superintended the siege of Khartoum, which fell in January 1885.[2] After the Mahdī's death 'Abd Allāhi's claims to the succession were by far the strongest. Not only did his nomination as Khalīfat aṣ-Ṣiddīq imply that he should succeed the Mahdī as Abū Bakr aṣ-Ṣiddīq had succeeded the Prophet, but on his deathbed the Mahdī appears to have designated 'Abd Allāhi as his successor.[3] After his election as the Khalīfat al-Mahdī, 'Abd Allāhi held a great oath-taking ceremony in the mosque beside the Mahdī's house. Here the Khalīfa administered the oath of allegiance and had proclamations and letters prepared informing the Anṣār of the Mahdī's death and the accession of 'Abd Allāhi. In addition, letters were sent to many high officials and tribesmen throughout the Sudan summoning them to attend a ceremony at the Mahdī's tomb on September 20, 1885, at which time they were to take the oath of allegiance to the Khalīfa.[4] Karam Allāh was naturally included in this group:

2. Hill, pp. 5–6.
3. Holt, *The Mahdist State in the Sudan*, pp. 119–20.
4. Ibid., p. 122.

From the servant of his God, Khalīfat al-Mahdī, peace be unto him, Khalīfa 'Abd Allāhi b. Muḥammad, Khalīfat aṣ-Ṣiddīq to his beloved in God Karam Allāh, Shaykh Muḥammad, Governor of the Baḥr al-Ghazāl. May God preserve him. Amen.

Peace be unto you with the mercy of God and His Blessing.

We inform you dearly beloved that your letter has been received and what it contains of the good news about your victory over the rebellious jihādīya and seizing what they had has been known. We thank and praise God for all this, and we have been very well pleased with your zeal in taking up the cause of the faith. May God reward you with all good things, bless you, and crown you with victory wherever you go in his service.

As our object, dearly beloved, is the victory of the true religion and drawing people nearer to God and the happiness of the next world, we have called all of the Anṣār in all the land to come to the Mahdī's tomb to see us and renew their oath of allegiance. Therefore, as soon as you receive this, hasten to come with all the Anṣār, jihādīya, and followers of Mahdism in that vicinity. Bring with you what you have plundered, all and everything; leave nothing behind which may draw your thought or care towards it, for by meeting and conversing together there is a great benefit and much enlightening of the mind and spirit. Start at once with all speed and delay not, for your presence is absolutely necessary. May God bless you and direct you to all things that please him. Amen.

P.S. Accompanying this is a copy of the proclamation which we sent abroad announcing the death of the Mahdī, a copy of the letter by the Khalīfa, the Ashrāf, and the rest of the emigrants and Anṣār, our proclamation to the inhabitants of the Nile districts and a letter to the people of your country asking them to come with you.[5]

Having put down the revolt of the jihādīya in the Baḥr al-Ghazāl, Karam Allāh, in response to the Khalīfa's summons, marched northward across the Baḥr al-'Arab with over 3,000 troops armed with rifles and an immense number of slaves.[6] Arriving at Shakkā

5. Khalīfa to Karam Allāh, Dhū al-Qa'da 12, 1302 (August 23, 1885), Mahdīya, I/33/12/6.

6. Slatin, pp. 411–12.

in October 1885, he was ordered by the Khalīfa to remain in Dār Fūr and watch the activities of Madībbū, chief of the Rizayqāt. It appears that Madībbū was reluctant to accept 'Abd Allāhi as the Khalīfat al-Mahdī and hoped to oust the Anṣār from Shakkā so that his Rizayqāt might again control the borders between Dār Fūr and the Baḥr al-Ghazāl, as in the past. Soon Madībbū was in open revolt and fighting took place between Madībbū, on the one hand, and Karam Allāh, who was upholding the Khalīfa's authority, on the other. Madībbū was defeated and fled but was subsequently captured near al-Fāshar and returned to Karam Allāh, who sent him to the Khalīfa. On the way to Umm Durmān, Madībbū was confronted at al-Ubaiyaḍ by the great Mahdist amīr, Ḥamdan abū 'Anja. Between these two there had long been bitter hatred, and abū 'Anja seized the opportunity of Madībbū's captivity to revenge himself. On a trumped-up charge the Rizayqāt chief was quickly executed and his head sent to the Khalīfa.

Since Karam Allāh had marched north of the Baḥr al-'Arab late in the year 1885, there were no longer any Mahdists in the Baḥr al-Ghazāl, and no further attempt was made by the Khalīfa to re-establish his control over the province. Within a short time the Baḥr al-Ghazāl returned to the pristine, tribal anarchy it had known before the coming of the Arab traders and the Egyptian Administration.

CHAPTER 2

THE SECOND MAHDIST INVASION OF THE SOUTHERN SUDAN

'Umar Ṣāliḥ Invades Equatoria

In the summer of 1888 the K͟halīfa 'Abd Allāhi ordered the invasion and conquest of Equatoria Province. Hitherto his attention had been diverted to the Mahdist campaigns in Abyssinia and Egypt, but the latest rumors from the South that a strong expedition led by Europeans had arrived in Equatoria alarmed the K͟halīfa.[1] He undoubtedly felt that the time had finally come to capture Emin Pasha, governor of Equatoria, and rid the Sudan of the last vestige of Egyptian authority.[2] He therefore ordered that an expedition under the command of 'Umar Ṣāliḥ should be immediately prepared to go to the South, and the letters of 'Umar

1. This expedition was the Emin Pasha Relief Expedition under the command of H. M. Stanley, who first arrived at the Albert Lake on December 14, 1887, and later met Emin on April 29, 1888.

2. Captain Count Gleichen, *Handbook of the Sudan* (London, 1898), p. 197.

leave no doubt that the capture of Emin Pasha and his province was the primary objective.[3] In October 1888 'Umar wrote from Equatoria to the Khalīfa: "As Emin and his Arab and Christian followers are the main concern, I have postponed the question of the Negroids and did not take anything from them except by exchange. When Emin is done with, we will treat the question of the Negroids with a view to their discipline, which is not now complete." [4]

This desire to deliver the Sudan from the last trace of Egyptian Administration, and thereby thwart any attempts by others to perpetuate it, appears to have been 'Abd Allāhi's sole motive for ordering the conquest of Equatoria. It was a political decision based on reports that Europeans had returned to Equatoria and not a religious decision to spread Mahdism in the Southern Sudan. Although 'Abd Allāhi experienced mystical visions and utilized the propaganda therefrom to associate himself with the sanctity of the Mahdī, he was not primarily motivated by religion.[5] Unlike the Mahdī, his Khalīfa was a military man, and although devout and filled with genuine religious enthusiasm, he did not make his decisions on purely religious grounds. There is no doubt that the Mahdist troops in the field regarded their cause as a mission to convert the enemy to Mahdism. It was a jihād, a holy war against the infidel, and the Mahdists in Equatoria made considerable effort to secure, by force if necessary, the adherence of the Negroid tribesmen to Mahdism. The Khalīfa certainly encouraged such religious fanaticism not only for its military value, which was great,

3. 'Umar Ṣāliḥ to the Khalīfa, Shawwāl 2, 1306 (June 13, 1888), Mahdīya, I/33/5; Ṣafar 1306 (October 1888), Mahdīya, I/33/19. 'Umar Ṣāliḥ (d. 1897) was a Ja'lī who had been reared at Shakkā in southern Dār Fūr. He was sent by the Khalīfa to Equatoria in 1888 with the intention of destroying the forces of Emin Pasha. He sent an ultimatum to Emin which was intercepted by Egyptian mutineers, who decided to fight. He then seized Rajjāf and killed Ḥamad Aghā, the mutineers' governor, but failed to capture Dufile. He was succeeded as the Mahdist amīr of Equatoria by al-Ḥājj abū Qarja and was killed in battle against the Congolese at Rajjāf in 1897.

4. 'Umar Ṣāliḥ to the Khalīfa, Ṣafar 21, 1306 (October 27, 1888), Mahdīya, I/33/12.

5. Sir Harold MacMichael, comparing the Mahdī and his Khalīfa, wrote of 'Abd Allāhi: "This was a man of altogether different type and one in whom the religious motive, however prominent, was subordinate to the militant." *The Sudan* (London, 1954), pp. 49–50.

but also to maintain the momentum of the Mahdist revolution, which was the best guarantee of the continuance of his personal power. Nevertheless, he himself was not a religious fanatic and did not base his military and political decisions on religious mysticism.

Although the lure of Equatorian ivory certainly aroused European interest, it appears to have had little influence on the decision of the Khalīfa to invade the South.[6] Indeed the question of ivory does not appear to have been even considered until 'Umar Ṣāliḥ wrote to 'Abd Allāhi after the Battle of Rajjāf (Rejaf) in 1888 requesting, with bored annoyance, instructions for disposing of all the ivory. Obviously the Khalīfa was pleased to receive ivory from the South, but although considerable amounts of it were shipped from Equatoria to Umm Durmān during the ensuing years, its procurement was an outgrowth of and not a reason for the second Mahdist invasion of the Southern Sudan.[7] Even if much of the ivory taken in Equatoria remained in the Sudan, the very low export figures would appear to indicate that its importance to the Mahdists was only secondary.[8]

The other principal commodity of Equatoria, slaves, was of much greater interest to the Khalīfa. He was anxious to increase whenever possible the number of his jihādīya, but it is necessary to make a distinction between the slave trade in the days of the Turkīya and that practiced under the Khalīfa. Private slave trading was prohibited, for a private trade in slaves would undoubtedly lead to traders, supported by their personal slave-army of bāzinqir, establishing their own authority in the districts in which they traded and thereby creating a threat to the position and personal rule of 'Abd Allāhi. Without a doubt his commanders and

6. H. M. Stanley, *In Darkest Africa, I* (New York, 1891), 52, 64.

7. 'Umar Ṣāliḥ to the Khalīfa, Ṣafar 21, 1306 (October 27, 1888), Mahdīya, I/33/10.

8. The value of all ivory exported from the Sudan via Aswān and Sawākin between 1892 and 1898 was E£14,194, against a total export trade valued at E£317,080. Thus ivory accounted for only 4.4% of the total value of goods exported. See Intelligence Reports, Egypt, 1892–98. It is doubtful whether much of Emin Pasha's vast store of ivory was captured by the Mahdists. It is related that 3,000 kantars of ivory were thrown into the Baḥr al-Jabal when Lado was evacuated, 1,000 kantars at Dufile, 700 kantars at Wadelai, 300 kantars at Muggi, 5 kantars at Labore, and 150 at the other river stations. This represents nearly 578 tons of ivory jettisoned into the waters of the Nile. See "Statement of Basili Bochtar," New York *Herald* (London Edition), May 5, 1890.

soldiers took prisoners of war as slaves for their own use or even to make a profit in small, private trades.[9] This, however, was a very different matter from the great caravans of slaves trekking overland under the eye of such slave-masters as az-Zubayr. Slatin mentions the great pomp and circumstance with which 400 male slaves were marched through Umm Durmān; a number which would have caused the great slave traders of the Turkīya to sneer in contempt.[10]

The Khalīfa was undoubtedly under pressure to send a force to the South. The Equatorial regions had always interested the Northern Arab, particularly the Danāqla and Ja'liyīn merchants who for many years had traded in the Southern Provinces for ivory and slaves. It was the Danāqla with their grievances against the anti-slavery policy of the Egyptian Government who had played such a vital role in the fall of the Baḥr al-Ghazāl and who had created such trouble in Equatoria. These same Danāqla had returned to Umm Durmān after the retreat of Karam Allāh in 1885 and must have been vociferous in their demands for a reconquest of the South, demands of which the Khalīfa must have been well aware.

Later, after the capture of Rajjāf (Rejaf), it was reported that the Mahdists there were suffering a great deal from the climate. The Khalīfa then decided to make it a place of exile to which he sent political prisoners.[11] Slatin wrote that from the time when a second expedition was sent to Equatoria, "Reggaf became a colony for the deportation of convicts, and of persons whose presence in Omdurman was considered dangerous by the state." [12] But this was a later development and appeared to have played no part in the Khalīfa's original decision to invade the province.

Thus on June 11, 1888, 'Umar Ṣāliḥ sailed from Umm Durmān

9. 'Umar Ṣāliḥ to the Khalīfa, Ṣafar 21, 1306 (October 27, 1888), Mahdīya, I/33/10.

10. Slatin, *Fire and Sword in the Sudan,* p. 507. Of these 400 male slaves, 300 were to be enlisted in the jihādīya. A. B. Theobald writes: "Here it should be noted that there was no revival of the slave trade on anything like the scale as that under the Turko-Egyptian Government." *The Mahdīya* (London, 1955), p. 184. 'Umar Ṣāliḥ was amazed and astonished at the number of slaves possessed by the officials of the Egyptian Administration in Equatoria. 'Umar Ṣāliḥ to the Khalīfa, Ṣafar 21, 1306 (October 27, 1888), Mahdīya, I/33/12.

11. Father Joseph Ohrwalder, *Ten Years' Captivity in the Mahdi's Camp* (London, 1892), p. 271.

12. Slatin, p. 470.

in command of three steamers, six barges, and 1,500 Anṣār, two thirds of whom were Arabs and the remainder jihādīya, and was supplied with letters written by the Khalīfa, Slatin, Georges Istānbūlīya, and the Copts of Umm Durmān, all appealing to the Governor of Equatoria, Emin Pasha, to surrender.[13] 'Umar had great difficulty in transporting this force to the South. The steamers *Bordein* and *Mansura* were overloaded, while the third steamer, *Muhammad Ali*, was so powerless that it had to be emptied and towed.[14] But the little task force managed somehow to proceed. The big, powerful steamer *Ismailia*, the most suitable for use in the *sadd* region, was added to 'Umar's fleet; but no sooner had it joined the other three steamers than it was requisitioned by the amīr of the *Bayt Māl al-'Umūm* (the Public Treasury) for more urgent business elsewhere. The loss of the *Ismailia* caused 'Umar to complain bitterly to the Khalīfa that he was left with inadequate steamers to fulfill his mission. His entreaties seemed to have earned him little sympathy, and he had no other choice than to commandeer some boats and proceed on his way.[15]

'Umar Ṣāliḥ and his force arrived at Lado on October 11, 1888,[16]

13. 'Umar Ṣāliḥ to the Khalīfa, Shawwāl 2, 1305 (June 13, 1888), Mahdīya, I/33/4; Shawwāl 15, 1305 (June 26, 1888), Mahdīya, I/33/6, 7; Ṣafar 21, 1306 (October 27, 1888), Mahdīya, I/33/8, 9. A. J. Mounteney-Jephson, *Emin Pasha and the Rebellion at the Equator* (London, 1890), p. 257. Holt, *The Mahdist State in the Sudan,* p 198. Slatin was the former governor of Dār Fūr who was now being held prisoner by the Mahdists at Umm Durmān. Georges Istānbūlīya (1840–1926), was a Syrian Christian merchant who was at al-Ubaiyaḍ when the Mahdists approached the town in 1882. Together with most of the inhabitants he went over to the Mahdist side before the siege of the town began. During the Mahdist regime he kept a shop in Umm Durmān and was a clerk to the Mahdī and the Khalīfa 'Abd Allāhi. He was considerate to the European captives at Umm Durmān. He survived the Mahdīya and died in Khartoum. See Hill, *Biographical Dictionary of the Anglo-Egyptian Sudan,* p. 187.

14. 'Umar Ṣāliḥ to the Khalīfa, Shawwāl 2, 1305 (June 13, 1888), Mahdīya, I/33/4.

15. 'Umar Ṣāliḥ to the Khalīfa, Shawwāl 15, 1305 (June 26, 1888), Mahdīya, I/33/7.

16. 'Umar Ṣāliḥ to the Khalīfa, undated, Mahdīya, I/33/22. The date of 'Umar's arrival at Lado was given by him in a letter to the Khalīfa dated Ṣafar 10, 1306 (October 17, 1888), and sent to Sawākin via 'Uthmān abū Bakr Diqna, where it was transmitted to Sir E. Baring at Cairo and forwarded to the Marquis of Salisbury in London on December 15, 1888. Palace Papers, I/3/9. Mounteney-Jephson related (p. 242) that the Mahdists had landed at Bor

and found it completely deserted. Unable to proceed by steamer because the river was very low, and reluctant to leave his boats undefended while the 1st Battalion of Equatorial troops was at nearby Rajjāf, 'Umar decided to send three Anṣār to Dufile with a letter calling upon Emin to surrender.[17] Similar letters were sent to the garrison at Rajjāf, which refused to capitulate and instead began immediately to prepare for the defense of the station. The surrounding ditches were widened, fortifications of wood and stone erected, and letters sent to Dufile and Wadelai requesting reinforcements.

The Mahdists soon besieged Rajjāf and cut the road to Dufile. The siege was pressed. On October 19 the garrison, although outnumbered, sallied from the fort and attacked the Mahdist positions. "The Anṣār made a counterattack and after a half hour defeated them [the Equatorial troops] and captured the fort." [18] Most of the garrison was taken prisoner, including the Egyptian officers, and all the arms and ammunition fell into the hands of the Mahdists. Those of the garrison who escaped capture or death fled either to Dufile to the south or to the Makaraka country to the west.[19] 'Umar lost sixty-eight men killed, thirteen wounded, and fifteen missing.[20] He seized a large supply of ivory and counted

some months previous to their arrival at Rajjāf. At Bor they had had a hard fight with the natives. If this is so, 'Umar did not mention it; and he certainly recorded no loss of men until after the Battle of Rajjāf.

17. 'Umar Ṣāliḥ to the Khalīfa, undated, Mahdīya, I/33/22. For an Arabic copy of the letter sent to Emin at Dufile and the English translation, see Mounteney-Jephson, pp. 481 and 245–53, respectively.

18. 'Umar Ṣāliḥ to the Khalīfa, undated, Mahdīya, I/33/22. Mounteney-Jephson gave two accounts of the battle of Rajjāf. The first, in a letter by 'Uthmān Lātīf, was based largely on hearsay. Mounteney-Jephson, p. 260. The second account was given by a fugitive from Rajjāf and was undoubtedly the more accurate although differing somewhat from the account of 'Umar. Jephson wrote, "He [the fugitive] said that at about five in the afternoon the Dongala [the Mahdists] accompanied by hundreds and hundreds of natives were seen approaching the station. They had marched round with flags flying and drums beating; they then made a dash at the postern gate, and took it in the first rush." Mounteney-Jephson, pp. 265–66.

19. "Statement of Basili Bochtar," New York *Herald,* May 5, 1890. "Report on Equatoria, 1890," Cairint, I/11/56.

20. 'Umar Ṣāliḥ to the Khalīfa, Ṣafar 21, 1306 (October 27, 1888), Mahdīya, I/33/9.

nearly 500 slaves.[21] These along with the battle flags, tarbushes, and a copy of the Khedivial decree, which officially acknowledged the abandonment of Equatoria by the Egyptian Government, were sent downstream to Umm Durmān under the supervision of Muḥammad Khair Bādī.[22] The Khalīfa later sent the captured copy of the Khedivial decree, as well as a dispatch from 'Umar Ṣāliḥ describing the situation in Equatoria, to General Grenfell commanding the Anglo-Egyptian forces at Sawākin.[23]

While 'Umar was achieving such rapid success at Rajjāf, the remaining garrisons in Equatoria had been paralyzed by discontent and mutiny. In August 1888, before the arrival of the Mahdists, the garrisons of Dufile and Labore had revolted against the leadership of the governor, Emin Pasha, who was supporting the pro-

21. 'Umar Ṣāliḥ to the Khalīfa, Ṣafar 21, 1306 (October 27, 1888), Mahdīya, I/33/10.

22. 'Umar Ṣāliḥ to the Khalīfa, undated, Mahdīya, I/33/22; and Ṣafar 1306 (October 1888), Mahdīya, I/33/19.

23. The decree and the dispatch were sent to General Grenfell via 'Uthmān Diqna, the Mahdist amīr besieging Sawākin. He interpreted the contents of 'Umar Ṣāliḥ's letter to mean that Emin had been captured and confidently stated as much in a covering letter to Grenfell. "The Khalīfa has informed me that the said Governor of Equatoria has fallen into our hands and is now one of the followers of the Mahdī." 'Uthmān Diqna to the British Officer Commanding at Sawākin, Palace Papers, III/10/192. In reality 'Umar had never said that Emin had been captured but rather that he was being held prisoner by his own officers and men. "We must thank the officers and men who made this conquest easy for us before our arrival. They caught Emin and a traveler [Mounteney-Jephson] staying with him and put them both in chains." 'Umar Ṣāliḥ to the Khalīfa, Ṣafar 10, 1306 (October 17, 1888), Palace Papers, III/10/192. Nowhere did 'Umar state that Emin himself had been captured by the Mahdists. He only implied that the conquest of the province would not be difficult. Wingate attempted to draw the following conclusions from 'Umar's implication: "Omar Salih having arrived, as far as is known, at Rejaf without fighting, leaves little doubt that the northern garrisons at once made terms with him. As regards the garrisons of the southern posts, there is also little doubt that numbers of officers had decided to adopt Mahdiism. Omar Salih, therefore, at the time he wrote his memorable despatch, was in all probability fully convinced that the officers were inclined to submit to him; and such would in all likelihood have been the case, had not the soldiers taken matters into their own hands and obliged the officers of the Rejaf garrison to lead them against the intruders." Wingate, *Mahdiism and the Egyptian Sudan,* p. 386. There is no evidence to substantiate this explanation.

posal brought by Stanley for all the officers and men of the Egyptian Administration to abandon Equatoria and, with the help of Stanley and his men, to retire through East Africa and thence to Cairo. Henry Morton Stanley, the most renowned explorer of his day, had been commissioned by the Emin Pasha Relief Committee of Great Britain to march into Central Africa and rescue the governor of Equatoria. With funds provided partly from private sources and partly by the Egyptian Government, Stanley and his selected band of English officers had journeyed to Zanzibar, where they hired over 600 Zanzibari porters. Then proceeding by ship around the Cape of Good Hope to the mouth of the Congo, the expedition was transported up river by steamer to the Aruwimi, a tributary of the Congo. Here Stanley left the main body of the expedition to push slowly forward, while he and an advance column hastened eastward to effect a meeting with Emin Pasha as rapidly as possible. Arriving at Kavalli's at the south end of the Albert Lake on December 14, 1887, Stanley could obtain no news of Emin. Unable to search for the Pasha without the portable boat, which had been carried in pieces as far as Ibwiri at the edge of the great rain forest of the Congo, Stanley had little choice but to retrace his steps and retrieve it.[24] Leaving the sick and disabled at Ibwiri, Stanley returned to Kavalli's on April 18, 1888, with the intention of sailing northward in search of the Pasha. At Kavalli's, however, word was waiting for Stanley that Emin, apprised of his coming, had his steamers ready to bring Stanley to him.[25] The two men subsequently met on April 29, and after several days of discussion between Stanley and the governor, it was agreed that Emin would collect his people in preparation to leave the province.[26] Stanley, on the other hand, was to return to his rear column, which was struggling through the rain forest of the Aruwimi, and bring it up to the Albert Lake.

In accordance with the agreement made with Stanley, Emin, accompanied by one of Stanley's officers, Mounteney-Jephson, proceeded to the various stations to inform the men of the impending evacuation of the province. At first all went well, but at Dufile

24. Stanley, *I*, 331–35.
25. Ibid., pp. 389–92.
26. Ibid., pp. 416–17.

and Labore the officers and men, upon being presented with the plan of evacuation, refused to leave the province, mutinied, and imprisoned Emin and Mounteney-Jephson. The mutiny was engineered at first by the Egyptian officers, many of whom were former 'Urabists who had no desire to return to Egypt, but they soon lost control of the mutiny to the Sudanese jihādīya, who, being for the most part southerners, were even more vehement against leaving their homeland.[27] A military council was established by the mutineers to administer the province and to deal with the governor and his close associates, the deputy governor and the province apothecary. Emin was deposed on September 25, 1888, and placed under house arrest, and the council summarily elected Ḥamad Aghā governor, and Salīm Bey deputy governor.[28] But having deposed Emin, the mutineers could not decide what to do with him. Characteristically, they postponed a decision by bringing the former deputy governor and the province apothecary to trial for the maladministration of the province. By October 15 the council had completed the trial and had returned to the question of Emin Pasha, when the news came from Rajjāf that the Mahdists had returned to Equatoria and were surrounding the station.[29] Two days later three Anṣār whom 'Umar had sent with letters demanding the surrender of the province arrived at Dufile.[30] The appearance of these Anṣār threw the council into utter confusion, which the nightly orgies of the officers and men only made worse, but on October 19 the news of the capture of Rajjāf by the Mahdists seemed to stir the mutineers to action. In a fit of revenge the Anṣār who had brought the letters were clubbed to death, and an expedition led by the new governor, Ḥamad Aghā, was forthwith assembled to march on Rajjāf.[31] Ḥamad was particularly anxious to recapture the station in order to rescue his family as well as other

27. Mounteney-Jephson, pp. 199–200.

28. *Tagebücher, 4,* 162–63, September 25, 1888. Mounteney-Jephson, pp. 214–15. "Report on Equatoria, 1890," Cairint, I/11/56.

29. Mounteney-Jephson, pp. 241–42.

30. Ibid., pp. 243–53, 481.

31. Ḥamad Aghā's force probably consisted of well over 200 men in spite of the fact that Mounteney-Jephson wrote that only sixty men and three officers left for Rajjāf (Mounteney-Jephson, p. 255). This number, however, was undoubtedly increased by men from the garrisons north of Dufile.

Sudanese officers' families who had fallen into the hands of the Mahdists.[32]

'Umar Ṣāliḥ learned through spies of the approach of the Equatorial troops, and so after morning prayers on November 12 the Mahdists marched out from Rajjāf and ambushed the force led by Ḥamad Aghā by the banks of the Baḥr al-Jabal. The Equatorials were routed in a half-hour fight, many being driven into the river and drowned. Ḥamad Aghā and all his officers were killed as well as half the noncommissioned officers.[33] Out of the total force, only about fifty men escaped to Dufile and probably the same number managed to fight their way through hordes of Bari tribesmen to the safety of the Makaraka country to the west. The Bari, who had been the constant victims of cattle and slave raids by the Equatorial troops, were only too pleased to seize this opportunity to exact revenge.[34] 'Umar lost only six men.[35]

The news of the annihilation of Ḥamad Aghā and his men reached Dufile on November 14 and threw the garrison into a complete panic. It was resolved that Salīm Bey, the most able of the Sudanese officers, should be made governor and that the women and children as well as Emin, Casati, and Mounteney-Jephson should be sent down to Wadelai as soon as possible. They left for the south on November 17.[36] While the evacuation of civilians was taking place, Salīm Bey ordered all the posts north of Dufile to be abandoned and the other stations to concentrate their forces there.[37] Salīm Bey had about 1,200 men under his command.[38] 'Umar's force probably did not exceed 1,400.[39]

32. 'Umar Ṣāliḥ to the Khalīfa, Rabī' al-'Awwal 13, 1306 (November 17, 1888), Mahdīya, I/33/32.

33. "The Statement of Basili Bochtar," New York *Herald,* May 5, 1890.

34. Mounteney-Jephson, pp. 285–86. The Mahdists had greatly impressed the Negroid tribes of Equatoria with their fighting qualities. Always anxious to be on the winning side, it is little wonder that they flocked to the Mahdist standard after the defeat of Ḥamad Aghā.

35. 'Umar Ṣāliḥ to the Khalīfa, undated, Mahdīya, I/33/26.

36. *Tagebücher, 4,* 182, November 17, 1888. Mounteney-Jephson, pp. 288–89.

37. 'Umar Ṣāliḥ to the Khalīfa, Rabī' al-'Awwal 13, 1306 (November 17, 1888), Mahdīya, I/33/33.

38. "The Statement of Basili Bochtar," New York *Herald,* May 5, 1890.

39. 'Umar left Umm Durmān with less than 1,500 men. Eighty-nine were killed or missing at Rajjāf and in the battle against Ḥamad Aghā. Other deaths due to climate, wounds, etc. would probably have reduced the force to less

'Umar Ṣāliḥ and his men marched on Dufile and laid siege to the station on November 25. Early on the 28th the Mahdists attacked.[40] 'Umar described the battle in his letter to the Khalīfa:

> After three days of hard siege, they [the garrison of Dufile] sallied forth in a square; but the Anṣār attacked them sharply and they fled back to their fortifications. On the fourth day we agreed to rush their station by night. Nine colors proceeded to carry out the plan; the leaders being Ḥabīb 'Alī Munīr, Nāṣra al-Karrār, Aḥmad abū an-Nakhīla, Adam qad ar-Rāb, Muḥammad Raḥma, Muḥammad Makbūl, Mūsā Tanakka, Muḥammad Nūr al-Aḥmār, and Idrīs as-Sharīf. Some besieged the fortress on the south and some on the west. At dawn, after prayers, they attacked the station in one body, and some who were near the river found an entrance and got in with difficulty; but the rest could not discover any passage to enter, because the station was well fortified and strengthened from the inside by wood and earth and having very strong doors, with trenches outside. The infidels, being well screened inside their fortress, began to fire on our brethren who were crowded at the door, striking it with axes and swords, but it was too strong and well covered with iron, while all the time the enemies were shooting at them. God did not wish the fall of the Post, and our brethren did not like to retreat and so the bearers of eight colors fell dead with those fighting under them. Our brave brethren could have been heard one saying to the other, "Forward to the infidels, I am dying." The other would answer him, "I am dying also." The wounded would also say to their stout companions, "Forward." When they despaired from getting in and being ashamed to have God see them retreating, you could have seen the one clasp his hands as in a state of praying and bow his head to the ground, being ashamed of heaven and remain so up to his death, until nearly all were killed and the colors with the gallant commanders fell on the ground lifeless. But God saved the ninth color of Adam qad ar-Rāb. Those who entered the sta-

than 1,400 troops. Although the Bari would on occasion aid the Mahdists, they could not be relied upon to give constant support in battle.

40. 'Umar Ṣāliḥ to the Khalīfa, Rabī' al-'Awwal 13, 1306 (November 17, 1888), Mahdīya, I/33/33.

tion, although few, crushed many of God's enemies and killed the Captain and those with him. The bugle was sounded and the enemies surrounded our friends and the majority were killed but some were captured.[41]

For the other side of the battle, Salīm Bey wrote less vividly to Emin Pasha an account which is striking for its similarities with that of 'Umar:

On November 25 the Donagla [the Mahdists] surrounded the station and shouted out on all sides, "We are the Mahdi's people." At 4 P.M. they sent us another letter, repeating their commands to us to surrender, but the soldiers threw the letter out of the station back at them. The bearer of the letter, when asked why the people had come, gave no answer except that the Donagla wished to have the station in their hands. On the 26th they approached, and firing went on between us from 9 A.M. to 3 P.M., when a body of soldiers sallied out and drove away the attacking party, and killed twelve of them, besides wounding many; among our soldiers there were no losses. On the 27th the Donagla again approached and a good deal of firing went on until dawn. On this day were wounded Achmet Aga el Assinti, Bachit Aga Ali, and Suliman Aga Soudan; some were shot, and others were wounded by sword thrusts in their hands and feet. Some few soldiers and non-commissioned officers were also wounded in the same way. In the midst of the affray some of the Donagla actually entered the station and killed Mahomet Effendi el N'djar, the captain of the Nyanza steamer and Ali Achmet, the engineer, Mooragan Deror, the pilot, Khanis Salim, the chief fireman, and Farajala Moru, second fireman, all belonging to the Khedive steamer. After these accidents we mustered up all our energy to try to kill the Donagla who had entered the station. Towards 8 o'clock A.M., the battle was won by our soldiers, and the enemy dispersed. They left behind them 210 killed, besides those we were unable to count, and such wounded people as reached their camp. We captured eleven flags, and among them that of the

41. 'Umar Ṣāliḥ to the K͟halīfa, undated, Mahdīya, I/33/6–1.

Emir, some Remington rifles, percussion guns, and a lot of swords and spears; we also took one prisoner.[42]

Following the unsuccessful assault, the Mahdists withdrew to continue their siege of the station. Two days later the garrison at Dufile, led by Salīm Bey, rushed out in a square in an attempt to overwhelm the Anṣār, but after a hard-fought battle they were forced to return to the protection of their fortifications.[43] 'Umar continued the siege in spite of the shortage of ammunition until his Negroid scouts brought the news that the troops who had previously fled to the Makaraka country were marching toward Rajjāf with the intention of cutting off the Mahdists from their base.[44] 'Umar therefore retreated to Rajjāf to await reinforcements from Umm Durmān.

Although one source claimed that "nearly all the Dervishes [Mahdists] were exterminated" in the six-hour battle at Dufile, it is more probable that 'Umar's losses were not as heavy as imagined.[45] In all probability he lost no more than the 250 men he himself claimed, for the figure corresponds with Salīm Bey's estimate.[46] But the Mahdists had been so chastened and weakened that they were unable to take the offensive against the Equatorial troops. They remained at Rajjāf, where they were able to keep a close watch, through spies, on the rapidly changing scene in Equatoria.

The Rebellion of Faḍl al-Mūlā Bey Muḥammad and the Departure of Stanley

When the news of Ḥamad Aghā's defeat had reached Dufile, Emin, Jephson, and Casati had been released from imprisonment and sent down to Wadelai. Here Emin was given a surprising welcome for one who had just spent the last three months in prison for the "maladministration of the province"; and, taking

42. Mounteney-Jephson, pp. 327–28.

43. 'Umar Ṣāliḥ to the K͟halīfa, undated, Mahdīya, I/33/6–1.

44. 'Umar Ṣāliḥ to the K͟halīfa, Rabī' al-'Awwal 13, 1306 (November 17, 1888), Mahdīya, I/33/33.

45. "The Statement of Basili Bochtar," New York *Herald,* May 5, 1890.

46. 'Umar Ṣāliḥ to the K͟halīfa, undated, Mahdīya, I/33/25.

command of the station, he began to prepare for the defense and for the reception of the refugees streaming south from Dufile and the northern stations.[1] On December 4, 1888, the commandant of the small station of Bora, north of Wadelai, came in with the news that Dufile and Fabbo had fallen to the Mahdists and that the Bari tribesmen, taking advantage of the Government's discomfiture, were pillaging the countryside.[2] A council was held, and it was decided that Wadelai should be abandoned and that the garrison should retire to Tunguru on the Albert Lake.[3] The evacuation began on December 6, but before it could be completed a steamer came from the north with the news that Salīm Bey and his troops had, in fact, beaten off the Mahdists, who had subsequently returned to Rajjāf. On hearing the news, many of the evacuees returned to Wadelai, but Emin decided to go on to Tunguru.[4] During the ensuing weeks Salīm Bey constantly sent to Emin reports of his activities, the purport of which was that he, Salīm Bey, was evacuating Dufile and going to Wadelai and he hoped Emin would return and resume his position as governor.[5] The evacuation was completed by January 15, 1889, but Emin remained inactive at Tunguru.

On January 26, 1889, news reached Tunguru that Stanley had arrived for the third time at the Albert Lake, on the 18th.[6] Nine months before, he had marched back from the Lake to Banalya on the Upper Aruwimi, where he had met what was left of his rear guard. All the officers were dead but one, Mr. Jameson, and almost half the porters had deserted or died. Stanley collected the remnants of this force and started again for the Albert Lake, which he reached after an arduous journey of five months.

The news of Stanley's return greatly disturbed the officers at Wadelai. They had rebelled against Emin, the Khedivial governor, and now feared that Stanley would march against them from the south while the Mahdists attacked from the north. Moreover the arrival of Stanley had made the hitherto remote possibility of go-

1. *Tagebücher, 4,* 182–85, November 18–December 3, 1888.

2. Mounteney-Jephson, pp. 315–16. "The Statement of Basili Bochtar," New York *Herald,* May 5, 1890. *Tagebücher, 4,* 185–86, December 4, 1888.

3. Ibid.

4. Mounteney-Jephson, pp. 331–32. *Tagebücher, 4,* 188–90, December 6, 1888.

5. "The Statement of Basili Bochtar," New York *Herald,* May 5, 1890.

6. *Tagebücher, 4,* 205–08, January 26, 1888.

ing to Egypt a definite reality and forced the officers and men to decide whether to remain in Equatoria or to leave for Cairo.[7] During the ensuing discussions the officers divided; one faction, led by Faḍl al-Mūlā Bey Muḥammad, was anxious to remain in Equatoria under any conditions, while the other, led by Salīm Aghā Bey, wanted to make peace with Emin and join Stanley in his forthcoming march to the coast. After a violent debate the party led by Salīm Aghā Bey prevailed, and it was decided by a vote of the officers' council to send a deputation to Stanley to inform the great explorer of their desire to join him and to discuss the preparations necessary for the march to Zanzibar.[8]

On February 17, 1889, the deputation reached Kavalli's, where Stanley was camped. On the following day a great council was held. It was decided that the evacuation of the province should be carried out with all possible speed,[9] and on February 26 Salīm Bey and his deputation departed northward to collect the people of Equatoria and bring them to Kavalli's. But before Salīm Bey was able to effect an evacuation, Faḍl al-Mūlā Bey Muḥammad, the commandant at Wadelai and the leader of those opposed to joining Stanley, "had suborned the greater part of the troops and with them, in the dead of night, he marched to the magazines, possessed himself of all the ammunition and left Wadelai for the hills." [10] Meanwhile, at Kavalli's the officers and men from Equatoria carried on one intrigue after another against the Relief Expedition. These machinations culminated on the night of April 4 in an attempt by the Egyptian officers to steal the rifles of Stanley's Zanzibaris. The following day Stanley in a fury addressed the whole assembly and stated that he would wait not a day longer than April 10.[11] True to his word, he marched out of Kavalli's on the appointed day with Emin Pasha and those people of Equatoria who had arrived at the station.

7. 'Umar Ṣāliḥ to the Khalīfa, Rabī' al-'Awwal 13, 1306 (November 17, 1888), Mahdīya, I/33/29.

8. Mounteney-Jephson, pp. 450–53. "The Statement of Basili Bochtar," New York *Herald*, May 5, 1890.

9. Stanley, 2, 151–55.

10. "The Report on the Arrival in Cairo of Twenty-one Officers and Non-Commissioned Officers with their Families from Equatoria via Mombasa, June, 1892," Cairint, I/35/205.

11. Stanley, 2, 198–206. Wingate, p. 463. *Tagebücher, 4*, 247–48, April 5, 1889.

The rebellion of Faḍl al-Mūlā had paralyzed all of Salīm Bey's hitherto feeble efforts to effect an evacuation; and after visiting Wadelai he returned to Tunguru.[12] Here on April 22, Salīm wrote to Stanley requesting him to await his arrival. Stanley replied that he would wait for him on the other side of the Semliki River and that if Salīm wished he could easily overtake the slow-moving caravan.[13] This was the last communication that passed between the Relief Column and Salīm Bey. Upon receiving this news, Salīm was presented with a dilemma. He could not return to Wadelai because of the presence of a well-armed force under Faḍl al-Mūlā in the hills; yet he himself had only a few men at Tunguru, while the rest were scattered along the road to Wadelai. While he was trying to decide what to do, deserters from Stanley's column returned to Kavalli's and pointed out to a small detachment of Salīm Bey's troops the spot where Stanley had buried eighteen boxes of powder and twenty-five boxes of ammunition.[14]

> The news of the find shortly afterward reached Fadl Maula Bey who on quitting Wadelai had encamped in the Wanzari and Asi Hills between Mswa and Wadelai and whose force had in the meantime been augmented by most of the troops and followers whom Salim Bey had been collecting and who had decided to throw in their lot with Fadl Maula when they learnt that Stanley had left the country. Fadl Maula at once despatched a party of 380 men with orders to seize the ammunition at Kavalli's; this they succeeded in doing, though the garrison at Kavalli's managed to secrete 5 boxes; this party on their return to Fadl Maula passed through Mswa where they ill-treated and imprisoned Salim Bey but subsequently released him and he returned with the few followers who still remained with him to Kavalli's. Here he planted the Egyptian flag and hoped that relief would eventually be sent him from the coast. His total garrison amounted to about 90 men with 300 women and children. Eight days after his arrival he was attacked by the natives and lost 50 of his men. This was a reprisal on the part of the Blacks on account of Stanley's recent

12. "The Report on the Arrival . . . from Equatoria," Cairint, I/35/205.
13. Stanley, 2, 223–27.
14. "The Report on the Arrival . . . from Equatoria," Cairint, I/35/205.

attack on them. After this severe loss, Salim Bey sought the assistance of Sheikh Kavalli who willingly came forward and warned the Blacks to desist from hostilities as, if Stanley returned, they would undoubtedly be all killed. After this Salim Bey remained in peace at Kavalli's, established a small settlement, and had little or no communication with Equatoria.[15]

Faḍl al-Mūlā, finding that he could not retain his large force in the hills, returned to Wadelai.

'Umar Ṣāliḥ in Equatoria, 1888–1890

After 'Umar Ṣāliḥ had established himself at Rajjāf, he took up the question of conquering the territory which spread east and west from the banks of the Baḥr al-Jabal. It was a vast country with large quantities of arms and ammunition in the hands of the Negroids, a fact 'Umar spared no pains to point out to the Khalīfa. Many of these Negroids had been induced to leave their tribes and follow former government officials, Danāqla merchants, or even deserters from the jihādīya who would set themselves up as local potentates with their own private armies. Often these private armies would number as high as a thousand well-armed men.[1] So attractive was the promise of loot, freedom from army regulations, and, in general, a free and irresponsible existence that not only Negroid tribesmen but fugitives from the government battalions swelled the ranks. Particularly after the revolts against the amīr Karam Allāh in the Baḥr al-Ghazāl, many jihādīya fled south into Equatoria, where they materially added to the power of those rulers who took them into their personal armies. These potentates often clashed with the local tribes in their raids for slaves and ivory, but more often they worked closely with the local people in depredations against more distant tribes. Indeed it is impossible to distinguish the private armies from the tribes, for more often than not the tribal head was a Turk, Arab, or former jihādī who had simply replaced the hereditary, tribal leaders and maintained his position of tribal chief by force and power. It was only the

15. Ibid.
1. 'Umar Ṣāliḥ to the Khalīfa, Ṣafar 21, 1306 (October 27, 1888), Mahdīya, I/33/12.

very largest and strongest tribes that were able to preserve their integrity against these marauders, who, unchecked by any authority, wandered throughout Equatoria hastening the distintegration of government, tribal as well as Egyptian, and creating anarchy, chaos, and disorder.

When 'Umar first came into the country, he had realized that if he was to achieve his primary purposes—capture of Emin Pasha and destruction of the Egyptian Administration—it would be necessary not only to show clearly the military might of the Anṣār but to treat the powerful local rulers with kindness and toleration. He was particularly careful not to take anything from the Negroid tribes without payment or exchange. Without a doubt it was this policy of toleration and the impressive fighting qualities of the Anṣār which led many tribes, such as the Bari, to join the Mahdists in battle against the hated Turk or, if not take an active part in the actual fighting, to hang on the flanks and the rear of the Equatorial troops and slaughter the stragglers and fugitives. This was not an unusual procedure. Frequently Negroid tribesmen would remain inactive during a battle until it was clear who would be defeated and then rush as a staunch ally to the side of the victor. But if the attitude of the Negroids was one of watchful aloofness, the general attitude of the Anṣār toward the natives was one of contempt. The sophisticated Arab with a culture and tradition centuries old felt, not unnaturally, that he was superior to the simple African who was created by Allāh to be a slave. Indeed, the letters of 'Umar Ṣāliḥ reflect this attitude. The words "slave" and "Negro" have been interchangeable in the Arabic language for centuries; the general Arab treatment of the Negroids in Equatoria appears to bear out this relationship, which still exists and is the most unfortunate legacy of the Mahdīya in the Southern Sudan. Certainly it is one of the major problems of the modern Sudan. But Anṣār-Negroid relations appear to have been satisfactory throughout 1888; and it was only after the Egyptian Administration had disappeared and left the Negroids and the Mahdists without a common enemy that the contempt of the Anṣār for the Negroid helped to produce the fighting which soon broke out when the Mahdists attempted to impose their rule and religion on the tribes.

The question of authority was paramount to the Negroid, who was, generally speaking, uninterested in Islam and Mahdism. To the Negroids, the defeat and dispersal of the Egyptian Administration signaled a return to the days before the Turkīya, when the tribe was left to its own devices to conquer and to defend itself as best it might in an Equatoria inhabited by a conglomeration of independent, sovereign tribes. The Mahdists did not look upon the matter in this way. The administration had been defeated by the soldiers of the K͟halīfa, and so, logically, the rule of the K͟halīfa should simply supplant that of the Egyptian Government. The Mahdists expected to impose their authority on the tribes just as the Egyptians had done before them, even if it required the force of arms to establish what they regarded as their right. Obviously, these very divergent views could only result in war. But a further Mahdist hope was the imposition of their religion as well as their rule.

Certainly, to 'Umar's disappointment, the Negroids were indifferent to Mahdism.[2] It is true that the primary aim of the Mahdist invasion of Equatoria was the destruction of the last vestige of Egyptian rule in the Sudan; but the driving force of Mahdism was religion, and if the capture of Emin Pasha and the destruction of his administraion were the goals of the campaign, the conversion of the people of Equatoria, which was a fundamental part of militant Mahdism, was synonymous with their conquest. Mahdism was uncompromising. If the Negroids had no faith in the religion of the Mahdists, it was only by the sword that conquest and conversion could become a reality. 'Umar wrote: "They [the Negroids] cannot be brought to surrender except by establishing stations from which patrols can be sent one after another to get hold of them and the arms which they have."[3] Even after the Mahdist victory at Rajjāf, it was necessary to march the whole force out of the station every time they foraged for food. If they had not, Negroid tribesmen would have fallen on the small detachments and cut them to pieces. Such tactics left the station with little protection and caused much anxiety to 'Umar. He urgently requested the K͟halīfa to send him sufficient men not only to protect the station

2. Ibid.
3. Ibid.

when foraging but also to disarm the Negroids, establish Mahdist rule over them, and convert them to Mahdism.[4] The disarming of the Negroids was the only way to conquer, administer, and convert the country.

After the defeat of Ḥamad Aghā and the destruction of his force, the attitude of the surrounding native tribes toward the Mahdists underwent a decisive change. Although the Negroids had viewed the coming of the Mahdists with hostile neutrality, the Anṣār's victories produced a greater respect for the powers of Mahdism.[5]

> [The Negroids] thought it a mystery to achieve victory by the use of spears against firearms. They asked how we could fight them with spears while the Turks claim that they are the masters of war and that the spears cannot compete with firearms. We the Anṣār told them that all of the Turks who were in the Sudan were killed by the Anṣār's spears and swords. They could not believe this until they saw it done before their eyes. They were astonished and claimed that this is not from the spears but from the words of the Mahdī.[6]

According to 'Umar, a great number of chiefs came in to declare their fealty to the Khalīfa, and they and their followers adopted the dress of the Anṣār and a few even adopted Islam.[7] It is unknown how deep this conversion went. Most probably it was superficial at best and confined only to the tribes in and around Rajjāf who had suffered most at the hands of government officials and who would most benefit by accepting the religion of the Mahdists.[8] The declarations of allegiance were also not to be taken seriously. The Negroids would fight at the first attempt by the Mahdists to disarm and to rule, let alone convert them. They knew well that once disarmed they were helpless against predators —Negroid, Arab, or European. To disarm was to conquer, and the Negroids, freed from one master, were not anxious to have an-

4. Ibid.
5. 'Umar Ṣāliḥ to the Khalīfa, undated, Mahdīya, I/33/22.
6. Ibid.
7. Ibid.
8. 'Umar Ṣāliḥ to the Khalīfa, Ṣafar 21, 1306 (October 27, 1888), Mahdīya, I/33/20.

other. The only alternative was to fight the Mahdists as they had fought the Turks before them and the neighboring tribes before that. Frequently, however, the Mahdists would ally with a powerful Negroid chief, particularly in their expeditions to western Equatoria, where they desired a base of operations. Such alliances were mutually beneficial. The chief would get assistance in destroying his troublesome neighbors, while the Mahdists would extend their control and gain much plunder. Often, however, when the Anṣār had finished with the services of a chief, he, too, would be stripped of his power and wealth just like his neighbors.

Throughout the year following the Battle of Dufile, 'Umar struggled constantly to disarm and to control both the Negroids and the irregular soldiers who had taken shelter in the tribal villages and who, in many cases, had imposed their will on the unfortunate inhabitants. The Mahdists were ill-trained and inadequate in numbers to bring these tribesmen and fugitive soldiers into subjection. Request after request was made to the Khalīfa in Umm Durmān for troops equipped with Remington repeating rifles and "trained as in the old days." [9] Occasionally, 'Umar would be able to incorporate local irregulars among his veterans, particularly when they were Arabs.[10] But such occasions must have been few indeed, for the size of the Mahdist army, after taking into account deaths due to the climate, showed little appreciable increase; consequently, progress in disarming the natives was painfully slow. It is doubtful if 'Umar ever really controlled much of the countryside surrounding Rajjāf, in spite of the fact that fear of the Mahdists spread far and wide. Certainly the letters of 'Umar during the next three years were a recitation of countless, futile skirmishes with the natives, of conquests and defeats, hardships and death in the cruel climate of Rajjāf.

The infrequent and tenuous communications with Umm Durmān did not help to alleviate 'Umar's difficulties. After the Battle of Rajjāf, 'Umar sent a steamer under the command of Muḥammad

9. 'Umar Ṣāliḥ to the Khalīfa, undated, Mahdīya, I/33/27. The phrase "trained as in the old days," probably refers to jihādīya of the Egyptian army, who were, all things considered, relatively well-trained troops. Many of these, of course, had been incorporated into the Khalīfa's army

10. 'Umar Ṣāliḥ to the Khalīfa, Muḥarram 22, 1307 (September 18, 1889), Mahdīya, I/33/36.

Khair Bādī with ivory and slaves to Umm Durmān.[11] The steamer started late in 1888 and had a long and arduous journey. It was probably detained by the sadd, for Father Ohrwalder does not report its appearance at Umm Durmān until June 1889, nearly seven months after leaving Rajjāf.[12] Muḥammad Khair Bādī had been instructed to relate to the Khalīfa what had taken place in Equatoria and to request the return of the steamer immediately with reinforcements. Consequently, after a few days the steamer again headed up the Nile to Equatoria, with several hundred men from the Khalīfa's own tribe, the Ta'ā'isha, as well as from the Banī Ḥusayn and the Kabābīsh—all under the command of 'Alī Mukhtār Bakrī.[13]

The steamer reached its destination in September 1889, for 'Umar wrote at that time that 'Alī Mukhtār Bakrī had arrived with a "number of Ta'ā'isha men" and that the ship was returning at once to the North with a load of ivory.[14] Again reports were carried back of the difficulties 'Umar had encountered. In spite of the reinforcements just received from Umm Durmān, 'Umar's force consisted of less than 1,400 men.[15] He reiterated to the Khalīfa the great difficulty which the Mahdists had encountered in trying to conduct military operations in the Southern Sudan. Equatoria was a vast country with much rain and grass and many rivers, streams, and dense woods, all making military operations ex-

11. 'Umar Ṣāliḥ to the Khalīfa, Ṣafar 21, 1306 (October 27, 1888), Mahdīya, I/33/14.

12. Ohrwalder, *Ten Years' Captivity in the Mahdi's Camp*, pp. 269–70. The Khalīfa, not hearing from 'Umar for over a year, feared that his force had been destroyed by Emin Pasha.

13. 'Umar Ṣāliḥ to the Khalīfa, Muḥarram 1307 (September 1889), Mahdīya, I/33/56, 57, 58. The Banī Ḥusayn and the Kabābīsh tribes had revolted against the rule of the Khalīfa and had been unmercifully crushed. The men sent to Equatoria under Mukhtār Bakrī were the pitiful remnants being sent into exile. The steamer probably carried no more than 300 men.

14. 'Umar Ṣāliḥ to the Khalīfa, Muḥarram 1307 (September 1889), Mahdīya, I/33/56, 57; Muḥarram 22, 1307 (September 18, 1889), Mahdīya, I/33/46.

15. 'Umar Ṣāliḥ to the Khalīfa, Muḥarram 22, 1307 (September 18, 1889), Mahdīya, I/33/47. To be exact there were 1,391 men of whom 915 were riflemen and 467 spearmen. If 'Umar had 1,142 men after the Battle of Dufile (November 1888) and a steamer arrived in September 1889 with 300 additional troops, his total force would be 1,442 not counting deaths from the climate and skirmishes with the Negroids.

tremely troublesome.[16] 'Umar requested donkeys, to facilitate marches through the countryside; currency for the Anṣār, so that they might buy wives; and clothes, for there were none in Equatoria.[17] Also, the small steamer *Muhammad Ali* was required for navigation in the narrow and sadd-choked channels of the Baḥr al-Jabal.[18] But 'Umar's greatest problem was the inability to recruit reinforcements. He wrote: "There is no possibility of any recruitment or increase of the army, as is the case in other places in the Arab countries. Those Negroids whom we conquer cannot stand our customs, nor can they practice our rules, for they find our life very strange. This religion of ours is very difficult for them to understand and follow and so they desert us." [19] Therefore, if local recruitment was impossible, it was necessary for the Khalīfa to send reinforcements to Rajjāf. But this was not the entire solution, for the reinforcements quickly died in the harsh climate. Of the Banī Ḥusayn and the Kabābīsh who came with Mukhtār Bakrī, one-third of the former and two-thirds of the latter died shortly after arriving in the South. The *rāyya* (flag) commanded by the amīr Rufā'a numbered ninety-one men; a year later there were only seventy remaining.[20] The death rate at Rajjāf was estimated by 'Umar at twenty a day, but this is undoubtedly an exaggeration. He calmly wrote to the Khalīfa: "Because of the severe climate, the men we need here must be very strong." [21] The only men who seemed sufficiently strong were, ironically, the Khalīfa's own tribesmen, the Ta'ā'isha.

The second steamer sent north by 'Umar in September 1889 arrived at Umm Durmān in midwinter of 1889–90. The Khalīfa, obviously pleased with the ivory and slaves, was encouraged by

16. 'Umar Ṣāliḥ to the Khalīfa, Muḥarram 1307 (September 1889), Mahdīya, I/33/58.
17. 'Umar Ṣāliḥ to the Khalīfa, Muḥarram 25, 1307 (September 21, 1889), Mahdīya, I/33/54.
18. 'Umar Ṣāliḥ to the Khalīfa, Muḥarram 25, 1307 (September 21, 1889), Mahdīya, I/33/50. The usual currency in the Southern Sudan was copper or iron.
19. 'Umar Ṣāliḥ to the Khalīfa, Muḥarram 1307 (September 1889), Mahdīya, I/33/58.
20. 'Umar Ṣāliḥ to the Khalīfa, Jumādā al'Ūlā 12, 1309 (December 14, 1891), Mahdīya, I/33/93.
21. 'Umar Ṣāliḥ to the Khalīfa, Muḥarram 1307 (September 1889), Mahdīya, I/33/58.

wad Bādī to outfit another expedition. But rather than waste his best troops in the enervating climate, he decided to make Rajjāf a place of exile to which would be sent all those who incurred his displeasure.[22] Therefore, he dispatched a steamer filled with convicts and political prisoners to the South under the command of Ḥasīb wad Aḥmad and Ilyās 'Alī Kannūna.[23] Making a slow journey up river, they seized many of the Shilluks who lived along the banks of the White Nile and plundered their villages, causing great destruction. Without a doubt it was the large supply of grain and the numerous slaves sent to Umm Durmān by the expedition as well as the reports of their predecessors who, returning from Rajjāf, had passed by these Nilotic villages that finally lured the Khalīfa to send a separate and very powerful expedition under Zākī Ṭamal to conquer the Shilluks.[24]

By the summer of 1890 'Umar's force had swollen to over 2,300 fighting men. This increase of nearly 1,000 troops over the number under 'Umar's command the year before was the result not only of the arrival in Equatoria of political exiles from Umm Durmān but of the success 'Umar was at last having with local recruitment. He wrote to the Khalīfa in August that over 500 of the nearby tribesmen had been enrolled as jihādīya in the Mahdist ranks.[25] This unaccustomed recruitment after the poor results earlier was not surprising, for 'Umar was slowly and inexorably taking over the country. After Emin and Stanley had withdrawn

22. See above, p. 58.

23. Slatin, *Fire and Sword in the Sudan,* p. 470. Ohrwalder, p. 271.

24. Zākī Ṭamal (d. 1893) was a member of the Mandala, a half-Ta'ā'isha serf community. He was made an amīr al-umarā' and saw much active service in Dār Fūr. Later he led the Mahdist invasion of Abyssinia and won a victory near Gondar in 1887. In 1889 he commanded the Mahdist army that won a decisive victory over a huge Abyssinian host at al-Qallābāt after King John, the Abyssinian commander, had been killed. In 1891 he commanded an expedition to the Shilluk country in which a large number of slaves were captured but no permanent conquest of the Shilluks made. Later he was accused by the amīr Aḥmad wad 'Alī Aḥmad of conspiring to hand over Kasala to the Italians. Summoned to Umm Durmān he was immured in a small stone hut and starved to death. See Hill, p. 389.

25. 'Umar Ṣāliḥ to the Khalīfa, Dhū al-Ḥijja 1307 (August 1890), Mahdīya, I/33/65; undated, Mahdīya, I/35/89. There were precisely 2,367 men at Rajjāf, of whom 1,518 were riflemen and 949 were spearmen. If 'Umar recruited locally 567 troops as jihādīya, this would leave 409 men to come by steamer from Umm Durmān—a not unreasonable number for a large steamer to carry

to the coast and Salīm Bey had settled himself at Kavalli's, there was only Faḍl al-Mūlā at Wadelai to concern the Mahdists. Consequently, 'Umar had his men occupy the former Egyptian stations between Rajjāf and Wadelai (i.e. Muggi, Kirri, Bedden, etc.). From these stations Mahdist expeditions went into the countryside to conquer the tribes, exact tribute in ivory and slaves, and disarm the scattered remnants of the Equatorial Battalions. These had largely dispersed to the native villages, where they joined a local ruler or set up their own miniature kingdoms supported by their guns. But the conquest was slow, painful, and costly to the Mahdists, who lost many men in the countless skirmishes and pitched battles. Fortunately for the Anṣār the Equatorial troops were often at odds with the Negroid tribesmen. In many cases the tribesmen, having suffered for years at the hands of the troops, would capture, disarm, and carry them to the Mahdists. If the Negroids were not forward in doing so, there was always the fear that they would be attacked in turn by the Anṣār and driven, for self-preservation, to submit to the fugitive soldiery.[26] In August 1890 'Umar declared to the Khalīfa that all the chiefs and sultans up to the borders of the Baḥr al-Ghazāl had surrendered to the Mahdists, but surely the vast majority of these submissions were at best nominal.

After the Battle of Dufile in November 1888, 'Umar sent powerful expeditions to the west, which, penetrating into the Makaraka country, occupied all the abandoned Egyptian stations and secured the support of Aya Tambia, the Chief of the Makaraka.[27] Aya Tambia not only supported the Mahdists, but he and his family became some of the few ardent converts to Mahdism. It was through his good services that the Anṣār were able to remain in the Makaraka country, for the chief not only supplied them with corn, but he and his men fought beside the Mahdists in many battles.[28] With his supplies and men, 'Umar was able to send expeditions over the Congo-Nile watershed into the valley of the Uele. But there the Mahdists

26. 'Umar Ṣāliḥ to the Khalīfa, Dhū al-Ḥijja 1307 (August 1890), Mahdīya, I/33/78.

27. R. P. L. Lotar, *La Grande Chronique de l'Uele* (Brussels, 1946), p. 138. 'Umar Ṣāliḥ to the Khalīfa, Jumādā al-'Ūlā 1309 (December 1891), Mahdīya, I/33/92.

28. 'Umar Ṣāliḥ to the Khalīfa, Jumādā al-'Ūlā 1309 (December 1891), Mahdīya, I/33/92.

were continually harassed by the Logos, who killed many of the Anṣār and, in one engagement, captured two flags and twenty Remington rifles.[29] In 1890 the revolt of a *kujur* (witch doctor) in Makaraka resulted in the recall of these expeditions fighting in the valley of the Uele. Again with the aid of Chief Aya, the Mahdists were able to suppress the uprising but so exhausted their ammunition that they were forced to retreat to Rajjāf, carrying the supplies and ivory plundered from the villages with them.[30] The chief, accompanied by his own troops, abandoned his territory and returned with the Anṣār to Rajjāf, but his men deserted one by one until only he was left. Still true to his new faith Aya Tambia swore allegiance to Mahdism and left for Umm Durmān on the next steamer, where he was presented to the Khalīfa.[31]

While the expedition to the west had failed to secure any permanent success, the Mahdist forces in the valley of the Baḥr al-Jabal had, between 1889 and 1890, achieved notable victories over the riverain tribes and had even won several battles over interior tribes east of the Nile, culminating in the conquest of the inhabitants of Jabal Warak on September 15, 1890.[32] But the continuous fighting and the unhealthy climate consistently took a large toll of 'Umar's force. After the disastrous fight at Wadelai in March 1891, in which the Mahdists were reported to have lost 700 men, 'Umar began to lose the supremacy over the riverain tribes which had been won the previous year, and by the autumn he was having great difficulty maintaining his position against the inexhaustible supply of hostile Negroid tribesmen.

Faḍl al-Mūlā and the Mahdists, 1889–1891

While the Mahdists were gradually occupying the stations abandoned by the Equatorial troops, Faḍl al-Mūlā, unable to support his large force in the hills, decided to return to Wadelai. He was en-

29. Lotar, *Chronique de l'Uele,* p. 138.

30. 'Umar Ṣāliḥ to the Khalīfa, undated, Mahdīya, I/33/94.

31. 'Umar Ṣāliḥ to the Khalīfa, Jumādā al-'Ūlā 1309 (December 1891), Mahdīya, I/33/92.

32. 'Umar Ṣāliḥ to the Khalīfa, undated, Mahdīya, I/33/87. To facilitate the Mahdist expeditions into the interior of Equatoria east of the Nile, 'Umar had erected a temporary zarība at Lokila. Jabal Warak appears to have been the Mahdist name for Jabal Lafon inhabited by the Berri tribe.

couraged to move by some seventy or eighty Danāqla who still remained with him. These Danāqla had for a long time been secretly communicating with the Mahdists at Rajjāf, and Faḍl al-Mūlā approved rather than discouraged this contact. There is little doubt that the return to Wadelai was merely part of a larger plot in which the Danāqla were to seize and destroy the ammunition at Wadelai and so enable the Mahdists to attack the station and capture the Equatorial troops. The plot was revealed, however, by a Dunqulāwī at Faḍl al-Mūlā's camp in the hills, and the Equatorial soldiers in their fury slaughtered all the Danāqla but their informant. As Faḍl al-Mūlā had been directly involved in the conspiracy, his position was extremely precarious; but the troops were reluctant to do away with the only superior governmental officer remaining in Equatoria.[1]

In spite of the insecure circumstances in which he found himself, Faḍl al-Mūlā persisted in communicating with the Mahdists. After the massacre of the Danāqla, he sent his steamer to Dufile, ostensibly to see if the station was clear of Mahdists; in reality, emissaries were on board "bearing a letter from Fadl Maula to the Dervish commander giving him full information as to his force and the events which had occurred and offering them his submission." [2] The emissaries proceeded to Dufile, where they disembarked and went overland to Kirri and finally to Rajjāf. "In reply the Dervish commander gave a full account of the Mahdi's and the Khalifa's victories, representing that the entire Sudan was in their hands, that they hereby nominated Fadl Maula an Emir and that they would shortly arrive at Wadelai." [3] Meanwhile, Faḍl al-Mūlā had succeeded in moving his men and their many camp followers to Wadelai, where he received 'Umar's reply. When the news of what their commander had done spread to the troops, they ignored Faḍl al-Mūlā's overtures to the Mahdists and prepared to resist. The Equatorial troops had no desire to be taken captive by the Anṣār, sent north to Umm Durmān, and enrolled in the jihādīya, and undoubtedly many believed that they were loyally defending the province for the Khedive against invading rebels. It was far better and, in the minds of the Equatorials, the only loyal course of action to risk a battle in order to retain their position in Equatoria as well

1. "The Report on the Arrival . . . from Equatoria," Cairint, I/35/205.
2. Ibid.
3. Ibid.

as the last vestiges of Egyptian rule than lose all to the Mahdists by uncontested capitulation. It is more difficult to understand the actions of Faḍl al-Mūlā. At first they appear to indicate that he was most anxious to join the Mahdists, but his later actions against them seem to belie any interest whatsoever in Mahdism. Most probably his intrigues with the Anṣār were only his way of ensuring his acceptance by them in the event of the destruction of his force. Faḍl al-Mūlā was an opportunist who by playing one party against the other hoped to win for himself the most favorable position possible. This attitude would explain not only his later alliance with the Congolese but also his hostile attitude toward the Mahdists after their defeat at Wadelai.

Thus when the Anṣār appeared before Wadelai, they were much surprised at being received with volleys of rifle fire instead of the joyful welcome they had anticipated. 'Umar, infuriated, ordered the assault of the station, but his force was driven off with a loss of 700 men, the Equatorials losing only eighty-nine.[4] The Mahdists retreated to Rajjāf, where 'Umar wrote an angry letter complaining, not unnaturally, of Faḍl al-Mūlā's bad faith. Meanwhile at Wadelai 800 Equatorial troops broke with Faḍl al-Mūlā and left in March 1891 with plenty of ammunition and 10,000 camp followers to join Salīm Bey at Kavalli's. 'Umar sent a detachment of Anṣār to overtake and destroy this horde, but "they failed to do so."[5] Faḍl al-Mūlā escaped to the south by steamer but later returned to Wadelai with his followers. The size of his force at this time is difficult to estimate. Certainly, when the Congolese came in 1892, he did not have over 500 men; but he had lost a considerable number, not only in fights with the surrounding tribes during foraging expeditions, but also in frequent encounters with the Mahdists.[6] Faḍl

4. The loss of 700 men on the part of the Mahdists is probably accurate. 'Umar, in December 1891, recorded the strength of his force as 1,338 ['Umar Ṣāliḥ to the Khalīfa, Jumādā al-'Ūlā 12, 1309 (December 14, 1891), Mahdīya, I/33/116]. This represents a loss of 1,029 men since the summer of 1890. If 700 were killed in the Battle of Wadelai, that would leave 329 deaths to be accounted for by the Battle of Jabal Warak, skirmishes with the natives, and the climate.

5. 'Umar Ṣāliḥ to the Khalīfa, Jumādā al-'Ūlā 1309 (December 1891), Mahdīya, I/33/84.

6. Lotar, *Chronique de l'Uele,* p. 140.

al-Mūlā did not remain long at Wadelai. After an epidemic of smallpox had swept through the station, he moved his camp two hours' march downstream to Bora.

The Arrival of al-Ḥājj Muḥammad abū Qarja in Equatoria

After the great loss at Wadelai, the Mahdists could no longer hold their own against the Negroids without reinforcements from the North. And these did not come. In December 1891 'Umar had only 1,300 men, of whom fewer than 500 possessed Remington repeating rifles.[1] This was an adequate force to control a few posts, but it was certainly insufficient to hold all the river stations, let alone those of the interior. The riverain tribes were only too well aware of this fact, and it was not long before they were in rebellion. The revolt appears to have begun when the amīr Ḥasīb was sent with two steamers to a landing two days' journey downstream from Rajjāf to collect ivory. Here the Mahdists were suddenly attacked by the Negroids, who killed all of Ḥasīb's men except a few who, led by the amīr himself, escaped in one of the steamers.[2] The other fell into the hands of the natives. Ḥasīb returned to Rajjāf and was later sent north to Umm Durmān in October 1891 with a load of ivory. Upon arriving and explaining to the Khalīfa the desperate situation in Equatoria, he was ordered to return immediately with reinforcements and to recover the missing steamer.[3] Some of the men who came to Umm Durmān with Ḥasīb said that the tribesmen had been stirred up by Emin Pasha, who had returned to Kavalli's in April 1891.[4] There seems, however, to be no foundation to this story, for Emin Pasha, after leaving Kavalli's, vanished into the heart of the Congo to the west, where he was later killed by an Arab slave trader.[5] Nevertheless, the rumors of Emin Pasha's return sufficiently disturbed the Khalīfa to cause him to send the Dun-

1. 'Umar Ṣāliḥ to the Khalīfa, Jumādā al-'Ūlā 12, 1309 (December 14, 1891), Mahdīya, I/33/116. 'Umar had under his command, to be precise, 1,338 men, 670 of whom had single-shot, breech-loading rifles, 173 had double-barreled rifles, and 495 had Remington repeaters.
2. Ohrwalder, p. 271.
3. Intelligence Report, Egypt, No. 1, April 1892, Appendix A.
4. Ohrwalder, p. 271.
5. "The Report on the Arrival . . . from Equatoria," Cairint, I/35/205.

qulāwī amīr Kunna Mujāhid in a special steamer in 1892 to ascertain if the news of Emin's return was correct.[6]

The revolt of the Negroids in Equatoria appears to have spread rapidly once it was known that the Anṣār did not have the means to suppress it. Soon most of the Negroid tribes were in rebellion, including those who had previously been loyal to the Mahdists. Indeed, even some of 'Umar's jihādīya mutinied and, taking their rifles, deserted to the tribes.[7] It was evident that 'Umar would have great difficulty in holding even the station at Rajjāf, and so he decided to transfer his troops downstream to Bor.[8] He wrote to the Khalīfa in October 1891 that he was doing this "as it became impossible for the steamer and boats to pass to Rajjāf." [9] This seems to be a clever fabrication for what in reality was a full-scale retreat, for there had been no steamers coming from the north to Rajjāf since the summer of 1890. Ironically, 'Umar blames this retreat on the absence of steamers and then justifies this absence because there are too many rocks and islands blocking the passage of steamers that never came.[10] The Khalīfa was no simpleton. One source reports that he became very angry with 'Umar because of this retreat and replaced him with the powerful Dunqulāwī amīr, al-Ḥājj Muḥammad abū Qarja.[11] Other sources, however, do not seem to

6. Intelligence Report, Egypt, No. 1, April 1892, Appendix A.

7. 'Umar Ṣāliḥ to the Khalīfa, Jumādā al-'Ūlā 12, 1309 (December 14, 1891). Mahdīya, I/33/96.

8. "Statement of Said Soghaiyer," Intelligence Report, Egypt, No. 60, Appendix 46. 'Umar Ṣāliḥ to the Khalīfa, Rabī' al-'Awwal 1309 (October 1891), Mahdīya, I/33/110.

9. 'Umar Ṣāliḥ to the Khalīfa, Rabī' al-'Awwal 1309 (October 1891), Mahdīya, I/33/110.

10. 'Umar Ṣāliḥ to the Khalīfa, Jumādā al'Ūlā 12, 1309 (December 14, 1891), Mahdīya, I/33/96. The Khalīfa probably had to use all available steamers to transport men and supplies to Zākī Ṭamal who was heavily engaged fighting the Shilluks.

11. "Statement of Said Soghaiyer," Intelligence Report, Egypt, No. 60, Appendix 46. 'Umar Ṣāliḥ to the Khalīfa, Muḥarram 2, 1311 (July 16, 1893), Mahdīya, I/33/116–1. al-Ḥājj Muḥammad abū Qarja, a Dunqulāwī amīr, was sent by the Mahdī after the fall of al-Ubaiyaḍ to lead the revolt in the Jazīra and to besiege Khartoum. During the ensuing siege he suffered a serious defeat at the hands of Gordon and was replaced by the amīr, 'Abd ar-Raḥmān wad an-Najūmī. In 1885 he occupied Kasala, where he remained until ordered by the Khalīfa to assist the amīr 'Uthmān abū Bakr Diqna in the Red Sea Hills.

support this story. It is probably true that the Khalīfa was extremely angry to hear of the retreat from Rajjāf. He became angry whenever he heard of a defeat or retreat of any of his forces. But whether this was the sole reason for sending Abū Qarja to the South to relieve 'Umar is doubtful. First, although the news of 'Umar's retreat reached Umm Durmān early in 1892, Abū Qarja was not dispatched until the autumn.[12] If the object was to replace 'Umar Ṣāliḥ, Abū Qarja would have been sent immediately with Ḥasīb, or most certainly with the amīr Kunna Mujāhid. Conversely, if 'Umar had incurred the intense displeasure of the Khalīfa, he would have been ordered to return to Umm Durmān; yet he lingered on in command at Bor and later at Rajjāf until June 1893.[13]

Abū Qarja was considered a source of danger in Umm Durmān.[14] The Khalīfa on April 23, 1892, had arrested nearly ninety Ta'ā'isha who had formed a conspiracy to kill him.[15] Although thirty of the conspirators were acquitted, the remainder were exiled to Equatoria in a special steamer.[16] It is not surprising, then, that the Khalīfa, surrounded by plots and intrigues, dared not risk the presence in Umm Durmān of such a powerful and hostile amīr as Abū Qarja. Furthermore, the constant rumors of a Christian force in Equatoria and the Baḥr al-Ghazāl undoubtedly made the Khalīfa more anxious than ever about his southern territories. He continually requested information regarding "the Christians and tourists" and urged his commanders to ascertain the validity of reports of their presence in the Southern Sudan.[17] Partly through fear and partly through jealousy, Abū Qarja was sent to Equatoria by the Khalīfa with the double object of protecting and re-establishing his authority there

---

He later returned to Kasala to thwart the Italian encroachment from Muṣawwa. In the autumn of 1892, he was sent to Rajjāf and was later imprisoned by 'Arabī Dafa' Allāh on the island of Rajjāf. In 1897, he escaped from Bor and surrendered to the Congolese forces which had captured Rajjāf.

12. "Equatoria," Intelligence Report, Egypt, No. 9, December 1892. Gleichen, p. 199.

13. 'Alī Mukhtār Bakrī to the Khalīfa, Dhū al-Qa'da 15, 1310 (June 1, 1893), Mahdīya, I/32/6.

14. Slatin, p. 496.

15. "Statement of Wad Dalil, a Jaali Merchant who left Cairo for Omdurman in February, 1892," Intelligence Report, Egypt, No. 4, July 1892.

16. "Equatoria," Intelligence Report, Egypt, No. 6, September 1892.

17. 'Alī Mukhtār Bakrī to the Khalīfa, Dhū al-Qa'da 23, 1310 (June 9, 1893), Mahdīya, I/33/11.

and of banishing this powerful amīr to the most distant part of the dominions.

In the years following the death of the Mahdī, the Khalīfa had endeavored to consolidate the victories won by the Mahdist revolution. The Mahdī had left little to guide his Khalīfa in the construction of the Mahdist state except his exhortations to model primitive Islam and, like the successors of Muḥammad, to carry the jihād beyond the borders of the homeland. Since both these aims required conditions which the Sudanese could not meet in the nineteenth century, the Khalīfa simply turned more and more to maintaining his personal power, ensuring the independence of his dominions and establishing a functional administration. To achieve these ends 'Abd Allāhi had adopted the mystical sanctions of Mahdism and turned them to his own use. He continued and expanded the jihād to maintain the momentum of the Mahdist movement, wherein lay the greatest security to his rule, and he brought under his tight control the tribesmen, particularly the Baqqāra Arabs of the west, whose inherent anarchy had been released by the destruction of Egyptian rule. The Rizayqāt, the Kabābīsh, and the Fūr were crushed. Hereditary tribal leaders were overthrown, recalcitrant tribes brought en masse to Umm Durmān where they could be carefully watched, and old tribal jealousies and rivalries exploited to weaken the tribes. The Khalīfa's rule was autocratic, resting on the might of the armed forces at his command. There is no doubt that he intended to transform the Mahdist state into an Islamic monarchy, the chief threat to which was the death of the Khalīfa himself by the intriguing, power-seeking factions in Umm Durmān. First there were the Ashrāf, the Mahdī's family and relations, who had never resigned themselves to the loss of power upon the death of the Mahdī, and in spite of the failure of their abortive rising in 1891 only awaited the suitable opportunity to reassert themselves. Then there were the hereditary tribal shaykhs who resided in Umm Durmān as hostages for the good behavior of their tribes. In addition to these two groups there were innumerable men who harbored personal grudges against the Khalīfa. Unsuccessful military commanders, incompetent administrators, and personal enemies lived in Umm Durmān feeding on their failures and conspiring against 'Abd Allāhi. Although the mass of Sudanese undoubtedly supported the Khalīfa and his Government, 'Abd Allāhi took steps to protect his person as well as to enhance the mystical concept of his sovereignty. He withdrew himself from the people, appearing publicly only four times a year closely surrounded by his bodyguard, and in 1893 he began the construction of a great wall around his residence. It was during this period of the Mahdīya that Equatoria became a penal colony for political prisoners and those considered by 'Abd Allāhi too dangerous to remain in Umm Durmān.

Al-Ḥājj Muḥammad abū Qarja was thus sent off to Rajjāf in October 1892 with two steamers and 250 men liberally supplied with arms and ammunition.[18] He was named amīr of Equatoria and commander of the rifle and spearmen; but at the same time Mukhtār Bakrī, one of the Khalīfa's relatives, who had gone to Rajjāf in the autumn of 1889, was appointed "to superintend" him.[19] But the Khalīfa took no chances. He secretly instructed several trusted Baqqāra amīrs, who accompanied Abū Qarja, to kill him at the earliest opportunity. As usual the plot was discovered. A fight ensued, and the Baqqāra were defeated, but nevertheless the victorious Abū Qarja fled overland with his followers to the Nūba Mountains in southeastern Kurdufān.[20] Nothing was known of his whereabouts until several months later.

Meanwhile at Bor, the Mahdists had been strengthened by the reinforcements brought by the amīrs Ḥasīb and Kunna Mujāhid as well as by the remnants of the force from which Abū Qarja had fled. On the other hand, these reinforcements did not greatly improve 'Umar's position, for the climate at Bor was not only worse than that of Rajjāf but the natives were more united and hostile than even those to the south. Therefore, upon receiving definite orders from the Khalīfa to return to Rajjāf, 'Umar did not hesitate to leave. On March 2, 1893, the steamers and boats departed with the supplies, and the men marched by land, stopping at Mongalla to rest and refresh themselves.[21] They reached Rajjāf on April 2, and here the Mahdists remained, inactive.

18. "Statement by Slatin on Equatoria," Intelligence Report, Egypt, No. 36 (March 1895), Part VIII.

19. 'Alī Mukhtār Bakrī to the Khalīfa, Dhū al-Qa'da 15, 1310 (June 1, 1893), Mahdīya, I/32/3, 5. Slatin, p. 496.

20. "Equatoria," Intelligence Report, Egypt, No. 13, April 1893.

21. 'Alī Mukhtār Bakrī to the Khalīfa, Ramaḍān 1310 (February–March 1893), Mahdīya, I/32/2.

Suddenly in June 1893 Abū Qarja appeared at Rajjāf with 141 amīrs and men.[22] This presented somewhat of a command problem. 'Umar Ṣāliḥ had been the amīr of Equatoria until Abū Qarja was ordered to replace him.[23] But the deputy commander both to 'Umar and later Abū Qarja was 'Alī Mukhtār Bakrī, a relative of the Khalīfa. Fortunately 'Umar and 'Alī Mukhtār had worked hand in hand, and their relations with one another were extremely cordial.[24] They had fought together in Equatoria and knew the country and the great problems facing the Mahdists. Abū Qarja complicated matters, however, for although he was appointed the amīr of Equatoria, he was to be closely watched and prevented from exceeding or usurping his authority. This appears to be a most curious arrangement, but presumably Abū Qarja was one of the few amīrs possessing sufficient prestige and abilities to rally the cause of Mahdism in Equatoria. The Khalīfa only wanted to be certain that it was his authority, not that of Abū Qarja, which was re-established throughout the Southern Provinces.

'Alī Mukhtār therefore appointed one Ṣiddīq Ṣāliḥ to build a special stone hut to store the arms and ammunition, and placed his most trusted men to guard it.[25] The Khalīfa had warned Mukhtār that he must be constantly on the alert so that the arms and ammunition should not fall into the hands of Abū Qarja.[26] There was certainly good cause for these admonitions. The Danāqla at Rajjāf had heard of the discriminations against their tribesmen in Umm Durmān at the hands of the Khalīfa's own tribe, the Ta'ā'isha. Therefore they had formed a secret society at Rajjāf to plot the overthrow of 'Umar Ṣāliḥ 'Alī Mukhtār, and their few Ta'ā'isha followers. The appearance of Abū Qarja admirably suited the Danāqla at Rajjāf, for here, in their midst, was one of the most powerful and best respected Danāqla amīrs, and it was only

22. 'Alī Mukhtār Bakrī to the Khalīfa, Dhū al-Qa'da 15, 1310 (June 1, 1893), Mahdīya, I/32/7, 9.

23. 'Alī Mukhtār Bakrī to the Khalīfa, Dhū al-Qa'da 15, 1310 (June 1, 1893), Mahdīya, I/32/6.

24. 'Alī Mukhtār Bakrī to the Khalīfa, Jumādā al-'Ūlā 12, 1309 (December 14, 1891), Mahdīya, I/32/1.

25. 'Alī Mukhtār Bakrī to the Khalīfa, Dhū al-Qa'da 15, 1310 (June 1, 1893), Mahdīya, I/32/4.

26. 'Alī Mukhtār Bakrī to the Khalīfa, Dhū al-Qa'da 15, 1310 (June 1, 1893), Mahdīya, I/32/5.

through constant alertness and careful precautions that Mukhtār and 'Umar were able to retain their position in the face of unceasing intrigues.[27] Naturally, the feud between the Ta'ā'isha and the Danāqla could not but influence the Ta'ā'isha amīr 'Alī Mukhtār Bakrī and his supporter 'Umar Ṣāliḥ, on the one hand, and the Dunqulāwī amīr Abū Qarja on the other. There was constant friction, bickering, and argument, particularly between Abū Qarja and 'Alī Mukhtār, which even the entreaties of the Khalīfa were unable to prevent.[28] But it was Abū Qarja himself who prevented mutiny and rebellion from breaking out in the Mahdist camp. Upon arriving at Rajjāf he had sought a reconciliation with the Khalīfa, and in order to prove his loyalty he restrained his fellow Danāqla and sent presents of ivory and slaves to Umm Durmān.[29]

In spite of the dissensions, intrigues, and counter-intrigues at Rajjāf, the Mahdists had managed to send an expedition into the riverain country to the south in order to reassert their prestige over the Bari. The latter had been reluctant to acknowledge again the supremacy of the Anṣār after their return from Bor, for Kiddein, a woman kujur (witch doctor), had convinced her tribesmen that her magic was strong enough to overcome the invaders.[30] Her power over the Bari chiefs was immense. Not only did she expect, and consequently receive, presents in ivory, but such was the confidence placed in her that the Bari stored their ivory at her home. When 'Umar Ṣāliḥ sent Ilyās 'Alī Kannūna with 400 men to seize Kiddein and the ivory, she gave black sticks to her forty followers and told them to run toward the Anṣār, shake the sticks at them and cry out to Allāh. Then the Mahdist rifles would not shoot and the enemy would fall to the ground. In spite of a gallant charge by her followers, Kiddein's magic was insufficient, for the Anṣār captured thirty of them, including the kujur herself, and over 100 pieces of

27. 'Alī Mukhtār Bakrī to the Khalīfa, Dhū al-Qa'da 15, 1310 (June 1, 1893), Mahdīya, I/32/8.

28. 'Alī Mukhtār Bakrī to the Khalīfa, Dhū al-Qa'da 15, 1310 (June 1, 1893), Mahdīya, I/32/3.

29. "Equatoria," Intelligence Report, Egypt, No. 20, November 1893.

30. 'Alī Mukhtār Bakrī to the Khalīfa, Dhū al-Qa'da 12, 1310 (May 30, 1893), Mahdīya, I/32/10. J. N. Richards, "Bari Notes," *Sudan Notes and Records, 16* (1933), II, 182.

ivory. So great was her influence, however, that even as a captive "she played evil on the minds of the Negroids and so was hanged."[31]

Throughout June and July 1893 the Mahdists remained at Rajjāf, building houses and storage huts for grain and ammunition.[32] They sent frequent raiding parties into the countryside to forage for food and ivory. Indeed, food in the surrounding areas was in such short supply that many Negroids moved south into Uganda. But life at Rajjāf was equally hard for the Anṣār. Frequent expeditions and constant skirmishes with the Negroid tribesmen, shortages of grain and other food supplies, and the many deaths from the debilitating climate all produced a demoralizing effect on the station.[33] It must have been with some relief that in August 1893 an expedition of 480 men was sent to the Makaraka country under the command of 'Alī 'Abd ar-Raḥmān and Muḥammad aṭ-Ṭarayfī, who were to follow an advance group led by Aya Tambia (now called 'Umar), the former Chief of the Makaraka, who had adopted Mahdism and visited Umm Durmān three years before.[34] The Mahdists had wanted to send this expedition in early June, for the Khalīfa had requested confirmation of the rumors which had reached Umm Durmān that Christians (i.e. the Congolese) were in the Southern Sudan. But such an expedition could not be sent without the aid of Aya Tambia, whose influence and prestige in the Makaraka country had to be utilized in order to ensure the Mahdists support for their expedition, and Aya Tambia required time to reassert himself in the country he had not seen since the summer

31. J. N. Richards related the following account regarding the death of Kiddein (or Kedeng): "The next day Arabi Dafalla summoned all the local Bari and had Kedeng up for trial as a witch. He asked whether she possessed such powers and she did not deny it. Arabi then told her that in that case a blow on the head would do her no harm and told her to squat on the ground. This she did, and one Mukhtar gave her a blow with a heavy stick on the back of the neck and she died in a few minutes. The body was handed over to the Bari for burial and they buried her about 200 yards east of the Rejaf stone Curi" (Richards, "Bari Notes," p. 183). There is no evidence to substantiate the fact that 'Arabī Dafa' Allāh was in Equatoria at the time of Kiddein's execution.

32. Unsigned, undated (probably June 1893) letter, Mahdīya, I/33/7.

33. In the summer of 1893 locusts had destroyed much of the grain crop in the Southern Sudan, and the Mahdists consequently had to rely on dura shipped from the north.

34. 'Alī Mukhtār Bakrī to the Khalīfa, Muḥarram 12, 1311 (August 11, 1893), Mahdīya, I/32/12.

of 1890.[35] For two months the Mahdists remained at Rajjāf and then, in spite of having no word from Chief Tambia, decided to march without delay for the Makaraka country. Upon arriving in Makaraka territory the Mahdists found the countryside deserted and were consequently forced to go further afield to gain any news of the Congolese and to collect supplies. They were soon joined by Aya Tambia and several Makaraka chiefs, who informed the Mahdists that their country had been conquered by the Congolese, who had then turned it over to their Azande allies to plunder.

> After the destruction, Zemio [a great Zande Chief] went with them [the Congolese] to Bora by road and brought the jihādīya [the Equatorial troops] who had been with Emin and had fled from us to the southern parts. They [the Congolese] have founded three zarības. In each zarība there are two Christians. Faḍl al-Mūlā, who had been with Emin and who came, through arrangements with Zemio, from Bora, is now in Milz's zarība at Ganda. The others are at Gumbari and Ndirfi. They are supported by Azande with rifles.[36]

When this news reached Rajjāf, a council of war was held by Abū Qarja, and it was decided that the Anṣār should drive the Congolese from the valley of the Upper Nile.

35. 'Alī Mukhtār Bakrī to the Khalīfa, Dhū al-Qa'da 23, 1310 (June 9, 1893), Mahdīya, I/32/11.

36. 'Alī Mukhtār Bakrī to the Khalīfa, Muḥarram 12, 1311 (June 11, 1893), Mahdīya, I/32/12.

CHAPTER 3

THE CONGOLESE IN THE UPPER NILE VALLEY

Faḍl al-Mūlā Bey [1]

Although he had visited Egypt in 1855, 1862, and again in 1864, the interest of Leopold II, King of the Belgians, in the Nile Valley appears to have been first aroused by General Gordon.[2] As early as 1880 Gordon was on friendly terms with Leopold and must have impressed on the King the need "to strike at the slave trade" at its

1. I am gratefully indebted, first to Mr. G. N. Sanderson of Khartoum University whose unpublished paper, "Leopold II and the Nile Valley, 1880–1906," has provided me with many valuable insights into Leopold's policy in the Upper Nile between 1880 and 1898, and second to the editors of *Zaïre* for permission to quote from my article "Anglo-Congolese Negotiations, 1900–1906," *Zaïre, 12* (1958), pp. 479–512, 619–54.

2. In June 1894 Baron Lambermont, the permanent head of the Belgian Foreign Ministry, told Sir Francis Plunkett, the British Minister in Brussels, that "it was General Gordon who had first put the idea into His Majesty's Head." Plunkett to Kimberley, June 23, 1894, London, Public Record Office, Foreign Office, No. 142, File 10, p. 616.

source—the Baḥr al-G̱hazāl.[3] But Leopold was not interested solely in suppressing the slave trade. To him "striking at the slave trade" and penetrating into the Nile Valley were one and the same problem; and most certainly the King's humanitarian motives were more than matched by his desire to acquire through military conquest or diplomatic maneuver as much as possible of the Southern Sudan. It cannot be doubted that Leopold, with his streak of megalomania, took such grandiose plans seriously, but he often caused the Great Powers intense irritation by his attempts "to combine the position of a second-rate power in Europe with a first-rate power in Africa." [4]

Leopold's first drive to the Nile was in the guise of the Emin Pasha Relief Expedition. Not only was Stanley in the pay of Leopold throughout the period of the expedition but upon rescuing the Pasha he offered Emin on May 3, 1888, the governorship of Equatoria as a Congolese province.[5] The offer was properly refused. But the attempt to seduce Emin was only the beginning of Leopold's schemes. Between 1887 and 1890, Belgian explorers had opened up the various river systems which take their rise on the Congo-Nile Divide. These preliminary explorations were accompanied by a corresponding diplomatic effort which was consummated by the "Mackinnon Treaty" of May 24, 1890, between the Congo Free State and the Imperial British East Africa Company. By this treaty the Imperial British East Africa Company agreed not to take politi-

3. B. M. Allen, *Gordon and the Sudan* (London, 1931), p. 166. Gordon in a communication to Sir E. Baring dated March 9, 1884, suggested that he should evacuate Khartoum and retire to the Baḥr al-G̱hazāl and administer that territory on behalf of the Free State. Allen, pp. 307–08.

4. Rosebery to the Queen, August 15, 1894, *The Letters of Queen Victoria, 2* (London, 1931), Series III, 420.

5. Van Eetvelde to Leopold, May 12, 1888, "Das Lado und Bahr el Ghazal—Pachtgebeit des Kongostaates," *Deutsches Kolonialblatt, 27* (1916), 141; Stanley, *In Darkest Africa, 1,* 411. While Stanley was in Africa with Leopold's proposal from Emin Pasha, the King obtained a diplomatic cover from the German Government for this first attempt to gain a foothold on the Nile. In June 1894 Van Eetvelde told Plunkett that Germany could raise no objection to the lease of the Baḥr al-G̱hazāl to the Congo State, "for there had been published in one of the German White Books a despatch which expresses the hope that the Congo State would occupy that district," and that "it was advice from Germany given in either 1887 or 1888 which first turned the attention of the King seriously in that direction." Plunkett to Kimberley, June 12, 1894, P.R.O., F.O., No. 119, 10/615.

cal action on the left bank of the Nile as far north as Lado and recognized the "sovereign rights" of the Congo State in the defined territory. On the other hand, the Congo State ceded to the Imperial British East Africa Company a corridor extending from Lake Albert Edward to the northern end of Lake Tanganyika.[6] Although the Mackinnon Treaty was never officially submitted to the British Government, Salisbury privately approved of it; and his assent was sufficient to create in Brussels the erroneous impression that Leopold had succeeded in clearing the way, diplomatically, for an advance to the Nile.[7]

Consequently, on October 3, 1890, Captain Van Kerckhoven left Belgium for the Congo in the greatest secrecy to prepare an expedition that was to march to Wadelai on the Baḥr al-Jabal and to ensure by occupation the claim of the Congo Free State to the Nile Valley.[8] He left Leopoldville with the main body of Congolese troops on February 4, 1891. On August 10, 1892, south of Mt. Beka on the Congo-Nile Divide, Van Kerckhoven was accidentally shot and killed by his gunbearer. The command of the expedition devolved on Lieutenant Milz, who was determined to push on to the Nile, where he hoped to enlist the soldiers of Faḍl al-Mūlā Bey in the service of the Congo Free State.[9] On August 12, Milz left his

6. "Das Lado und Bahr el Ghazal . . ." 142; "Mémoire sur l'arrangement du 12 mai 1894," quoted in T. Simar, "Léopold II et le Soudan," *Congo* (November 1924), 509–11.

7. *Deutsches Kolonialblatt* prints two personal letters dated May 21 and June 9, 1890, from Lord Salisbury to King Leopold. In the first of these, Salisbury says that "no objection will be raised on the part of the Foreign Office," and in the second that "there is nothing [in the Mackinnon Treaty] to which the British Foreign Office is entitled to object." Moreover, the final clause of the Treaty itself asserts that it was signed "after it had been ascertained that the British Government have no objection to it." "Das Lado und Bahr el Ghazal . . ." p. 142. Certainly, Hatzfeld thought that the British might come to some arrangement with Leopold ("Das Lado und Bahr el Ghazal . . ." p. 143). And Lugard, who was always well-informed, intimates in an anonymous article in 1894, that Salisbury approved of the treaty "The New African Crisis with France and Germany," *Blackwood's Magazine, 156* (July 1894), 145–58.

8. *Biographie Coloniale Belge, 1* (Brussels, 1948), 568–69.

9. Jules Milz was born at Virton on September 10, 1861. A second lieutenant in the 4th Lancers, he enlisted in the service of the Free State in 1888 and led the advance guard of the Basoko expedition. Later, he was *chef de poste* at Upoto, Yambinga, Basoko, Bomaneh, and Bassoa. He accompanied Roget to Djabir on the lower Uele and on January 10, 1890, was made *chef de poste* of

camp at Mt. Beka and continued his march to the east. Two days later the exhausted column pitched camp on the River Arave. Milz, thinking that the river was a tributary of the Baḥr al-Jabal, sent a reconnaissance party downstream on the 17th. In the evening the party returned accompanied by guides and a boy who had been with Faḍl al-Mūlā and spoke a little Arabic.[10]

With the information received from these guides, Milz judged that he was only a two days' march west of the Baḥr al-Jabal. Therefore, he sent a messenger to establish contact with Faḍl al-Mūlā and to propose a meeting with him. Then Milz marched northward in search of the Kibbi River. On August 19 he reached the remains of the former Egyptian zarība situated only a short distance from the Kibbi. Nearby was the village of Chief Lahmin, who assured Milz of the submission of the Kakwa and the Kaliko. But the other neighboring tribes, the Lugwaret and the Lubari, appeared hostile. Milz therefore ordered the construction of a zarība, which he named Camp Kibbi, on the ruins of the Egyptian station. Here he remained, patiently awaiting Faḍl al-Mūlā and his followers.

The Equatorials did not appear. Finally, on September 15, Milz sent another party of twenty men in search of Faḍl al-Mūlā.[11] They were entrusted with a long letter written by Milz and addressed to Faḍl al-Mūlā, in which the Congolese commandant explained in detail that Leopold II, by the rights vested in him by the Congress of Berlin, had the authority to extend his rule throughout the Congo and "to stretch it further"; and that, after learning that Faḍl al-Mūlā and his men had been abandoned by the Egyptian Government and were without essential supplies, His Majesty was willing to take the Equatorials in to the employ of the Free State.[12]

that station. He joined the Van Kerckhoven expedition as second in command on January 1, 1891. At the death of Van Kerckhoven, Milz successfully led the expedition to the Nile. He returned to Europe on November 25, 1893. In 1900 he returned to Africa with the mission to delimit the Kivu frontier. Returning to Europe in 1901, he died at Brussels on October 1, 1902. See *Biographie Coloniale Belge, I,* 697–701.

10. Lotar, *Chronique de l'Uele,* p. 135.

11. Ibid., pp. 136–37.

12. Lt. Milz to Faḍl al-Mūlā, September 15, 1892, Mahdīya, I/34/92. This letter came into the possession of the Mahdists after the defeat of Faḍl al-Mūlā in 1894. It was then sent to Umm Durmān, where it was found by the British after they captured the city in 1898. There is absolutely no mention or intimation that Milz was prepared to repatriate the Equatorials to Egypt as Lotar

Although Milz appears to have taken a very broad interpretation of the Berlin Convention, which did not expressly authorize Leopold to stretch his rule beyond the Congo, the letter was certainly designed to appeal to Faḍl al-Mūlā and his men. They had had no contact with the outside world for many years and were in exceedingly short supply of European goods ranging from clothes to ammunition. Furthermore, Milz had 800 trained troops under him as well as the military strength of the Congo Government behind him—a fact which the Equatorials must well have appreciated. Faḍl al-Mūlā needed no encouragement. After receiving the first messenger sent by Milz at his camp on the River Arave, he had decided to join the expedition and had marched out with his men from their station at Bora. Near Mt. Wati, however, they were attacked by the Lubari and the Lugwaret, who killed sixty men, captured fifty guns, and forced the Equatorials to retreat to Bora. Here they remained until the arrival of the twenty men sent by Milz from Camp Kibbi.

On September 29 these twenty men returned to Camp Kibbi accompanied by two of Faḍl al-Mūlā's officers, Maḥmūd Aghā and Aḥmad al-Dinka, and two clerks. They declared, in the name of Faḍl al-Mūlā, that the Equatorials were prepared to enter into the service of the Congo Free State if given supplies of food, clothing, arms, and ammunition.[13] Therefore, on October 4, Milz, accompanied by the four representatives of the Equatorials, Zemio, and 400 men, left Camp Kibbi and after a five-day march reached Faḍl al-Mūlā's camp at Bora.[14] Here were drawn up and signed on October 19 an Alliance and a Contract defining the exact terms under which Faḍl al-Mūlā and his men agreed to serve the Free State.[15]

maintained in his *La Grande Chronique de l'Uele,* p. 137. For a translation of the Arabic text of the letter, see Appendix A.

13. Lotar, *Chronique de l'Uele,* pp. 136–37.

14. Ibid., p. 139. Lotar relates that Faḍl al-Mūlā was stationed at Wadelai. This is highly improbable. The Equatorial troops had moved to Bora long before the arrival of the Congolese. Here they remained until their attempt to join Milz's expedition was frustrated by the Lubari and the Lugwaret. Following this defeat, the Equatorials undoubtedly retreated to their well-fortified zarība at Bora rather than Wadelai which must have been dilapidated from disuse. It was at Bora that the Alliance and the Contract between Faḍl al-Mūlā and the Representative of the Free State, Milz, were signed.

15. The Arabic texts of the Alliance and the Contract have long been considered lost (Lotar, *Chronique de l'Uele,* p. 140). In reality, they were captured

The Alliance was a straightforward, voluntary incorporation of Faḍl al-Mūlā's men into the service of the Free State. They agreed to obey the laws and precepts of the State and "to serve it in a pure heart under all circumstances and in all services, and to submit willingly to the orders of the above-mentioned [Congo] Government." [16] If Milz had been a better judge of his new employees, he would have realized that such a declaration would be largely forgotten before the ink on the treaty was dry.

The Contract, which followed as a supplement to the Alliance, reveals more accurately the aspirations and desires of both parties. On the one hand the Congo Government was interested not only in the military possibilities of Faḍl al-Mūlā's force but in its commercial potentialities. Sections III and IV, providing for the establishment of trading stores at the stations of the Equatorials and for the collection of ivory, rubber, and ostrich feathers, clearly demonstrate the underlying importance to the Free State of making a march to the Nile commercially profitable. Section VI, requiring all illegitimate children to be sent to Bora, appears to be an attempt to increase the fighting efficiency of the Equatorials by the elimination of the vast horde of camp followers. It is doubtful whether such a provision was a great success. On the other hand, Section VII, obliging the Congo Government to provide the necessary supplies and arms, was, of course, to the Equatorials the sine qua non. The vagueness of the wording, probably not diminished by translation, allowed ample room for the difficulties of interpretation which later arose.[17] The Contract was valid for one year beginning on November 1, 1892. The remaining Sections (I, II, V, VIII) pertain to the application and procedure of the Contract itself and are of only secondary importance.[18]

Faḍl al-Mūlā's reasons for joining the Free State with such alacrity are not hard to discern. The Congolese possessed a force superior in fire power and training to any he had seen, which, when sup-

after the defeat of Faḍl al-Mūlā and sent to Umm Durmān, where they fell into the hands of the British following the Battle of Kararī in 1898. For a translation of the texts see below, Appendices B and C.

16. Mahdīya, I/34/79.

17. The Contract and the Alliance were drawn up in Arabic and translated into the French by Sulaymān, the official interpreter of the expedition, whose competence was later questioned by the Congolese.

18. Mahdīya, I/34/89.

ported by the military resources of the Congo State, would be more than a match for the Mahdists. Furthermore, the Free State was in a position to supply Faḍl al-Mūlā and his men with a constant stream of supplies which had been denied them for so long. This security undoubtedly more than offset any qualms of loyalty to the Khedive such as had touched Salīm Bey on the arrival of Lugard.[19] It was a temptation and an opportunity that did not happen twice in Central Africa. Certainly Faḍl al-Mūlā himself had nothing to lose and everything to gain. He was officially designated "Governor of Equatoria," a title never conferred upon him but one he had long claimed; and armed with this ill-befitting aura of respectability, he issued a pompous document entitled "Instructions to be Followed at the Present Time and in the Future."[20] Taken at face value the Instructions appear to be a sincere attempt to carry out the spirit of the Contract and the Alliance, but the later actions of the Equatorial troops clearly indicate that they were disregarded. This document is all the more ludicrous and futile when one realizes that Faḍl al-Mūlā's hold over his men was based largely on the prestige acquired as the last remaining Khedivial officer in Equatoria, a prestige which gained for him the nominal leadership over the men who had every reason to distrust him. Twice before he had attempted to betray them, and it is doubtful whether the lapse of time had allayed their suspicions.[21] Certainly Faḍl al-Mūlā's prestige had been enhanced by his successful negotiations with the Congolese, but his leadership was still insufficient to elicit obedience from his troops.

It is more difficult to understand why the Congolese employed this motley force. Milz had his orders, which were probably drafted in Brussels by men who knew little of the condition of Faḍl

19. In spite of past events, many of the Equatorial troops regarded themselves still in the Khedive's service. When Lugard arrived at Kavalli's on September 7, 1891, he was most impressed with Salīm's "unbreakable loyalty to the Khedive." Indeed, Salīm Bey and his men gave in and joined Lugard only after much persuasion and assurances by the latter "that the Khedive was now one with the British." M. Perham, *Lugard: The Years of Adventure, 1858–1898* (London, 1956), pp. 275–78.

20. Mahdīya, I/34/75. For a translation of the text of the "Instructions" see below, Appendix D.

21. See above, pp. 81–82.

al-Mūlā's troops and recognized only the fact that here was a virtual army to be had for the asking.[22] It was acquiring an army on the cheap but what an army! The military effectiveness of the Equatorials was hampered not only by their complete lack of discipline and training but by hundreds of camp followers, who undermined any latent soldierly qualities they may have possesed. Furthermore, since they had revolted against Emin Pasha and later against their own military officers, it was doubtful that they would submit to any orders of the Free State that were not to their liking. Faḍl al-Mūlā and his men were a collection of debauched, ill-fated opportunists whose only virtue was a certain stubborn courage in the face of adversity. Milz and his superiors, as well as their successors, showed a definite want of judgment in placing any confidence whatsoever in these troops.

But the most interesting document signed by Faḍl al-Mūlā was a general declaration regarding his conduct should the British suddenly appear in the valley of the Baḥr al-Jabal and attempt to seduce him into joining their service. It is a most illuminating document:

Protestation Given by Faḍl al-Mūlā in Arabic for the English if They Come to the Nile

I, Faḍl al-Mūlā Bey, Chief of the Troops in Equatoria, affirm, having taken service on the 1st of November, 1892, with the Independent Free State and having at the same time put the country and the natives of Khaṭṭ al-Istiwā' [Equatoria] that I command under the domination of the same State, that the Congo State, who have made a Contract with me, have declared to me that a convention has been made between the Independent Free State and the Imperial British East Africa Company in 1890, which establishes the Nile as the eastern frontier of the Independent Free State. I have not received any other instructions, and I have not received information that this convention has been changed; your [i.e. the British] presence in the territory which I have received the command of from the Independent

22. One would have thought that after Stanley's experience with the Equatorials Leopold would have been more cautious in employing them. Perhaps he reasoned that if he did not employ them the Mahdists would.

> Free State is a violation of the Treaty of 1890 with the Imperial British East Africa Company, and I can only inform my Government of the action you [the British] have taken.[23]

Such was Leopold's attempt to ensure the validity of the Mackinnon Treaty in Central Africa if not at Whitehall.

After the negotiations had been completed, Milz immediately began to dispose of the new additions to his expedition. Faḍl al-Mūlā and the majority of his followers were sent downstream to Dufile, where they could detect any possible Mahdist advance up the valley of the Baḥr al-Jabal. The remainder of the Equatorial troops, 150 strong under the command of Maḥmūd Aghā, accompanied Milz westward to Camp Kibbi.[24] From Camp Kibbi the expedition marched north to the former Egyptian zarība of Ganda situated at the headwaters of the River Ayu. Arriving there on October 23, Milz temporarily divided his force until the organization of the supplies permitted the erection of an intermediate post between Dufile and Ganda. Lieutenant Gustin and 125 Congolese troops were ordered to remain at Ganda while the Equatorial troops of Maḥmūd Aghā were sent further north to the former Egyptian station of Korobe located on the slopes of the mountain bearing the same name.[25] Having completed his initial task, Milz, accompanied by Zemio and fifty-six Azande warriors, left the expedition in command of Lieutenant Gustin and retraced his steps to the valley of the Dungu. Zemio was ordered to remain at Ndirfi, to secure the line of communications between Ganda and the Upper Dungu. Milz continued downstream, however, to the village of the

23. Mahdīya, I/34/75. The British did not arrive on the Upper Nile however until February 1894 when Major E. R. Owen with a picked crew set out from the eastern shore of Lake Albert and rowed up the Nile to Wadelai, raised the Union Jack, and then immediately returned to the lake.

24. Lotar, *Chronique de l'Uele,* p. 140.

25. Ibid., p. 141. Gustave Gustin, born at Luxemburg on April 7, 1867, was a second lieutenant of the 2nd Infantry Regiment when he enlisted in the service of the Free State in 1891. Upon arriving in the Congo, he joined the Van Kerckhoven expedition and accompanied it to Ganda where he was left in charge of 125 Congolese troops. He returned later to the valley of the Uele, but was sent again to the Nile on a reconnaissance expedition. He returned to Europe in June 1894, but enlisted for a second, third, and fourth term of service at Bangalas and Kasai respectively. He died at Pania Mutombo on April 28, 1911. See *Biographie Coloniale Belge, I,* 465–68.

Logos Chief, Faradj, where he established nearby a military post on the ruins of the former Egyptian station of Mundu.[26] On December 18, Milz finally reached the confluence of the Dungu and the Kibali Rivers, where he again established a new station, which he appropriately named Dungu. Here he met Florimond Delanghe; and the two left Dungu on January 20, 1893, and traveled downstream to Niangara, where Milz officially handed over to Delanghe the command of the stations of the Uele and of the Nile.[27]

On February 20, 1893, Milz and Delanghe learned that Lt. Gustin had left Ganda because of the difficulties encountered by him from the insubordination of the Equatorial troops and from the lack of supplies and had marched to Ndirfi, where, collecting Zemio and his Azande, he proceeded to Dungu.[28] At the same time, Faḍl al-Mūlā had moved from Dufile to Ndirfi via Ganda with the greater part of his men. The remainder under Aḥmad al-Dinka were at Mundu near Faradj. Actually Delanghe had expressed the opinion, in discussions with Milz at Dungu during the preceding month, that the stations in the valley of the Baḥr al-Jabal ought to be evacuated as there were insufficient military forces to support them. His opinion was now confirmed by a fait accompli. On March 15 Gustin and Zemio arrived at Niangara. There had been no news of the Mahdists.

After learning of the withdrawal from the Nile, Delanghe left Niangara on March 20 in order to ascertain the situation in the valley of the Nile. On the 26th he arrived at Dungu and was informed that there were simply insufficient military forces for an expedition to the Baḥr al-Jabal. Furthermore, Faḍl al-Mūlā had little control over his men, who had returned to Ganda, and it was rumored that he was scheming with Kabarega, King of Unyoro, to

26. Chief Faradj of the Logos ruled all the Logos and the Abukaias in the Upper Dungu.

27. Lotar, *Chronique de l'Uele,* pp. 143–44. Florimond Delanghe was born at Bruges on July 25, 1861. A lieutenant in the engineers, he joined the service of the Free State and left for the Congo on April 6, 1892. On January 31, 1893, he took over command of the Nile Expedition from Lt. Milz and led it again to the Nile. On July 16, 1894, he relinquished command of the District of the Uele to Francqui in order to assume the duties of Resident at the home of Zemio. He fell ill in the spring of 1895 and embarked for Europe on May 1, 1895. On May 30, he died on board ship off the coast of Sierra Leone. See *Biographie Coloniale Belge, 2,* 250–54.

28. Lotar, *Chronique de l'Uele,* p. 146. *Biographie Coloniale Belge, 1,* 466.

overthrow the authority of the Free State in Equatoria.[29] In their present condition he and his men would only be a hindrance and a burden to any expedition. But Delanghe was determined to re-establish the stations in the Nile Valley. To meet the deficiency of troops he sought to enroll as irregulars the Azande warriors of Chief Renzi.[30] To win over the Equatorials he sought to satisfy their demands by further concessions.

In the first instance, Delanghe was successful in establishing contact with Renzi, who promised sufficent irregular troops and porters to enable the Congolese to reach the Baḥr al-Jabal. In return Renzi asked for and received guns and ammunition to fight his neighbor and enemy, Yambio.[31] In the second instance, Delanghe was equally successful, though he had to pay a much higher price. Although Faḍl al-Mūlā had consistently refused to obey orders, had surreptitiously increased his force by arming without authority the Makaraka irregulars, and had turned the natives against the Free State by his plundering raids, he held a trump card with which to bargain successfully with Delanghe.[32] Hoffman, during a reconnaissance from

29. Lotar, *Chronique de l'Uele,* pp. 147–48.

30. Renzi, a Zande sultan, was the second son of Wando and nephew of Yambio. His village of Duru was situated near the River Duru, a tributary of the Uele. He supported both the Mahdists and the Free State depending on which appeared to be the stronger at the time.

31. Yambio, or Mbio (d. 1905), a Sultan of the Azande and the son of Basimbe and the uncle of Ndoruma. About 1860 he, his father, and a large Azande following, then living west of the River Yubo, migrated east to the area around the present-day town of Yambio situated in the Sudan near the Congo-Nile watershed. In 1881 he totally defeated a mixed force of government troops under 'Uthmān Badawī and the Azande irregulars of Ndoruma, but the following year, 1882, he was defeated and captured by Rifā'ī Aghā az-Zubayr, an officer of Lupton Bey, Governor of the Baḥr al-Ghazāl. He was taken to Wau but subsequently returned to re-establish his power. He defended his territory energetically against the Mahdists, and in January 1897, after a fierce engagement, he forced a strong Mahdist expedition under 'Arabī Dafa' Allāh to retire from western Equatoria to Rajjāf. After the fall of the Mahdīya, Yambio was equally hostile to both the Congo Free State and the Sudan Government. Although defeated by the former, it was not until he was wounded by a Sudan Government patrol near his village in February 1905 that he was captured. Taken to a hospital, he died three days later, and on his death his sultanate was divided among his descendants. See Hill, *A Biographical Dictionary of the Anglo-Egyptian Sudan,* p. 383.

32. Lotar, *Chronique de l'Uele,* pp. 149, 151.

Ganda, had learned that the Mahdists had returned to their station in the Makaraka country southwest of Rajjāf.[33] Consequently, Delanghe now needed all the support he could muster.

After completing the negotiations with Chief Renzi, Delanghe on June 1 left Ndirfi for Alema, where he intended to meet the Equatorials and discuss the question of grievances. He ordered Faḍl al-Mūlā, who had returned to Ganda with his men, to meet him at Alema on June 27, but this date was subsequently changed to the 25th.[34] Faḍl al-Mūlā had no intention, however, of discussing any questions with the officers of the Free State except in his own well-fortified station among his own troops. He refused to come to Alema, and Delanghe had no choice but to go to Ganda. He and his officers were greeted courteously and accorded sumptuous hospitality by the Equatorials.[35] After the formalities were completed, the negotiations began in earnest. Lieutenant Laplume, one of Delanghe's officers, described the conference: [36]

33. William Hoffman was born at Bornberg, Germany, on October 10, 1867. The former cook of H. M. Stanley, he joined the Van Kerckhoven expedition on December 10, 1891, and accompanied the expedition to the Nile. He remained at Ganda from which he made several exploratory expeditions, taking part in the Battle of Mundu in 1894. He returned to Europe in October 1894 but subsequently served a second term in the Congo as *chef de poste* at Yambuya, and returned again to Europe on July 2, 1897. He served a third term in the Congo in the Aruwimi District from July 11, 1898 to March 11, 1900. See Lotar, *Chronique de l'Uele,* p. 311.

34. Gustin to Faḍl al-Mūlā, June 22 and 23, 1893, Mahdīya, I/34/103 and 105 respectively. For a translation of these two letters see below, Appendix E.

35. Lotar, *Chronique de l'Uele,* pp. 152–53.

36. Jules Laplume was born at Salm-Château on November 16, 1866. He joined the service of the Free State and left Europe for the Congo on November 6, 1892. He joined the Nile Expedition on June 1, 1893, and in April 1894 took part in the campaign against Bili. He was made *chef de poste* of Gumbari on May 27, 1894. In 1895 he accompanied the expedition against Bafuka and was promoted to *chef de poste* of Niangara on August 26, 1895. In September 1895 he participated in the expedition against the Arabs in the territory of Mbelia. On December 14, 1896, he joined the Chaltin Nile expedition and fought at the Battle of Rajjāf on February 17, 1897. After serving as *chef de poste* at Dungu, he embarked at Boma for Europe on November 23, 1898. He served a second term in the Uele from 1899 to 1903, and a third term as *chef de poste* at Api from 1904 to 1907, during which time he took part in the campaign against Djabir in 1905. He served a fourth term from 1908 to 1911 at the elephant-training camp. Returning to Europe, he died at Spa on June 1, 1929. See *Biographie Coloniale Belge, I,* 584–87.

> Delanghe reproached them for being in such a condition for soldiers of the Congo Free State and for conducting themselves as robbers, bad soldiers, and thieves, and for supporting the acts which the irregulars had committed. The Bey and his officers, seated on mats, dropped their rosaries and pretended not to understand. They cast questioning looks among themselves. Suddenly, the officer, Aḥmad al-Dinka, spoke, agreeing completely with Commandant Delanghe and reproaching the others for pretending not to understand. They then made a flood of *salam 'alaykums* [Peace Be With Thee].[37]

It appears that the main controversy arose over the Contract signed by Milz and Faḍl al-Mūlā at Bora on October 19, 1892. In translating the Arabic text of the Contract into French, Sulaymān, the interpreter, seems to have made errors of such a serious nature that they appear almost intentional. Delanghe wrote:

> The infamous half-wit Sulaymān had translated into French the Arabic Treaty made by Milz in September [*sic*], 1892. In the French text, the work of Sulaymān, it is stipulated that the treaty was to receive the approval of the Government of the Congo State. In that of the Turks, nothing like this is mentioned. Moreover, in the Contract it is written that we have to furnish them arms and ammunition; in mine, nothing about this was said. These are the two considerations which forced me to make concessions in order not to place the Sudanese against us.[38]

A careful reading of the Arabic text appears to justify Delanghe's contentions. First, there is certainly no mention of the necessity to secure the approval of the Congo Free State.[39] Second, Section VII of the Contract does maintain that the "Congo Government is obliged to give and to equip them [the Equatorials] with all the necessary stores of arms and the like." [40] Therefore, Delanghe had

37. Quoted in Lotar, *Chronique de l'Uele,* pp. 153–54.

38. Ibid., p. 154. The Arabic treaty made by Milz was actually signed in October, not September as Delanghe indicates.

39. For a translation of the text of the Contract see below, Appendix C.

40. Contract made between Faḍl al-Mūlā and the representatives of the Congo Free State, Mahdīya, I/34/89.

to concede these two points "in order not to place the Sudanese against us." [41]

After Delanghe had restored harmony in the Equatorial camp, he decided that his position was sufficiently secure to start for the Baḥr al-Jabal. On July 13 he left Ganda for the station of Labore. Lieutenant Delbruyère, one of Delanghe's officers, was already on his way to occupy Muggi, and Lt. Gustin was to leave Alema for Kirri on the 16th.[42] After eighteen days of the most difficult marching, Delanghe reached the Baḥr al-Jabal at Muggi. A few days later he moved south to Labore, where all the forces of the Congo Free State had concentrated to establish a new station called Fort Leopold on the remains of the former Egyptian post.[43] But Fort Leopold was to be only a temporary camp from which a more permanent station was planned at Loufire, south of Dufile, for the eventual occupation of the Albert Lake.[44] Meanwhile, 300 Equatorials under the command of Maḥmūd Aghā and 350 Congolese regulars and irregulars were stationed at Labore.

While at Labore, Delanghe had contemplated an expedition against the Mahdists, but this plan had to be abandoned in order to send foraging parties to intimidate the Kukus into relinquishing supplies and to try to still the mounting discontent among the irregulars and the troublesome Equatorials.[45] He had some success, but this was of no consequence, for on August 17 he was ordered to leave Labore for the Uele Valley, where he was to hand over his command to Ernest Baert.[46] Most of the Congolese troops ac-

41. Quoted in Lotar, *Chronique de l'Uele,* p. 154.

42. Louis Delbruyère was born at Trazegnies on October 27, 1860. A lieutenant in the 2nd Artillery, he joined the service of the Free State in 1892 and took part in the Van Kerckhoven expedition of the same year. In 1893 he accompanied the Delanghe expedition to the Nile and was later placed in command at Mundu on March 10, 1894. He died at Dungu on August 24, 1894. See *Biographie Coloniale Belge, I,* 290–92.

43. Lotar, *Chronique de l'Uele,* pp. 155–56.

44. Delanghe to Fiévez, August 28, 1893, Lotar, *Chronique de l'Uele,* p. 157.

45. Delanghe to Fiévez, undated, Lotar, *Chronique de l'Uele,* pp. 157–58.

46. Ernest Baert was born at Brussels on August 12, 1860. A second lieutenant in the 1st Artillery Regiment, he joined the service of the Free State in 1885 and served in the lower Congo. From 1889 to 1892 he served as the successor to Van Kerckhoven as the District Commissioner of Bangalas. He returned to Europe in 1892 but went out again to the Congo to command the Nile Expedition,

companied Delanghe back over the Congo-Nile Divide to the Uele, and only a small contingent of regulars under Delbruyère and the Equatorials under Maḥmūd Aghā remained behind.[47] Arriving at Ganda on August 21 or 22, Delanghe again had sharp words with Faḍl al-Mūlā about the latter's procrastination in marching to the Baḥr al-Jabal. Delanghe then proceeded to Gumbari, which he reached in the early evening. A few hours later a special messenger arrived from Faḍl al-Mūlā with the news that the Equatorials had received four pompous letters from the Mahdists exhorting them to betray the Christians and to join their cause. Furthermore, Faḍl al-Mūlā reported the presence in the area of two Mahdist spies who were traveling through the countryside exciting the population against the Europeans.[48]

This news deeply disturbed Delanghe. The following day he sent a strong reconnaissance party northward; returning several days later, it confirmed the reports that the Mahdists had a post four or five days' march from Gumbari. Delanghe, after reinforcing Gumbari, immediately retired to Ganda and from there to Alema, which he reached on August 31. Here he remained until September 20, when the news of continuous and bitter quarrels between the officers of the Free State and the Equatorials in the stations on the Baḥr al-Jabal reached Delanghe and forced him to make his way again to Ganda to try to work out with Faḍl al-Mūlā a solution to end these bickerings. During the march Delanghe's column came under heavy attack from the local natives, who, angered by the marauding raids of the Equatorials and incited to rebellion by Mahdist agents, realized the weakened position of the Congo State forces and so attacked them.[49]

At this point the position of the Congo State was not very satisfactory. Wearied by endless marches and countermarches, the troops were weak and demoralized. The Azande irregulars were impossible to control and looted and pilfered at every opportunity. The Equatorial troops, no better, harassed the local natives for supplies and women and refused to cooperate with the officers of the Free

---

then under the leadership of Delanghe. He died at Dungu on August 16, 1894. See *Biographie Coloniale Belge, I,* 54–57.

47. Lotar, *Chronique de l'Uele,* p. 158.

48. Ibid., p. 159.

49. Ibid., pp. 159–60, 162.

State. More important, the Mahdists were again in the country and slowly infiltrating into the valley of the Uele. They had sent spies and agents to stir up the native tribes, who needed no excuse to attack the vulnerable columns of the Congolese. More than ever the Free State needed the services of Faḍl al-Mūlā and his men.

Delanghe and his officers, upon arriving at Ganda, were again cordially received by Faḍl al-Mūlā; but after days of negotiations the primary question of the authority of the Europeans still remained unresolved. Consequently, Delanghe broke off negotiations and decided to await the coming of Baert.

In late September 1893 news came from Labore that Delbruyère, on a reconnaissance patrol, had had an encounter with the Mahdists, in which both sides had withdrawn after some hours of desultory fighting. A few days later orders arrived from Baert for Delbruyère to withdraw from Labore with all the regular troops, leaving only the two Equatorial companies. He left on September 30 and marched up the River Ayu to the base of Mt. Moya, where the expedition camped. During the march an Abyssinian noncommissioned officer and a group of his countrymen deserted to the Mahdists, who were camped a few days' march to the north.[50]

No news having come from Baert for several weeks, negotiations between Faḍl al-Mūlā and Delanghe were begun again. Faḍl al-Mūlā was most anxious that the Equatorial troops at Labore be evacuated, particularly after the departure of the Congolese. He argued, quite logically, that Labore was too weak to resist a Mahdist attack, but more probably he desired the two companies of Equatorials to rejoin him at Ganda, so that he would have numerical superiority over the Congolese. On the other hand, Delanghe argued that Labore was a shield for Dufile and Loufire, which he was most anxious to occupy and to develop. Finally, Faḍl al-Mūlā suggested that the Congo State should occupy Labore and that the Equatorials should hold the stations to the south, i.e. Dufile and Loufire. Delanghe agreed, to the surprise of Faḍl al-Mūlā, who, faced with the thought of moving from Ganda, quickly changed his mind. Delanghe did not insist. It was for Baert to decide.[51]

Meanwhile the Contract signed the year before between Faḍl al-Mūlā and Milz had expired, and the Equatorials demanded the

50. Ibid., pp. 164–65.
51. Ibid., pp. 165–66.

payment due them. Delanghe did not have the necessary goods at Ganda and could only suggest that the Equatorials go to see Baert at Magora to receive their pay. Again discussions were broken off, and Faḍl al-Mūlā proclaimed himself a free agent. He no longer flew the Congo State flag and ordered the two companies of Equatorial troops still at Labore to march to Ganda. Delanghe protested bitterly but to no avail. Maḥmūd and his two companies arrived at Ganda on November 9. The last Congolese station on the Baḥr al-Jabal had been evacuated.[52]

Finally, on November 15, news arrived from Baert that he would not be able to move beyond Magora because of desertions and mutinies among his irregular troops. Delanghe was ordered to maintain or evacuate, whichever he thought best, the stations of the Equatorials and to retire to Magora. He could do nothing about the former, but he could at least retire with his own forces. Therefore, he left Ganda on November 23—accompanied, however, by a contingent of Equatorials, who were seeking their back pay. He arrived at Magora on December 4, where, after suppressing another mutiny of the irregulars, he paid off the Equatorials, who subsequently returned to Ganda. On December 9, Delanghe and the whole company at Magora left to join Baert, who had established his headquarters at Mundu.[53] Accompanying Delanghe were the representatives of the Equatorials, if not Faḍl al-Mūlā himself, to discuss the possibilities of a new contract between themselves and the Free State.

On December 11, 1893, Delanghe arrived at Mundu and negotiations regarding a new contract were opened shortly afterward with the representatives of the Equatorials. A contract was completed and signed on January 1, 1894, to become effective immediately for the duration of one year.[54] The dominant feature of this Contract is the independence given to the Equatorials. One would think that the Congolese would have been only too pleased to jettison Faḍl al-Mūlā and his men, but exactly the reverse was true. The preceding year, when Milz had signed the first contract, it was the Congo State that was in a strong position while the Equatorials were desperate and destitute. In December 1893 the positions were

52. Ibid., p. 168.
53. Ibid., pp. 168–70.
54. For a translation of the text of this Contract see below, Appendix F.

reversed: the Free State had evacuated its stations from the valley of the Baḥr al-Jabal, the irregulars had mutinied and deserted, and the native tribes were soon to rise against the Congolese. And, of course, the Mahdists were somewhere on the Congo-Nile watershed. Baert, in order to keep the Equatorials out of the Mahdist camp, was willing to pay the price necessary to keep them attached to the Free State. He therefore could do little but accede to the terms pressed upon him by the representatives of the Equatorials: although ineffective as soldiers, they were still an armed force which could be used to impede a Mahdist advance.

Regarding the Contract itself, Sections V and VI stress, as in the preceding agreement, the importance of trade. In the new Contract, however, all the articles of exchange were to be provided by the State. Sections I and VIII emphasize that the conduct of the Equatorials is to be governed by their officers and no longer by the laws and precepts of the Congo State. Certainly, such clauses put in writing what was already an accomplished fact, but nevertheless this is very different from the spirit and wording of the contract of October 1892. Sections III and VII deal with the supply of arms and ammunition. Not only does the Congo State supply the arms but also the type and number are specifically stated. It appears that the only concession on the part of the Equatorials is the pledge, which was probably worthless, not to move out from the stations to maraud, plunder, or attack the natives (Section II). Moreover, the State was able to ward off any demands for an increase in the actual cash and kind payment (Section X). The Contract was to become effective at once regardless of the approval or disapproval of the Free State Government (Section XII). Certainly, the Equatorials appear to have gotten the best of the bargain.[55]

Thus the valley of the Nile had been evacuated. Most certainly it was not due to the Mahdists, for they had only succeeded in sending a few pompous letters to Faḍl al-Mūlā demanding his surrender. In fact, the Congo State had not only failed to consolidate its position in the Uele before pushing on to the Baḥr al-Jabal, but had neither the organized system of communication and supply nor the men necessary to maintain such a system. By the end of 1893, the Congolese had stretched their resources to the limit and early in the following year they nearly lost everything. Niclot's column

55. Mahdīya, I/34/71.

was assaulted; Bonvalet and Devos were massacred; the Logos and the Faradj went to war against the Congolese; Niangara, the powerful Zande Chief, tried to form a coalition to overthrow the Free State and seize the arms and ammuntion; the irregulars mutinied and fled with their arms and supplies to harass future expeditions; and the Europeans were ill, disheartened, and overworked.[56] They were hardly in a condition to repulse the Mahdist attacks which were soon to penetrate deep into the territory of the Congo State. But the officers of the Free State were determined to resist, and it was only through the energetic courage of these few European officers supported by the Azande warriors of the loyal Zemio that the Congolese were able to turn near defeat in January 1894 into certain victory by January 1895.

Arrival of 'Arabī Dafa' Allāh at Rajjāf and the Defeat of Faḍl al-Mūlā Bey

While Leopold II was making his bid for the control of the Upper Nile Valley, the rumors of the successive Congolese expedi-

56. Jean-Baptiste Niclot (1864–1911) had accompanied the Delanghe expedition to the Nile in 1893 and was at Labore until the Congolese withdrew from the station in September. In December 1893 he was made *chef de poste* at Niangara. While making his way toward Dungu in January 1894, his escort mutinied and attacked him. He saved himself by plunging into the bush and later came upon a column of regular soldiers coming from Dungu. In 1895 he accompanied the Francqui expedition against Bafuka and commanded the camp at Kabassidu before departing for Europe on November 17, 1895. He served a second and third term in the Congo at Kirundu and Camp Lisala respectively and died at the latter place on October 14, 1911. See *Biographie Coloniale Belge,* 2, 734–36. Gaston Bonvalet (1856–94) and Achille Devos (1869–94) were leading a Congolese column toward Tambura on the Yubo when they were ambushed by the Azande of Bili on March 2, 1894. Bonvalet and all the men except the rearguard were massacred on the spot, but Devos was captured and carried to the village of Bili, where he was tortured to death. Lotar, *Chronique de l'Uele,* pp. 177–80. Niangara was the great Zande Sultan in the Central Uele Valley. He had close relations with the Egyptian Administration which had established a post at Tingazi in his territory. After the fall of the Administration, he was attacked by the Arabs coming from Stanley Falls, and so quickly submitted to the Government of the Congo State. In March 1892 Milz established a post at the village of Niangara. After the danger from the Arabs had subsided, Niangara, disgruntled under the rule of the Free State, tried to form a coalition to overthrow its rule, but died in December 1894 before his plans had matured.

tions of 1892 and 1893 had raced northward to Umm Durmān, where they caused no little concern to the Khalīfa. It was true that the Mahdist garrison at Rajjāf had been recently reinforced and in the early autumn of 1893 had even decided to march against the forces of the Free State in the Uele Valley. But the Khalīfa neither trusted Abū Qarja, the Mahdist commander, nor felt that there were sufficient troops to combat the Congolese. He therefore ordered to Equatoria his relative, 'Arabī Dafa' Allāh, who had incurred his displeasure by urging the release of Zākī Ṭamal, the great Mahdist amīr who had been immured in a stone hut and left to die for alleged conspiracy against the Khalīfa.[1] 'Arabī left Umm Durmān on August 12, 1893, with two steamers and 300 men.[2] The majority of the men were political prisoners going into exile. Indeed so great was the number of prisoners that the steamer, when taking on wood, had to anchor in midstream to avoid a mass escape.[3] Upon arriving in the territory of the Shilluks, against whom the Anṣār had been fighting for two years, 'Arabī and his men joined the Mahdist forces at Fashoda in an expedition against the Shilluks which resulted in

1. "Equatoria," Intelligence Report, Egypt, No. 26, May 1894. 'Arabī Dafa' Allāh (d. 1916), was a Mahdist amīr of the Ta'ā'isha Baqqāra related to the Khalīfa 'Abd Allāhi. One of the first to join the cause of Muḥammad Aḥmad al-Mahdī, he was in Dunqulā during the earlier part of the Mahdīya. In August 1893 he was appointed amīr of Equatoria with headquarters at Rajjāf. He ably defended the southern approaches to the Sudan, reorganized the Mahdist forces in Equatoria, held down the native tribes, and ambushed and killed Faḍl al-Mūlā Bey. After invading the valleys of the Dungu and Uele and causing serious harm to the Congolese in those areas, he was defeated at Bedden and Rajjāf by a Congolese force under the command of Captain L. N. Chaltin. Since the way to the North was blocked by the advancing Anglo-Egyptian army, he and his followers fled westward to Mandua in Dār Ta'ā'isha near the present borders of French Equatorial Africa, and from there conducted an abortive parley by letter with the Sudan Government. After an unsuccessful attack on French outposts in the region, he surrendered, in 1902, to 'Alī Dīnār, the Sultan of Dār Fūr. He then lived in al-Fāshar but was continually under suspicion by the Sultan, and in 1903 was imprisoned for alleged intrigue. He continued, however, to take part in many of the Sultan's military expeditions. After the withdrawal of the Fūr forces from the Jabal al-Ḥilla in 1916, he was executed by the Sultan for attempting to correspond with the Sudan Government. See Hill, p. 58.

2. 'Arabī Dafa' Allāh to the Khalīfa, Jumādā al-'Ākhira 12, 1311 (December 21, 1893), Mahdīya, I/32/22.

3. Ibid., Ṣafar 1, 1311 (August 14, 1893), Mahdīya, I/32/2.

the capture of several important Shilluk chiefs and twenty-five guns.[4] But 'Arabī did not remain long at Fashoda. By September 20, he was at the mouth of the Sūbāt River, where he met Bashīr Maqbūl with two boats coming from the Baḥr al-Ghazāl.[5] Finally on October 22, 1893, 'Arabī arrived at Rajjāf and immediately took command of the station.[6]

The Mahdists at Rajjāf had been on the defensive since the great losses suffered in 1891 at the Battle of Wadelai. Even after reinforcements had arrived in the spring of 1893, the Mahdists had been hamstrung by the quarrels, intrigue, and plots between Abū Qarja and his Danāqla, on the one hand, and 'Umar Ṣāliḥ and Mukhtār Bakrī and the Ta'ā'isha on the other.[7] It was not until August 1893 that they were able to launch their first offensive in nearly two years. But the arrival of 'Arabī changed all these activities. Carrying out his instructions from the Khalīfa, 'Arabī made an investigation into the conduct of Abū Qarja. It appears that Abū Qarja claimed to have borrowed $600 from the Public Treasury for use of the army but in reality simply pocketed the sum for his personal use.[8] Upon learning of Abū Qarja's attempt to defraud the Government, 'Arabī Dafa' Allāh imprisoned him on the island of Rajjāf, where he was thrown into chains and all his property confiscated.[9] 'Arabī's next task was to solve the problem of the Bayt Māl al-'Umūm itself. Hitherto all plunder and supplies had been kept in the house of the commander, thereby creating an irresistible temptation to filch government property. 'Arabī reorganized this system so as to prevent such malpractices in the future. He ordered the construction of a building for the Bayt Māl al-'Umūm and entrusted this task to the faithful Ta'ā'isha amīr, Ṣiddīq Ṣāliḥ, the supervisor of the arms and ammunition. Ṣiddīq constructed a special hut enclosed by a zarība and introduced a system of registration and bookkeeping.[10]

4. Ibid., Rabī' al-'Awwal 10, 1311 (September 21, 1893), Mahdīya, I/32/19.

5. Ibid., Rabī' al-'Awwal 9, 1311 (September 20, 1893), Mahdīya, I/32/5.

6. Ibid., Jumādā al-'Ākhira 12, 1311 (December 21, 1893), Mahdīya, I/32/22.

7. Above, pp. 88–89.

8. 'Arabī Dafa' Allāh to the Khalīfa, Jumādā al-'Ākhira 12, 1311 (December 21, 1893), Mahdīya, I/32/9.

9. Ibid., Mahdīya, I/32/8, 18. The following goods were taken from the possession of Abū Qarja: 8 Remington repeating rifles, 48 pieces of ivory, 1 Italian rifle, 1 sheet, 2 irons, 6 double-barreled rifles, 1 ring of iron, and 2 pistols.

10. Ibid., Mahdīya, I/32/13.

Equally important, however, were the complaints of many of the loyal Ta'ā'is̲h̲a who, having served their tour of duty in Equatoria, wished to return to the North. 'Arabī satisfied many by dispatching 200 of them northward with the next steamer.[11] Then Muḥammad aṭ-Ṭarayfī was removed from his post as the Mahdist commander in Makaraka and replaced by 'Alī 'Abd ar-Raḥmān, who was ordered to keep a close watch on the movements of the Congolese.[12] 'Arabī even proposed to the K̲h̲alīfa that the headquarters should be moved from Rajjāf to Lado, but well aware of the displeasure incurred by 'Umar's precipitous flight to Bor in 1891, he was careful to consult the K̲h̲alīfa in advance.[13] Certainly 'Arabī had strong reasons for his proposal. Between Lado and Rajjāf the steamers had to pass through rapids which were very difficult to navigate. It was for this reason that the Egyptians had built their headquarters at Lado and not farther upstream. Furthermore, the countryside around Rajjāf had been denuded of supplies while the area a half-day's march to the north was still "fruitful." [14] But nothing ever came of 'Arabī's recommendation to move to Lado, for the Mahdists were still at Rajjāf three years later.

'Arabī's greatest task was to weld a discontented and mutinous force into a fighting unit. The quarrels and hatreds had to be allayed and the differences of the leaders resolved.[15] It appears that 'Arabī had some success in achieving unity, for by the middle of November he claimed that the garrison was ready to fight. There were nearly 1,500 men with rifles. Therefore, on November 11, 1893, the Mahdists marched out of Rajjāf toward the Latuka country in the east. After three days they reached the Imatong Mountains, where many of the tribe had taken refuge.[16] These mountains rise to a height of 10,000 feet and form a natural barrier to the heart of the country beyond. Here the Latuka had taken up defensive positions, and a great battle ensued in which the Mahdists were victorious.[17] The fighting continued from morning until midday, but finally the Latuka were routed, their women and chil-

11. Ibid., Mahdīya, I/32/12.
12. Ibid., Mahdīya, I/32/7.
13. Ibid., Mahdīya, I/32/6, 16.
14. Ibid., Mahdīya, I/32/6.
15. Ibid., Mahdīya, I/32/16.
16. Ibid., Mahdīya, I/32/22.
17. Ibid., Jumādā al-'Āk̲h̲ira 13, 1311 (December 22, 1893), Mahdīya, I/32/21.

dren captured, and large amounts of corn seized. After the chief of the Latuka submitted and accepted Mahdism, he was given "the bestowal of peace," and the Anṣār then returned to Rajjāf.[18]

This great victory over the militant Latuka brought the ready submission of the Bari and other riverain tribes. Seven great chiefs came in to make their submission and were accordingly sent down to Umm Durmān under Maqbūl 'Abd Allāh in command of a steamer taking 290 pieces of ivory, ninety of which had been given to the Mahdists by the chiefs as tribute.[19] Not only had the supremacy of the Mahdists been re-established by the submission of the chiefs, but their departure for Umm Durmān deprived the tribes of their natural leaders without whom revolt against the Mahdists would be considerably more difficult. But 'Arabī left nothing to chance. The zarība at Rajjāf was completed and strengthened. He boasted that it was so strong that if the Mahdists left on an expedition, the zarība could be held with less than fifty men.[20]

After the great Mahdist success in the Nile Valley, 'Arabī turned his attention to the Congolese. Before he had arrived in Equatoria, Abū Qarja had decided to attack the forces of the Free State and had even sent to Faḍl al-Mūlā in August 1893 four letters demanding his surrender and the betrayal of the Christians.[21] This appeared to the Congolese to be a prelude to a general Mahdist offensive. And so it was meant to be. But the arrival in October of 'Arabī delayed these plans. First of all there were the quarrels to reconcile and the station to put in order. Then there were the expedition to the Latuka country and the acceptance of the submission of the riverain tribes. When these had been completed, 'Arabī was at last free to deal with Faḍl al-Mūlā. Since the threatening letters of August 1893 had not resulted in the expected Mahdist assault, Faḍl al-Mūlā, in order to feed the incredible number of camp followers, had continued, with increasing frequency and carelessness, his depredations against the local tribes. Even the Congolese could not stop him. By the end of 1893 such was the

18. Ibid., Jumādā al-'Ākhira 12, 1311 (December 21, 1893), Mahdīya, I/32/22.
19. Ibid., Mahdīya, I/32/11, 15.
20. Ibid., Mahdīya, I/32/10.
21. Lotar, *Chronique de l'Uele,* p. 159.

character of his raids that many of the chiefs who had once paid nominal allegiance to the Mahdists began to look to Faḍl al-Mūlā. 'Arabī rightly foresaw that the Anṣār might lose what little support they possessed in the interior if Faḍl al-Mūlā was not crushed.[22] Therefore, on January 10, 1894, 'Arabī and the whole Mahdist garrison moved out of Rajjāf toward Ganda, where Faḍl al-Mūlā was camped.[23]

Faḍl al-Mūlā had returned to Ganda after having successfully completed the negotiations with Baert pertaining to a new contract. When he left Mundu immediately after the first of the year 1894, he carried orders from Baert to move to Dufile on the Nile and to raise there the Free State flag before the British "concentrate and disputes arise." [24] Consequently, on January 14 he and his Equatorials marched out of Ganda with all their followers.[25] It is well known that Baert had long desired to push on to the Nile and had been frustrated only by the internal difficulties of the Free State. Furthermore, the British were moving northward from Uganda into the valley of the Baḥr al-Jabal, a fact of which Baert was well aware.[26] It is surprising that Faḍl al-Mūlā ever stirred at all from his well-prepared defenses at Ganda. He had successfully resisted for many months the orders of Delanghe to go to the Nile, and the only explanation for his change of heart lies in the very favorable contract he had made with the Free State. Certainly, if he had known that a large Mahdist force was moving rapidly over the watershed, he would not have exposed himself as he did.

On January 25 the Mahdists arrived at Ganda, only to discover that Faḍl al-Mūlā had left eleven days before. They quickly followed and by forced marches covered in four days the same distance that had taken Faḍl al-Mūlā fifteen. Near Wadelai the Mahdists surprised, encircled, and in a half-hour battle virtually annihilated the Equatorials.[27] Only 200 survivors managed to make

22. 'Arabī Dafa' Allāh to the K͟halīfa, Jumādā al-'Āk͟hira 12, 1311 (December 21, 1893), Mahdīya, I/32/20.
23. Ibid., Mahdīya, I/32/32.
24. Ibid., Mahdīya, I/32/31.
25. Ibid., Mahdīya, I/32/32.
26. "Equatoria," Intelligence Report, Egypt, No. 29, August 1894.
27. 'Arabī Dafa' Allāh to the K͟halīfa, S͟ha'bān 29, 1311 (March 7, 1894), Mahdīya, I/32/32.

their way to Wadelai and thence south to Kavalli's, where the British Officer, Captain Thruston, eventually found them.[28] Faḍl al-Mūlā, his clerk, and the interpreter Sulaymān were killed. The amount of captured guns and supplies was, for Equatoria, enormous. Over 300 rifles, two brass field guns, large quantities of ammunition, and 150 jihādīya were taken and incorporated into the Mahdist ranks.[29] There were also forty-five communications (twenty-seven in Arabic; eighteen in French) between Faḍl al-Mūlā and the Congolese, including a copy of the Mackinnon Treaty and a photograph of King Leopold II.[30] These and eleven guns of Belgian manufacture, tarbushes and flags, 710 slaves, and three Abyssinians were all sent to Umm Durmān as proof of 'Arabī's great victory.[31]

The news of the Mahdist victory soon spread throughout the length and breadth of Equatoria. The Congolese, weakened and reportedly concerned for their stations, rapidly fortified their post at Mundu. Hearing of these fortifications, 'Arabī sent 'Alī 'Abd ar-Raḥmān with 700 men to besiege Mundu.[32] Why 'Arabī did not advance with his whole force remains a mystery. Certainly, with the whole of the Mahdist contingent, he stood a very good chance to capture Mundu. On the other hand, such a maneuver would have left his base at Rajjāf and his line of communications exposed to potentially hostile tribes. In any case the remainder of the Mahdist force, approximately 700 strong returned to Rajjāf, which

28. Gleichen, *Handbook of the Sudan,* p. 202. On February 4, 1894, only a few days after the defeat of Faḍl al-Mūlā and his men, Major E. R. "Roddy" Owen with a picked crew in a steel boat arrived at Wadelai from Lake Albert. He was to ascertain the truth of rumors that the Van Kerckhoven expedition had reached the Nile. Owen found Wadelai abandoned, raised the British flag, and then retired at once to the Albert Lake. Although Owen must have learned of the rout of Faḍl al-Mūlā from a local chief with whom he talked, there is no evidence that he knew of the defeat, or if he knew of it, realized its significance.

29. 'Arabī Dafa' Allāh to the Khalīfa, Sha'bān 29, 1311 (March 7, 1894), Mahdīya, I/32/28. Slatin to Ohrwalder, July 18, 1894, Intelligence Report, Egypt, No. 31, October, 1894.

30. 'Arabī Dafa' Allāh to the Khalīfa, Sha'bān 29, 1311 (March 7, 1894), Mahdīya, I/32/31, 28.

31. Ibid., Mahdīya, I/32/34, 28, 24.

32. Ibid., Mahdīya, I/32/27.

they reached on February 9.[33] Here the only problem for the Mahdists was to find proper female companions for the victorious Anṣār. Many had been away a long time from Umm Durmān but were still reluctant to take as concubines the local Negresses, who were considered ugly. Even the harem of Faḍl al-Mūlā, which amounted to over forty women, was insufficient to satisfy their needs.[34]

The Battle of Mundu

While the Mahdists were advancing across the Congo-Nile watershed, the Congolese were frantically trying to consolidate their position, which they had hitherto neglected, in the valley of the Uele. Throughout January and February 1894 not only were they fortifying their stations in the Uele, attempting to keep the peace with the local tribes and disarming the mutinous irregulars, but they were also waging a desultory campaign against the Tanganyika Arabs, who had infiltrated into the valley of the Bomokandi.[1] Desertion, revolt, and mutiny were everywhere, and the authority of the Free State existed only around the small number of isolated stations.

It is extremely difficult to ascertain if the penetration of the Mahdists into the Uele Valley precipitated the revolts of the local tribes against the Free State. Certainly, Mahdist agents, aided by the news of their victories, were everywhere attempting to stir the local tribes to rebel against the Congolese. It is doubtful, however, whether the activities of these agents were really necessary, for the depredations of Faḍl al-Mūlā and the weakness of the Congolese gave ample motivation and opportunity for the local tribes to overcome their fears and revolt. Of course, the efforts of the Mahdist agents must not be discounted, but they were not the primary cause of rebellion in the Uele Valley.

In February the revolts and mutinies spread throughout the territory of the Free State. At Bomokandi the irregulars massacred the regular soldiers and took over the station. Niangara attempted to

33. Ibid., Mahdīya, I/32/32.
34. Ibid., Mahdīya, I/32/26.
1. Lotar, *Chronique de l'Uele,* p. 163. Sir Gerald Portal wrote in November

organize a coalition against the Free State with the intention of killing the Europeans and seizing the arms and ammunition.[2] At the beginning of March, the Bonvalet-Devos column was massacred by the people of Bili.[3] The situation in the Uele Valley was becoming extremely precarious for the Congolese.

After the defeat of Faḍl al-Mūlā, the Mahdists turned westward and a column of 700 armed men under 'Alī 'Abd ar-Raḥmān moved over the watershed toward Mundu. Delanghe had fortified the station with a ditch and a palisade, but he still had no information regarding the whereabouts of the Mahdists. This lack of information is indicative of the isolation of the posts of the Free State and almost led to disaster. Two days before the arrival of the Mahdists at Mundu, Delanghe left the station to proceed with Hoffman and fifty men to apprehend the murderers of the loyal chief of the Logos, Gamango. By so exposing himself without proper reconnaissance, Delanghe very nearly committed the same fatal error as Faḍl al-Mūlā. Mundu itself was left in the command of Delbruyère with the assistance of Niclot, Ray, Wtterwulghe, Baras, Ligot, and Dautzenberg. They had 210 regular troops, 325 guns, and 100,000 rounds of ammunition.[4]

On March 12, 1894, the Mahdist forces suddenly appeared before Mundu, besieged the station, and prepared to attack. Ray gave the following account of the battle: [5]

> On the 12th, in the morning, the station of Mundu was attacked by a party of Mahdists, our former Makaraka irregulars,

1893 that "it is now known that frequent communications pass from the Arabs of Tanganyika and Tabora to the Fanatical Muhammadans [the Mahdists] . . ." (Parliamentary Papers, C-7303, pp. 29–30). There is nothing, however, to substantiate this claim, and it is extremely doubtful if the Mahdist offensive from the north over the Congo-Nile watershed was ever coordinated with a push from the south by the Tanganyika Arabs.

2. Lotar, *Chronique de l'Uele,* pp. 175–76.

3. Ibid., pp. 177–81.

4. Ibid., p. 181.

5. Henri Ray was born at Brussels on December 28, 1870. A sergeant of the 7th Infantry, he joined the service of the Free State in 1892 and was ordered to the Upper Uele. In March 1894 he took part in the defense of Mundu, where he was wounded in the leg. In December 1895 he accompanied the expedition against Sokoi. On March 29, 1896, he left the Congo for Europe. He served a second term from 1896 to 1899, during which time he was *chef de poste* at Niangara and later at Suronga and Poko. See Lotar, *Chronique de l'Uele,* p. 324.

> and the principal native chiefs from the area of the station. We estimated the force which attacked us at nearly 3,000 men. Our losses were considerable enough. Twenty-four thousand rounds of ammunition were expended; Sergeant Ligot, having lost his reason following a sunstroke, died at the head of his platoon. The station had by this time been four days without a drop of water. This caused great privation for the soldiers and cattle. The First Sergeant, Ray, was in charge of the construction of the trenches. During the supervision of this work he was wounded by a bullet which passed through his leg, and seventeen men were killed.[6]

Laplume, who received a firsthand account of the battle from Baras,[7] wrote:

> One morning, they ascertained that the station was on the point of being surrounded by the Dervishes [the Mahdists]. For two days they remained blockaded unable to make a sortie. The natives, who knew that the station was encircled, said nothing, thinking to make common cause with the Dervishes and to divide the spoils.
>
> Delanghe, on the way, learned through the messengers who had not been able to re-enter Mundu that the station was attacked by the Dervishes. Returning by forced marches with his soldiers, he found himself face to face with the attackers. From the zarība, they recognized the soldiers of the commandant, and the Whites decided to make a sortie. Ligot was one. He was firing away from a prone position when a bullet entered his shoulders and came out his back. Realizing that he was dying, he cried out to Baras and, holding his hand, he said, "Good-by, Baras, I am finished." Ray was shot in the leg while supervising the digging of a trench. The Dervishes were commanded by Coffe Mohammad, who that night during the lulls

6. Quoted in Lotar, p. 183.

7. Edward Baras was born on December 16, 1864, at Noville-les-Bois. He joined the service of the Free State in September 1891 and was ordered to attach himself to the Van Kerckhoven expedition. In September 1893 he was sent to Magora and later went on to Mundu. Here he took part in the defense of Mundu in March 1894, after which he returned to Europe. He served a second term in the Congo with the Henry expedition but returned to Belgium in 1899 and died at Huy on March 20, 1902. See *Biographie Coloniale Belge, 1*, 86–87.

> [in the fighting] cried that all the Whites would be killed except his friend Hoffman. The soldiers will not be killed if they come over with their arms.
>
> It was this same Mohammad who had told our troubles to the Dervishes and had advised them to attack. The Dervishes had come in full force; on the way, they had taken Ganda, defended by the Turks, and a few of these were captured. At Ganda it appears to have been a veritable slaughter. The Bey, Faḍl al-Mūlā, his Bimbās̲h̲īs [officers], and Sulaymān were massacred without pity.
>
> Attacked sharply by the troops of Delanghe, the Dervishes took shelter; at the moment when the commandant advanced, a contingent of armed Azande of the Sultan Zemio, sent by Baert and commanded by Pimpurniaux, made a junction with the troops of Delanghe. Instead of re-entering the zarība, these aided by the Azande (of Zemio) and the troops making the sortie, swept the Dervishes from their cover and, after killing many of them, forced them to fight while retreating. It was a wonderful victory. It was quickly known everywhere. The natives astounded, became humble and pleasant. They made the mistake of not pursuing the Mahdists.[8]

Actually the garrison was so weakened by the siege and its victory that it, too, was unable to pursue the Mahdists, who retreated hastily to the village of their late enemy, Chief Gamango of the Logos.

Shortly after the retreat of the Mahdists the Congolese decided to abandon Mundu and Akka and to concentrate the garrisons at Dungu. Lack of supplies, desertion, low morale, and the constant threat of treachery on the part of the Azande chiefs all played a part in this decision. Furthermore, Baert desired to withdraw the garrisons in order to protect the interior as well as to cover his flank during the projected march to the Albert Lake by way of the Kibali.

8. Quoted in Lotar, *Chronique de l'Uele,* pp. 183–84. It is not known to whom Laplume refers when he writes that the Mahdists were led by Coffe Mohammad. The Mahdists were in reality led by 'Alī 'Abd ar-Raḥmān. Laplume only indicates that Coffe Mohammad was an Arab who had once been with the Congolese but had deserted to the Mahdists.

By April 9 the Congolese had arrived at Dungu.[9] Here they remained throughout the spring and summer fortifying the station and making expeditions into the countryside mainly in support of their ally Ukwa against the Zande Chief Renzi, who was openly aiding the Mahdists. In June, however, news reached Dungu that the Mahdists were again moving down the valley of the Uele and were at that time situated at the village of Palembia near Faradj.[10]

The retreat of the Congolese from the Nile Valley could hardly have been known in Europe during the spring of 1894, when Leopold was carrying on delicate negotiations with Great Britain and France. He could still claim that the Free State flag was flying on the banks of the Baḥr al-Jabal. But as the summer wore on, the bad news could no longer be concealed. Leopold's Nilotic dreams were in ruins. Not only had his forces suffered military defeat, but by the end of the summer of 1894 the French and the Germans had crushed his diplomatic victory of the spring—namely the Anglo-Congolese Agreement of May 12, 1894—and the Congo State itself was on the verge of bankruptcy.

Deterioration of Leopold's Diplomatic Position in the Upper Nile [1]

In 1892 Leopold's diplomatic position in the Upper Nile Valley began to crumble. The British, whose good will Leopold believed he had secured in 1890, performed an about-face. On March 1, 1892, Lord Vivian, the British Minister in Brussels, formally requested an assurance that the Congo State would not advance beyond the frontiers announced in her declaration of August 1, 1885, and would make no attempt to enter the British sphere as defined by the Anglo-German Convention of July 1, 1890.[2] Leo-

9. Lotar, *Chronique de l'Uele,* pp. 188–89.

10. Ibid., p. 200.

1. Collins, "Anglo-Congolese Negotiations, 1900–1906," pp. 482–85.

2. This request was repeated in a memorandum by M. Gosselin to S. E. M. le Comte de Grelle-Rogier, March 24, 1892. Ministère des Affaires Etrangères, A.F.l. -40, Lado, No. 12516. In a proclamation of August 1, 1885, Leopold defined the northeastern boundary of the Congo Free State as the 4° of latitude to its intersection with the 30° of longitude and thence south along the 30° of longitude to the Albert Edward Lake. R. S. Thomson, *Fondation de l'État Indépendant du Congo* (Brussels, 1933), pp. 299–302.

pold, taken aback, appealed to Lord Salisbury's approval of the Mackinnon Treaty. The British Government replied that it considered the Mackinnon Treaty void, on the following grounds: Lord Salisbury's opinion had been strictly personal and not the official decision of Her Majesty's Government; the Treaty had never been formally communicated, and was therefore "unknown" to Her Majesty's Government; the Imperial British East Africa Company had no powers to cede political rights; and one of the conditions of the Treaty, the cession of the Tanganyika strip, had never been consummated.[3] This reply was final. Leopold could do nothing but find another way to secure a diplomatic hold on the Upper Nile Valley. And that he immediately proceeded to do.

In July 1892 Leopold, through Van Eetvelde, suggested that the Congo State should hold part of the Nile Valley on a lease, but this proposal was rejected and the negotiations were finally abandoned without result in August 1893. Leopold then turned to the French. Equally fruitless negotiations were carried on more fitfully but with greater hope than in those with Great Britain.

In the spring of 1894, however, there arose the opportunity for which Leopold had been waiting: a Franco-German rapprochement against England on African questions. The Franco-German Cameroon Agreement of February 4, 1894, drew the frontier between the Cameroons and the French Congo so as to leave France with free access to the north and east—ultimately to the Nile.[4] The effect of this treaty was not lost on the British Foreign Office, for not only had Monteil been one of the French plenipotentiaries, but the treaty appeared to imply another Monteil expedition.[5] On March 10 Lugard reported that "Monteil means to march on Lado

3. "Das Lado und Bahr el Ghazal," pp. 144–45. One of the articles of the Mackinnon Treaty provided for the cession by the Congo to the Imperial British East Africa Company of a corridor extending from Lake Albert Edward to Lake Tanganyika. The I.B.E.A. never made any attempt to occupy this strip of territory. See above, pp. 93–94.

4. For the text of the Franco-German Cameroon Agreement see E. Hertslet, *The Map of Africa by Treaty* (London, 1909), 2, 657–60.

5. Plunkett to Rosebery, February 11, 1894, No. 18, Anderson's Minute, P.R.O., F.O., 10/614. A. J. P. Taylor, "Fashoda, the Question of the Upper Nile, 1894–5," *English Historical Review, 65* (1950), 54. J. R. Rodd, *Social and Diplomatic Memories, 1884–1893* (London, 1922), pp. 346–47.

or Fashoda with an exceptionally well organized expedition."[6] Therefore, Rennell Rodd, whose instructions had already been drafted, was summarily whisked off to Brussels. Here he laid the foundation for the final agreement, which was reached in London between Van Eetvelde and the British Foreign Secretary, Lord Kimberley, on April 12, 1894.[7]

Great Britain agreed to lease to the Congo Free State for the duration of the reign of King Leopold the left bank of the Nile as far north as Fashoda and as far west as latitude 30° east. In addition, the territory of the Baḥr al-G̲hazāl within the boundaries of 25° east, 10° north, and 30° east was to be held by the Congo "so long as the Congo territories as an Independent State or as a Belgian Colony remain under the sovereignty of His Majesty and His Majesty's successors." In return Leopold recognized the "British Empire" as defined in the Anglo-German Agreement of July 1, 1890, and leased to Great Britain a strip of territory connecting British East Africa with the north end of Lake Tanganyika.[8]

While Leopold had been concluding the Anglo-Congolese Treaty, he had been dickering with the French through Count de Grelle-Rogier. But the best that the French would offer was not nearly so much as had already been obtained from Great Britain. Negotiations were broken off on April 23. Meanwhile, the British Government had been urging early publication of the April 12 Treaty. This request alarmed Leopold, for if the French learned of the farce that the Belgian king had been making them play in Brussels, they might well bring up embarrassing questions about Belgium.[9] Consequently, in response to Leopold's pleas the British

6. "Lugard's Memorandum," March 10, 1894, P.R.O., F.O., 83/1310.

7. Rodd, p. 345. Taylor, p. 54.

8. For the text of the April 12 agreement see Foreign Office to Plunkett, April 18, 1894, Africa, No. 29, P.R.O., F.O., 10/613.

9. If Hanotaux at the break off of the Franco-Congolese negotiations had threatened to bring the Belgium question before Europe, he might very well have carried out this threat if he had learned of the successful Anglo-Congolese negotiations going on behind his back. On April 24, 1894, Van Eetvelde told Plunkett that Hanotaux had used the "most offensive and even threatening" language and added that "the French delegate maintained that this was a European, not merely an African question." Plunkett to Kimberley, April 24, 1894, Africa, No. 52, P.R.O., F.O., 10/614. M. Blanchard, "Français et Belges sur l'Oubanghi, 1890–1896," *Revue d'Histoire des Colonies, 37* (Paris, 1950), 26–27.

agreed to cancel the original agreement of April 12 and substitute another for it, substantially identical but bearing the signature date of May 12.[10]

The publication of the agreement aroused a storm of indignation in both France and Germany. The Germans were furious at the corridor behind their East African sphere, and despite Rosebery's blustering there was nothing Leopold could do but give up this clause of the agreement.[11] Having given way to the Germans, he could not resist the claims of France. On August 14 Leopold was forced to sign the Franco-Congolese Treaty agreeing not to exercise his rights as lessee north or west of an area bounded by 5° 30′ north and 30° east, the Lado Enclave.[12] Leopold's schemes for the acquisition of the Nile Valley were shattered. Defeated diplomatically and militarily, the coup de grâce was the financial insolvency of the Congo State. Long on the verge of bankruptcy, the Congo, it was agreed in negotiations with the Belgian Ministers in January 1895, must be ceded to Belgium as a colony. Such a development would, of course, end the Nilotic adventure, for the careful, penny-wise burghers of Belgium would most certainly not continue the expensive schemes of their King. But Leopold's luck was not finished. The cession of the Congo to Belgium was not consummated at this time, the financial situation improved, and the possibility of the Congo becoming the neutral solution to Anglo-French rivalry all combined to leave Leopold free again to dabble, more cautiously however, in his quest for the Nile.

Struggle for the Uele Valley

The Anglo-Congolese Agreement of May 12, 1894, had been a great diplomatic victory for Leopold. It was now only necessary for him to occupy the large block of territory ceded to him by

10. For the text of this May 12th Agreement see Hertslet, 2, 578–82.

11. Rosebery to the Queen, June 14, 1895, *Letters of Queen Victoria, 2,* 404–05. M. B. Hornik, "The Anglo-Belgian Agreement of 12 May, 1894," *English Historical Review, 57* (1942), 238–41. The British Cabinet did nothing to help Leopold in his negotiations with the French, merely informing the King that Her Majesty's Government would raise no formal objection to the Franco-Congolese Agreement but expressly declining to be a party to it.

12. For the text of the Franco-Congolese Agreement of August 14, 1894, see Hertslet, 2, 569–70.

Britain. Consequently, Captain Francqui was sent out to the Congo with instructions to prepare yet another expedition to march to the Nile.[1] But this expedition was to march not by way of Dungu but through the Baḥr al-G͟hazāl.[2] The plans for such an expedition had probably been formulated in the early spring, when Leopold believed that the Congo State flag flew on the banks of the Baḥr al-Jabal. In reality the Free State forces in the Uele were in no position to undertake another expedition to the Nile. By the early summer their situation had only just begun to improve, but by then the Mahdist threat loomed larger than ever. Faced with a renewed Mahdist offensive, Francqui was ordered to Dungu. He left Zemio's and proceeded to the Uele, where on July 16, 1894, he succeeded Delanghe. When Baert died a month later, Francqui was also placed in command of the Nile Expedition and began an exasperating search for sufficient troops and supplies to ensure his expedition some chance of success.

The Congolese were not the only ones short of supplies and men. 'Arabī Dafa' Allāh, trying to maintain his long line of communications through hostile country, required additional troops. In the summer of 1894 he sent a plea to Umm Durmān for reinforcements. The K͟halīfa complied. A steamer towing eleven barges of jihādīya and Baqqāra was dispatched southward from Umm Durmān on November 23.[3] Meanwhile in the Uele Valley the Mahdists, who had been stationed near Faradj, were slowly moving forward pushing out expeditions into the countryside for supplies, allies, and converts. By the beginning of August the Anṣār had passed the deserted station of Mundu and had pushed as far as the right bank of the Akka, where the amīr aṭ-Ṭāhir had established a

1. Lucien Francqui was born at Brussels on June 25, 1863. He joined the service of the Congo Free State in 1885, when a second lieutenant of the 2nd Infantry. He served a second term of service in the Katanga from 1888 to 1893. In 1894, he was sent to Zemio's with the intention of undertaking an expedition to Daym az-Zubayr, but events at Dungu demanded his services in the Uele. He succeeded Delanghe and was ordered to lead a new expedition to the Nile in December 1894, in place of the expedition to the Albert Lake projected by Baert. He participated in the Battles of Akka and the Nageru against the Mahdists, and returned to Brussels in 1896. See Lotar, *Chronique de l'Uele,* p. 308.

2. Lotar, *Chronique de l'Uele,* p. 200.

3. "Translation of a letter written on January 17, 1895 by Secret Agent No. 1," Intelligence Report, Egypt, No. 34, January, 1895, Appendix A.

zarība.[4] The spies of Ukwa reported that they were only waiting for the end of the rainy season before marching to Dungu, Niangara, and Zemio's, hoping not only to drive all the Christians from the valley of the Uele, but to punish Zemio for his long record of cooperation with the enemies of Mahdism. Ukwa, alarmed at this dangerous and threatening attitude—which might bring his enemy, Renzi, back into power in the Uele—offered Baert 2,000 spearmen and 150 riflemen to fight alongside the Congolese against the Mahdists.[5] Baert accepted, and with these reinforcements decided to send a reconnaissance in force under Millard, Swinhufvud, and Wtterwulghe, with 165 regular troops and a Nordenfeld cannon, toward the Mahdist camp on the Akka.[6] On August 21, they marched out from Dungu.[7]

4. Lotar, *Chronique de l'Uele,* p. 207; aṭ-Ṭāhir was an amīr under 'Alī 'Abd ar-Raḥmān.

5. Ukwa, a Zande Chief and son of Wando, was in continuous competition with his brother Renzi for the hegemony of the Uele Valley between Niangara and Dungu.

6. Albert Millard was born at Bouillon on June 30, 1860. A sergeant in the 1st Infantry Regiment, he joined the service of the Free State in 1892, was appointed *chef de poste* of Akka in March 1893, and participated in the Battle of Akka. On May 11, 1895, he left the Congo for Europe but returned to serve a second term as *chef de poste* of Niangara in November 1896. He died a month later on December 19, 1896; see *Biographie Coloniale Belge, I,* 695–96.

Axel Swinhufvud was born at Westerås, Sweden, on August 18, 1867. He joined the service of the Free State on October 6, 1893, and arrived at Niangara on April 13, 1894. He was commandant of the military training camp at Niangara from May 26 to July 2, 1894. He participated in the Battles of Akka and the Nageru. He accompanied the Francqui expedition against Bafuka in February 1895, and a second expedition against the Zande chief in the summer of 1895. He was commandant of Camp Kabissidu from September 6, 1895 to August 1, 1896, after which he returned to Europe; see Lotar, *Chronique de l'Uele,* p. 328.

Georges Wtterwulghe was born at Ghent on December 24, 1871. A second lieutenant in the 3rd Infantry Regiment, he joined the Congo Free State in 1892, and was made *chef de poste* at Mundu on December 1, 1893. Participating in the defense of the station, he later took part in the Battles of Akka and the Nageru. He was *chef de zone* of the Dungu District from July 1895 to April 1896, at which time he returned to Europe. He served a second term as *chef de zone* of Makaraka from 1900 to 1902, and a third term at Yei, during the course of which he died on May 8, 1904; see *Biographie Coloniale Belge, I,* 1003–06.

7. Lotar, *Chronique de l'Uele,* pp. 202–03. Baert died on August 16 before the expedition left Dungu.

It was the worst possible time to undertake such an expedition. Not only was it the height of the rainy season, but the route was blocked with marshes and many deep-flowing streams. Moreover, the irregulars of Ukwa were ill-trained and nearly worse than useless. It was bad judgment on the part of Baert, who should have played a defensive role, to take the offensive during the rainy season and particularly to rely on Ukwa's warriors for support. On September 2, not far from the Akka, the column was ambushed by the Mahdists, who completely routed the Congolese. Swinhufvud wrote of the battle:

> On September 2 in the morning, we marched in battle order as always, when we were suddenly attacked by the Mahdists. At the first shots fired by the enemy, all the men of Ukwa, their chief at their head, turned back . . . and dragged away with them our flankers. Our porters threw their loads, the cases of ammunition, and even the pieces of the cannon into the tall grass. It was a catastrophe.[8]

A fierce battle took place in spite of the flight of Ukwa's irregulars. Fifty Congolese troops remained with Wtterwulghe and Millard while Swinhufvud managed to find the parts to his cannon in the high grass, assemble it, and fire about ten shots. Wtterwulghe rallied 150 men and slowly beat a retreat, though abandoning the cannon and five boxes of shells. The Mahdists, satisfied with their success, did not follow. They had lost thirty-five men but had captured fifty Belgian rifles and ten boxes of cartridges as well as the cannon and shells.[9] After the news of the defeat of the Congolese reached Niangara, reinforcements were rushed to Dungu, which was now the farthest outpost of the Free State. The victory of the Mahdists greatly encouraged Renzi to aid the Anṣār, and it was soon learned that Mahdist expeditions were pushing in all directions from the Akka—to the Dungu, the Upper Bomokandi, and the Kibali—accompanied by the troops of Renzi as well as many Fadjelu tribesmen.[10]

The Mahdists under the amīr aṭ-Ṭāhir had established a string

8. Quoted in Lotar, *Chronique de l'Uele,* p. 203.

9. "Statement of Said Soghaiyer," Intelligence Report, Egypt, No. 60, Appendix 46.

10. Lotar, *Chronique de l'Uele,* pp. 204–05.

of zarības between the Nile and the Dungu. On the Nageru they had a strong zarība; on the Oigiga, a tributary of the Akka, they had another which was directly connected with their semipermanent base in the Makaraka country. There were even rumors that the Mahdists were trying to suborn Ukwa and Niangara to turn against the Free State and cut off the supplies for the station of Dungu. In early October two men of Renzi came into Dungu with a message from the amīr aṭ-Ṭāhir stating that Allāh had given the Mahdists the victory at Akka and calling upon the representatives of the King of the Belgians to embrace Mahdism and submit to the Anṣār. He further announced that he was being joined by 'Arabī Dafa' Allāh with 500 guns and 2,000 spearmen and a large quantity of ammunition. In December 1894 Christiaens, the commander at Dungu, sent Swinhufvud and Laplume upstream to see if the Mahdists had pushed farther west than their zarība on the Nageru.[11] They shortly returned with the information that the Mahdists, probably awaiting reinforcements, had not moved. Francqui decided to march against them. He could not begin his expedition into the Baḥr al-Ghazāl until January 1895, when the dry season was well-advanced; and consequently, during the interim, he decided to remove the Mahdist threat to his flank by driving the Anṣār from the Uele Valley.[12]

Francqui arrived at Dungu on December 10, 1894, and formed a column to march on the Mahdist zarība on the Nageru consisting of two platoons of Zemio's irregulars and five platoons of seventy-five regulars apiece, commanded by Wtterwulghe, Swinhufvud, Laplume, Frennet, and Niclot respectively.[13] Christiaens was second

11. Emile Christiaens was born at Diest on May 26, 1858. He joined the service of the Congo Free State on June 6, 1892, and was assigned to the Upper Uele. Wounded at Adaba in a battle with the Adaba Bakongo, he convalesced at Yakoma until February 1893. He was appointed commandant of the Rubi-Uele Zone on April 1, 1893, and of the Makua District on November 15. He took part in the Battle of the Nageru, in which he was very seriously wounded. Recovering, he led the expedition against Bili after the massacre of the Bonvalet-Devos column. He took part in the Francqui expedition against Bafuka in 1895. He returned to Europe in May 1895. Later he became director of the Société Equatoriale. He died on February 13, 1909. See *Biographie Coloniale Belge, I*, 234–36.

12. Lotar, *Chronique de l'Uele*, pp. 205–07.

13. Victor Frennet was born at Ixelles on February 11, 1868. A second lieutenant in the French Foreign Legion, he joined the service of the Free State

in command. The Mangbettu and Azande irregulars, who had proved themselves unreliable, were left behind. Francqui and his force of 525 men marched out from the station of Dungu on December 18. The route was less difficult than that of the preceding September, for many of the marshes had dried up and the rivulets and streams had shrunk. Near the Nageru on December 23 the column met the Mahdist force consisting of 700 men supported by 2,000 Azande tribesmen under Renzi. Swinhufvud described the battle:

> We left Dungu on December 13 and returned on the 23rd after winning a great victory on the same day. We decimated the enemy—their total strength amounted to 1,100 men—and destroyed their zarība. The Mahdists left a great number of their dead on the field of battle, as well as guns, Remingtons, and flags. They were expelled forever from the territories of the State, thanks to Francqui, to whom one should give high praise, and to the brave Christiaens, seriously wounded in the right shoulder, who lost a finger of the left hand. We had only twenty-six soldiers killed and fifty wounded. During the battle, Renzi, with his men, held back a certain distance, ready to throw himself on us in the event the Mahdists carried the day.[14]

The Mahdists retreated to the village of Renzi, who, impressed by the Congolese victory, proclaimed his neutrality. Francqui was now free to march into the Baḥr al-Ghazāl.

On February 1, 1895, 700 regular soldiers and the auxiliaries of Zemio marched out from Niangara and advanced northeastward toward the Nile across the country occupied by Bafuka, brother of Renzi. Bafuka, like Renzi, had been paying nominal allegiance to the Mahdists, who had furnished him with arms and ammunition. Although the Anṣār had withdrawn, it still did not make him amenable to the Congolese, who were ardently supported by Ukwa

---

on June 6, 1893. He joined the Nile Expedition at Dungu on September 1, 1894, and took part in the Battle of the Nageru on December 23, 1894. On February 11, 1895, he was killed in action while accompanying the Francqui expedition against Bafuka. See *Biographie Coloniale Belge, I*, 387–89.

14. Quoted in Lotar, *Chronique de l'Uele*, p. 208; "Statement of Said Soghaiyer," Intelligence Report, Egypt, No. 60, Appendix 46.

and Zemio, two of Bafuka's oldest enemies. Therefore, Bafuka planned to ambush the column. While marching with unloaded guns through a gallery forest on February 11, the Congolese fell into the trap. The advance guard was annihilated and the center square was badly mauled. If it had not been for the rear guard coming quickly to the rescue, the whole column might have been wiped out. There were over fifty-four soldiers killed, forty rifles lost, and countless wounded. The column was obliged to give up the projected march to the Baḥr al-G͟hazāl and the Nile. It retreated slowly to Dungu, whence minor expeditions were sent out against Bafuka during the spring and summer. In September 1895 Francqui relinquished his command to Captain Chaltin, who had come to take command of the Uele and to lead yet another expedition to the Nile.[15]

Although the defeat of Francqui frustrated Leopold's fourth attempt to occupy the Upper Nile Valley, he was not discouraged. During the spring and summer of 1895 the Congo State, for the first time, began to show the possibility of a profit, and the proposed annexation had aroused such bitter opposition among Belgian public opinion that the government was happy to back out even at the price of meeting the financial needs of the Congo State. A free agent once more, Leopold ordered the preparation of yet another Nile expedition to occupy the Lado Enclave. With the Enclave firmly in his grasp, who could know what opportunities might arise for him to extend his empire farther down the Nile?

To command Leopold's greatest Nile expedition two men experienced in fighting the Arabs were chosen: Baron Dhanis and Captain Chaltin.[16] Dhanis was named commander-in-chief of the

15. Lotar, *Chronique de l'Uele,* pp. 209–12. A small patrol of Mahdists was at the home of Bafuka but rapidly retreated to the Yei upon the approach of the Congolese.

16. Francis Dhanis, Baron, was born in London, England, on March 11, 1862. A second lieutenant of the 8th Infantry Regiment, he joined the service of the Free State and took part in the fifth expedition which explored the eastern frontier of the Congo State from October 1884 to March 1885. He served a second term from 1886 to 1889, during which time he established the camp at Basoko. During his third term he took part in the expedition to Kwango in 1890 and 1891. In 1892 he was named commissioner of the Luabala-Kasai District and carried out successful campaigns against the Tanganyika Arabs. He returned to Europe in October 1894. He was dispatched to the Congo for

expedition and was ordered to build up a strong column at Stanleyville and march from there to the Nile via Lake Albert. Chaltin, on the other hand, was given command of the Uele with orders to assemble a second and smaller expedition to support Dhanis. Chaltin was to march to the Nile along the route pioneered by Van Kerckhoven, Milz, and Delanghe. But Chaltin, unlike his predecessors, knew that before marching to the Nile he must pacify the tribes of the Uele and consolidate his position. This task was to take him over a year.

In December 1895, Chaltin began a tour of the Uele during which he settled the intratribal disputes among the sons of the newly deceased Azande sultan Niangara, and in March 1896 he moved against the recalcitrant Azande princes, Bili and Ndoruma.[17] After a month of marching and fighting, Chaltin routed the Azande in a fierce battle on April 5, 1896, in which he himself was wounded. The Uele was pacified and secured. Chaltin returned to Ibembo, where he remained until his wound was healed.[18] Suddenly, on October 31, 1896, Chaltin received orders to march immediately to Lado without waiting for the main column under Dhanis, which had not yet left Stanleyville. The news had reached Europe that General Sir Herbert Kitchener, the Sirdār of the Egyptian army, had completely defeated the Mahdists at Farka on June 7, 1896,

---

a fourth term of service as commander of the Nile Expedition. On April 11, 1897, he was appointed vice-governor-general of the Free State. He returned to Europe in 1900 and died on November 13, 1909; see *Biographie Coloniale Belge, I,* 311–25. Louis-Napoleon Chaltin was born at Ixelles on April 27, 1857. A lieutenant of the 3rd Infantry Regiment attached to the Institut Cartographique, he joined the service of the Free State in 1891 and was appointed District Commissioner for the Aruwimi. In 1892 and 1893 he took part in the campaign against the Arabs in the Aruwimi, where he was wounded. He returned to Europe in 1894, but in 1895 he was placed in command of the Uele. He led the punitive expeditions against Bili and Ndoruma and then commanded the Nile expedition to Rajjāf, where he defeated the Mahdists in February 1897. In 1899 he was appointed State Inspector and organized the administration of the Uele and the Lado Enclave. He left the service of the Free State in 1902 and rejoined the Belgian army at the rank of major. In 1905, a riding accident forced him to retire, but during World War I he commanded a volunteer unit during the siege of Namur. He was captured by the Germans but later was exchanged. He died at Uccle on March 14, 1933. See *Biographie Coloniale Belge, I,* 229–32.

17. Above, p. 110.

18. Lotar, *Chronique de l'Uele,* pp. 229–46.

and was advancing south toward Dunqulā. Kitchener had received his orders to advance up the Nile and reoccupy Dunqulā on March 13, 1896. This decision of the British Government to reoccupy permanently this most northern of Sudanese provinces had been ostensibly motivated by appeals from the Italian Government for a diversionary movement to relieve Mahdist pressure from the Italian flank at Kasala after the disastrous defeat of the Italian forces at Adua on March 1. Actually the British Government was alarmed by reports that a French expedition was preparing to march to Fashoda to secure the Upper Nile for France. Consequently, Kitchener was sent into the Sudan. He advanced unopposed to 'Akāsha and then marched on to Farka, where he routed the Anṣār. By September the Northern Sudan from Wādī Ḥalfā to Marawī was occupied by Egyptian forces, and at the end of the year Kitchener received authorization to continue the advance.

'Arabī Dafa' Allāh at Rajjāf

The Mahdist defeat on the Nageru and the subsequent retreat to the home of Renzi had seriously weakened 'Arabī Dafa' Allāh's already depleted force. He sent off Bashīr Maqbūl to take command of the Mahdists at Renzi's and to reorganize this force in order to obstruct the anticipated Congolese advance.[1] He then sent 'Umar Ṣāliḥ to the North with a frantic plea for men and supplies. 'Umar proceeded as far north as Shambe, where he found the river blocked by the sadd. So thick was the blocked area that "animals cross the river walking on the sadd." [2] After some months a passage was eventually cut, and 'Umar managed to get two boats through the obstruction. He arrived at Umm Durmān in July 1895.[3]

The news of the Mahdist defeat and retreat must have disturbed the Khalīfa greatly, for shortly after the arrival of 'Umar at Umm Durmān, he gave the alarming orders that one man out of every three should prepare to go to the south. He also took strict measures to try to keep the news of the Mahdist defeat a secret, and it was

1. "Statement of Said Soghaiyer," Intelligence Report, Egypt, No. 60, Appendix 46.
2. 'Umar Ṣāliḥ to the Khalīfa, Dhū al-Qa'da 17, 1312 (May 12, 1895), Mahdīya, I/33/124/1.
3. "Equatoria," Intelligence Report, Egypt, No. 40, July 1895.

reported only that a steamer was stuck in the sadd and needed many men to extricate it. It is unbelievable that one-third of the male population of Umm Durmān left for the south, but the Khalīfa did dispatch to Rajjāf both 'Umar Ṣāliḥ and Muḥammad Hamdān Allāh, with the steamers, *Ismailia, El Fashar,* and *Muhammad Ali,* together with one sandal and seven boats—all full of troops.[4] The flotilla proceeded to Fashoda, where it was diverted by Makk 'Abd al-Faḍīl for a campaign against the Shilluks.[5] After some months of fighting in the Shilluk country 'Umar Ṣāliḥ and his men again set out for Rajjāf, only to be blocked once more by the sadd near Shambe in January 1896. Here the reinforcements remained for several months, enduring great privations while attempting to open the way to the south. Hunger and disease reduced the number of men to less than 300 of the original force.[6] Yet a way had to be opened, for 'Umar well knew that if the Negroids did not see a steamer come from the north for a long time, they would become emboldened and attack Rajjāf.[7] But such were the difficulties and so great was the loss of men that 'Umar advised the Khalīfa to reinforce the Mahdist garrison in Equatoria by sending a strong army overland rather than by the river route.[8]

Meanwhile, 'Arabī had become alarmed about his position at Rajjāf. The delay of 'Umar Ṣāliḥ's flotilla at Fashoda and in the sadd had cut off Rajjāf from reinforcements or even news for over a year and a half. Consequently, he withdrew all the Anṣār from Renzi's and the Makaraka country to Rajjāf and sent Ilyās 'Alī Kannūna with 100 Anṣār and 600 jihādīya with 300 rifles to try to force a way overland to Umm Durmān along an abandoned road used in the days of the Turkīya.[9] This force marched northward to the vicinity of Tonj; here, at the end of January 1896, they

4. These reinforcements probably numbered close to 1,000 men. A sandal is a narrow two-masted boat used on the Nile.

5. "Equatoria," Intelligence Report, Egypt, No. 48, May and June 1896; 'Umar Ṣāliḥ to the Khalīfa, undated, Mahdīya, I/33/unnumbered.

6. 'Arabī Dafa' Allāh to the Khalīfa, Ṣafar 12, 1314 (July 23, 1896), Mahdīya, I/32/42.

7. 'Umar Ṣaliḥ to the Khalīfa, Rabī' al-'Awwal 10, 1313 (September 30, 1895), Mahdīya, I/33/130.

8. Ibid., undated, Mahdīya, I/33/135.

9. 'Arabī Dafa' Allāh to the Khalīfa, Shawwāl 12, 1313 (March 27, 1896), I/32/36.

were attacked by the Nuer. Ilyās was killed, his arms and ammunition captured, and most of his force annihilated. Those who managed to escape fled to Rajjāf with the news of the defeat. Meanwhile, a letter had arrived from Makk 'Abd al-Faḍīl informing 'Arabī that 'Umar Ṣāliḥ and his force could not cut their way through the sadd. Both the news of 'Umar's plight and the tale of defeat at Tonj prompted 'Arabī to leave half his troops at Rajjāf under the command of Aḥmad abū an-Nūkhayla and to proceed northward with the remaining half to Bor.[10]

Here he received a letter from 'Umar Ṣāliḥ, who informed 'Arabī that after the greatest efforts he had succeeded only in passing the small steamer *Muhammad Ali* through the sadd. When the steamer arrived at Bor in May 1896, it brought the news of the pitiful condition of the Anṣār and many complaints against the amīr Ḥamdān Allāh. Consequently, 'Arabī himself, accompanied by 150 men, returned in the *Muhammad Ali* to appraise the situation. At Shambe the Mahdists were truly in a wretched condition. Only 300 men remained of the original force and of these half were too ill to work while the other half were too weak from hunger to make much progress. Therefore, 'Arabī left supplies and 150 able-bodied men under the direction of Sa'īd Sūghaiyār to help in the cutting of the sadd, and took 150 sick men of 'Umar back with him to Bor.[11]

'Arabī spent the rest of May and June 1896 at Bor. At the beginning of July he received a letter from Sa'īd Sūghaiyār informing him that the rainy season had rendered it impossible to cut through the sadd. Consequently, 'Arabī again made his way to Shambe to inspect the situation. He found that most of the men he had left there two months before were ill and exhausted. A council of war was held, and it was decided to abandon during the rainy season at least the attempt to cut through the sadd. 'Arabī sent the boats back to Rajjāf to collect the slaves, ivory, and other loot taken from the Congolese which was awaiting shipment to Umm Durmān.[12] All these goods were brought to Shambe, car-

10. "Statement of Said Soghaiyer," Intelligence Report, Egypt, No. 60, Appendix 46.

11. 'Arabī Dafa' Allāh to the Khalīfa, Ṣafar 12, 1314 (July 23, 1896), Mahdīya, I/32/42.

12. Ibid., "Statement of Said Soghaiyer," Intelligence Report, Egypt, No. 60, Appendix 46. The loot taken to Umm Durmān consisted of 1,082 tusks, 1,020

ried across the sadd, and loaded onto the steamers *Ismailia* and *El Fashar,* which under the command of Sa'īd Sūghaiyār started northward to Umm Durmān. Sa'īd had not proceeded a great distance, however, before the steamers were stopped by another sadd obstruction so large that even after six hours of marching the end of it could not be reached. He remained for twenty-four days before this barrier trying to cut a passage through it. Finally, taking the *Ismailia* and three boats, he went in search of an open passage. In the evening of the first day Sa'īd came across a small channel through which it was possible to pass a steamer. The following morning he returned to the *El Fashar.* In the meantime, however, fresh sadd had formed behind the steamer, isolating her and making movement impossible. After loading the *Ismailia* to capacity with the goods from the *El Fashar,* the latter was sunk and the *Ismailia* proceeded northward, arriving at Umm Durmān in September 1896.[13]

Meanwhile, 'Arabī had received at Bor a letter from Kabarega, King of Unyoro, informing the Mahdist commander that the Christians had driven him out of his country into exile and implying that they were moving northward up the Baḥr al-Jabal.[14] Fearing for the garrison at Rajjāf, 'Arabī returned in order to put the station into a state of defense.[15] Although Kabarega had been referring to the British activities in Uganda, his warning was timely, for Chaltin was making his final preparations for the march to the Upper Nile.

The position of 'Arabī at Rajjāf in the autumn of 1896 was precarious. Not only was he completely cut off from the North,

---

slaves, 400 spears, 200 shields, one Nordenfeld cannon, 33 Belgian rifles, 500 jars of honey, 3 Belgian tents, and 5 boxes of artillery shells.

13. 'Arabī Dafa' Allāh to the Khalīfa, Ṣafar 12, 1314 (July 23, 1896), Mahdīya, I/32/40.

14. Ibid., Mahdīya, I/32/42.

15. Ibid., Dhū al-Qa'da 15, 1313 (April 28, 1896), and Ṣafar 12, 1314 (July 23, 1896), Mahdīya, I/32/39 and 41 respectively. Of the 1,500 men at Rajjāf in 1893, 90 had been killed in the Uele Valley in the campaigns against the Free State and 250 had been killed in various battles against the Negroids. Of the 1,160 men remaining, 150 of these had been sent to Shambe to work in the sadd. This left 1,000 men at Rajjāf, 150 at Bor recovering from illnesses, and some 300 at Shambe. Undoubtedly some of these returned to the North in the steamer of Sa'īd Sūghaiyār.

but of the 1,500 men under him at Rajjāf in 1893, only 1,000 remained to defend the station.[16] Equally serious was the deficiency of ammunition, particularly for the Remington repeating rifles. Large quantities of this ammunition had been expended in the continuous fighting and had not been replaced from Umm Durmān. The situation was so serious that each man was armed with a spear in addition to his rifle.[17] Certainly the Mahdists were in no condition to assume the offensive once more against the Congolese.

16. Ibid., Dhū al-Qa'da 15, 1313 (April 28, 1896), Mahdīya, I/32/39.
17. Ibid., Dhū al-Qa'da 5, 1313 (April 18, 1896), Mahdīya, I/32/38.

CHAPTER 4

THE CONGOLESE EXPEDITIONS INTO THE BAḤR AL-GHAZĀL

Although the Mahdist invasions of the Southern Sudan during the rule of the Khalīfa 'Abd Allāhi had primarily followed the course of the River Nile, the Congolese advance of 1893 and 1894 deep into the Baḥr al-Ghazāl elicited Mahdist expeditions overland from Dār Fūr and Kurdufān. It is true that there was never a clash between the forces of the Free State and those of the Mahdists, but although the Congolese troops were ultimately withdrawn for reasons of European diplomacy, the presence of the Anṣār precluded the Congo Free State from establishing a permanent post in the northern Baḥr al-Ghazāl. To the Khalīfa the Congolese expeditions were further proof of the need to defend more energetically the inviolability of the Sudan from European invaders. To the Congolese the expeditions were an assertion of their rights to the Baḥr al-Ghazāl, a claim which in the first decade of the twentieth century was to cause great difficulties between England and the Congo Free State. The expeditions into the Baḥr al-Ghazāl must be viewed simply as another attempt by Leopold II to secure the Upper Nile Valley, and consequently the reaction against these expeditions on the part of the Khalīfa must be regarded as a precautionary measure to defend his southern frontier.

When the amīr Karam Allāh was recalled to Umm Durmān in 1885, the Mahdist forces were withdrawn from the Baḥr al-Ghazāl, and the province returned to much the same conditions that had existed prior to the Egyptian occupation. The tribes, again independent and free, reverted to their ageless intertribal warfare. The chiefs basked in a new-found anarchy devoid of taxes or corrupt administrators. There is, however, very little known about events in the Baḥr al-Ghazāl during this period until the coming of the Congolese in 1894 and later the French in 1895. The first Mahdist invasion had swept past the Nuer and, after 1885, little is known of the Dinka. Only of the tribes in the western Baḥr al-Ghazāl, thanks to the tireless inquiries of Father Santandrea, is there any record at all.[1]

Two tribes in the western Baḥr al-Ghazāl, the Feroge and the Njangulgule, had been expanding southward from the Baḥr al-'Arab at the time of the Egyptian occupation. Here they slowly established their hegemony over—and, in some cases, absorbed—the minor tribes. After the Mahdists had withdrawn north of the Baḥr al-'Arab, it was inevitable that these two expanding tribes would clash, but before any decisive victory had been won by either the Feroge or the Njangulgule, the Azande hordes of Zemio had easily disposed of the weak tribes on the Congo-Nile watershed and had driven all the way to Daym az-Zubayr. At one point the son of Zemio, Gubere, pushed northward, driving the small tribes (the Sere, the Golo, the Ndogo, and the Bai) who paid allegiance to the Njangulgule into a fortified zarība on the Ngoku. Here the Njangulgule forces under Durub came to relieve the besieged and enabled them to break through the Azande and flee to safety. After a brief period of peace, the Azande of Zemio again came northward in 1890, this time led by another son, Gbudue. An extensive campaign against the Njangulgule culminated in the capture of Sarago and the siege of the Ndogo stronghold of Zaka. The Njangulgule were defeated and driven to their westernmost settlement of Bora before the Azande withdrew.[2]

1. Above, p. 23.

2. Santandrea, "A Preliminary Account of the Indri, Togoyo, Feroge, Mangaya, and Woro," *Sudan Notes and Records, 34* (1953), II, 241–49.

Meanwhile to the west of the Baḥr al-G͟hazāl, Rabīḥ Faḍl Allāh, better known as Rabīḥ Zubayr, had carved out for himself such an extensive kingdom that he was known in European diplomatic circles as "the Napoleon of the desert." [3] It is difficult to determine how great was his influence in the Baḥr al-G͟hazāl. Probably his raiding parties penetrated well into Dār Fūr and Dār Fartīt, but they never remained for any length of time.

After Karam Allāh had left the Baḥr al-G͟hazāl in 1885, the Mahdist forces retired to S͟hakkā. Here a small force under 'Ut͟hmān Ganū occasionally made raids to the south and west to gather slaves, ivory, and information. On the death of the amīr 'Ut͟hmān, Abū Maryam succeeded him as the commandant at S͟hakkā.[4] He sent continuous reports to Umm Durmān of the activities in the Baḥr al-G͟hazāl and beyond, including those of Rabīḥ Zubayr.[5] In 1892 Mahdist agents reported the arrival of the Congolese on the Upper Bomu and their subsequent alliance with Zemio.[6] In

3. Rabīḥ Faḍl Allāh, also called Rabīḥ Zubayr (1845–1900), slave trader and freebooter, was born, probably of Hāmaj origin, in an undesirable quarter on the southeast side of Khartoum named Salāmat al-Bās͟ha. Here he received the elements of a Qur'ānic education and went to the Baḥr al-G͟hazāl while a young man as assistant head of a slave-trading concern. When the Government took over his firm, he worked for Zubayr Raḥma Manṣūr, greatest of all the freebooters in the Baḥr al-G͟hazāl, and was in service with Zubayr's son Sulaymān when the latter was defeated by R. Gessi Pasha in 1879. Taking with him some of Sulaymān's men, he fled to the country of the Azande, where he founded a sultanate 1880–84. In 1885, dressed in the patch clothes of the Mahdist warrior, he invaded Dār Banda and lived on the country. In 1891 he massacred the French mission of P. Crampel but then, marching northward into Wadā'i, he was beaten in battle by the sultan. Moving farther west, he set himself up over the pagan people of the Chad. Appearing in Bornu in 1894, he was joined by Ḥaiyātu, ruler of the Adamawa, who married his daughter but who was killed by Rabīḥ's son Faḍl Allāh in a quarrel in 1899. In this year he destroyed another French mission, that of Naval Lieutenant Bretonnet, at Togbao. The French now took effective steps to overcome him, and he was killed by a force under E. Gentil, governor of the S͟hārī near Lake Chad. See Hill, *A Biographical Dictionary of the Anglo-Egyptian Sudan,* pp. 312–13.

4. "Statements Made by Slatin on Equatoria and the Bahr el-Ghazal," Intelligence Report, Egypt, No. 36, March 1895, Part VIII.

5. "Bahr el-Ghazal," Intelligence Report, Egypt, No. 8, November 1892.

6. Ḥag͟hurḍaḥa to Abkar 'Umar, undated (probably 1892), quoted in Armand Abel, "Traduction de documents arabes concernant le Bahr-el-Ghazal (1893–94)," Institut Royal Colonial Belge, *Bulletin Des Séances, 25* (1954), II, 1408–09. This letter from the Mahdist agent Ḥag͟hurḍaḥa was intercepted by Zemio and sent to the resident general of the Bomu.

response to these reports, the Khalīfa sent in the early winter of 1892 an expedition under Ḥājj Zubayr wad al-Faḍl not only to ascertain their validity but also to collect ivory, slaves, and the jihādīya who, fleeing from the Khalīfa's armies, had established a small colony in the western Baḥr al-Ghazāl.[7] Disturbances in the Nūba Mountains prevented wad al-Faḍl from proceeding beyond al-Ubaiyaḍ for some months.[8] Eventually, however, he was able to move to Shakkā and beyond across the Baḥr al-'Arab, but his force had been so badly decimated by disease and frequent skirmishes with the Nūbas that it accomplished virtually nothing. The following year two expeditions were sent by Maḥmūd Aḥmad, the Mahdist governor in the west, to the Baḥr al-Ghazāl. One under al-Khatīm wad Mūsā was sent into the western Baḥr al-Ghazāl, while the other was ordered to march into the Dinka country and retrieve the jihādīya who had fled from the Mahdist army. The Dinka expedition was commanded by Abū Maryam, the Mahdist commandant at Shakkā, who was to lead the expedition against the Dinkas before the rainy season of 1894.[9] Advancing into the Dinka country, the Mahdists were heavily attacked, defeated, and virtually annihilated. Abū Maryam himself was killed, and the few survivors hastily retired to Shakkā.[10] It was at this time that al-Khatīm wad Mūsā and his men returned from the western Baḥr al-Ghazāl to al-Ubaiyaḍ with the news that the Congolese were definitely in the province. Maḥmūd immediately sent out orders for the Dār Fūr sultans to come in with their followers, and the Khalīfa began to prepare a strong force to repel the Congolese during the next dry season.

The Nilis-de la Kéthulle Expedition to the Baḥr al-Ghazāl

Leopold's drive to acquire the Upper Nile Valley was not confined to the expeditions of Van Kerckhoven and Delanghe to the

7. "Bahr el-Ghazal" and "Appendix A," Intelligence Report, Egypt, No. 9, December 1892.

8. "Bahr el-Ghazal," Intelligence Report, Egypt, No. 11, February 1893, and Intelligence Report, Egypt, No. 27, June 1894.

9. "Statements Made by Slatin on Equatoria and the Bahr el-Ghazal," Intelligence Report, Egypt, No. 36, March 1895; Part VIII. "Bahr el-Ghazal," Intelligence Report, Egypt, No. 27, June 1894, and Intelligence Report, Egypt, No. 22, January 1894.

10. "Bahr el-Ghazal," Intelligence Report, Egypt, No. 22, January 1894.

Baḥr al-Jabal. In 1894, two expeditions were to be sent into the Baḥr al-Ghazāl. One under the command of Lieutenant Nilis and de la Kéthulle was to march due north from the village of the Zande chief, Rāfa'i, toward Ḥufrat an-Naḥās.[1] The other, commanded by Lieutenant Fiévez, was to advance northward from Zemio's toward Daym az-Zubayr. In December 1893 Nilis and de la Kéthulle established their headquarters at the village of Rāfa'i in preparation for their march into the Baḥr al-Ghazāl. Rāfa'i not only welcomed the expedition but agreed to support it; for the

1. Theodore Nilis was born at Brilon in Westphalia on June 27, 1851. He entered the military school in 1870, and was commissioned a second lieutenant on April 8, 1872. He left Europe for Africa on February 1, 1882, and upon arriving in the Congo was made second in command of Morianga Post. He returned to Europe on December 7, 1883, with his health seriously impaired. He remained in Europe for four years, but on March 19, 1888, he again joined the service of the Free State and was placed in charge of repatriating the Zanzibaris of the lower Congo. Returning to Europe from Zanzibar, he did not go out to the Congo until 1893, at which time he was placed in command of a reconnaissance expedition to the Baḥr al-Ghazāl. Back in the Bomu, he was placed in command of the Ubangi-Bomu District on January 1, 1895, but left the Congo in May 1895 for Europe. In June 1901 he received his military pension and died four years later on April 23, 1905. See *Biographie Coloniale Belge, I*, 732–36.

Charles de la Kéthulle de Ryhove was born at Louvain on December 6, 1865. A lieutenant in the riflemen, he joined the service of the Free State in December 1890 and in August 1891 was ordered to accompany the Van Kerckhoven expedition. Arriving at Bomokandi, Van Kerckhoven ordered him to the village of Rāfa'i. Several months later he reached Rāfa'i's, where he was welcomed by the Zande sultan, who agreed to give his support to the Free State. From Rāfa'i's he made a reconnaissance expedition north of the Bomu and in 1892 traveled to the station of Zemio erected by Lieutenant Milz. He accompanied Nilis on the expedition into the western Baḥr al-Ghazāl. Returning to the Bomu, he traveled to Europe on the expiration of his term of service in October 1894. Back in the Congo, he was appointed district commissioner of Bangala in December 1895 and was raised to the rank of governor in 1898. He returned to Europe in 1901 and died at Limbourg on January 14, 1903. See *Biographie Coloniale Belge, I*, 573–77.

Rāfa'i (1850–1910), was a Zande chief and son of Kasango. He was also chief of the Banda, a large Sudanic and Bantu tribe which, although keeping its own chiefs of the Baza clan, adopted the Zande language and customs. With the help of Djabir, the great Banda chief to whom he was the lieutenant, he strengthened his position among the Anzakara, Azande, and other tribes of the River Shinko, tributary of the Bomu. He later won the support of Rabīḥ Zubayr during the latter's brief sultanate, 1880–84. He had died before 1912, when the expedition of the Duke of Mecklenburg found his son 'Uthmān ruling in his place. See Hill, p. 313.

Dongo, undoubtedly encouraged by the Mahdists, had invaded his territory the preceding summer, and the presence of the Congolese would help to offset any Mahdist influence.[2] On February 8, 1894, the expedition departed from Rāfa'i's for the north. After a month of difficult marching they reached Katuaka, situated a few miles south of the River Adda. Here the local chief gave them an excellent reception and raised the Free State flag which de la Kéthulle had sent to him some months before.[3] Nearby the Congolese erected a post which they named Fort Adda. From this post emissaries were sent to Ḥufrat an-Naḥās, where they met with Ḥusayn, the self-styled Sultan of Dār Fūr, and requested that he accept the protection of the Congo Free State.[4] Ḥusayn, who was at odds with the Mahdists, not only accepted the protection of the Free State but surrendered the property of the copper mines at Ḥufrat an-Naḥās to King Leopold. An agreement was subsequently concluded and signed by Ḥusayn on May 18, 1894, with the stipulation that even if the influence of the Congo State ceased in these territories, the mines would pass in full right to the person of Leopold II and his heirs.[5] This clause of the agreement was to have far-reaching consequences, for during the Anglo-Congolese dispute over the Baḥr al-Ghazāl between 1900 and 1906, Leopold used his rights to the copper mines to support his claims, commercial and territorial, to the whole of the province.

At the end of March 1894 Nilis and de la Kéthulle received an invitation from Hanolet, who was then exploring the Ubangi-Shari District of the former French Equatorial Africa, to join him at

2. The Wakīl of Rāfa'i to 'Abbās Mūsā, July 11, 1893, and 'Abbās Mūsā to Ḥamad Mūsā, July 13, 1893, Abel, pp. 1396–97 and 1394–96, respectively. The Dongo are a small tribe in the western Baḥr al-Ghazāl who now have come completely under the influence of the Feroge. There is only a handful of the tribe remaining today.

3. R. P. L. Lotar, *La Grande Chronique du Bomu* (Brussels, 1941), pp. 82–84. The name Katuaka is derived from Koti-Waka, a Kreisch clan, but the local chief, designated as Ahmed Curcia by Lotar, has been forgotten by the few old residents of Katuaka. See S. Santandrea, "The Belgians in the Western Bahr el-Ghazal," *Sudan Notes and Records, 36* (1955), II, 190.

4. Lotar, *Chronique du Bomu*, pp. 153–56.

5. "Landeghem-Royaux Mission, 1902," Intelligence, V/5/51; "Memorandum by Van Eetvelde," A.F.l. -40, Lado, No. 13016. In a letter to the Governor of the Bomu from Ḥamad Mūsā dated Dhū al-Qa'da 9, 1311 (May 9, 1894), [Abel, pp. 1403–05], it is stated that the Congolese are at Ḥufrat an-Naḥās.

Dabago.[6] Unable to proceed beyond the Adda because of the flooded condition of the countryside, Nilis and de la Kéthulle left Lieutenant Gerard and fifty men at Fort Adda and marched to Dabago, which they reached on April 27.[7] Here orders were waiting for them to return to the Bomu. Hanolet, however, proceeded northward to Mbelle, where he remained until November 1894, but his expedition was too far to the west to have any contact with the Mahdists.[8]

6. Leon Hanolet was born at Mehaigne-Eghezée on November 25, 1859. A second lieutenant in the 13th Infantry, he joined the service of the Free State in 1888 and was attached to the fourth Ubangi expedition. He was left in charge of Zongo Post for two years after which he returned to Europe. Returning to the Congo in 1892, he joined the Ubangi-Bomu expedition under the command of Le Marinel. On April 19, 1893, he succeeded Bulat as the commandant of the Upper Ubangi–Bomu District and later made a reconnaissance expedition northward to Mbelle in 1894. In April 1895 he returned to Europe but volunteered for a third term of service with the Free State and left from Anvers on June 6, 1896. He succeeded Chaltin as commandant at Rajjāf in November 1897 and successfully repelled a Mahdist attempt to recapture the station. In the engagement he was seriously wounded. On January 2, 1899, his term expired and he left Rajjāf for Europe. Promoted to Inspector, he again returned to the Congo in 1901 to replace Chaltin, whose term of service had expired, as the commandant of the Lado Enclave. He returned to Europe in 1903 and died on December 1, 1908. See *Biographie Coloniale Belge, 2,* 446–52.

7. Lotar, *Chronique du Bomu,* p. 84. Auguste Gerard was born at Warisoulx on May 10, 1871. A second lieutenant, he joined the service of the Free State in 1890 and was ordered to the Ubangi-Bomu District. He accompanied the Nilis–de la Kéthulle expedition and was left in charge of Fort Adda near Katuaka. Threatened by the Mahdists, he was rescued by a relief column; abandoning the post, the column returned to the Bomu, where Gerard was made *chef de poste* at Imese. He returned to Europe in June 1896 and again took service with the Free State, becoming *chef de zone* of Dungu. In an expedition against the Bokoyo he was seriously wounded and returned to Europe in 1899. He was appointed commandant of the Ubangi District in 1900 and, in 1904, commandant of Bangalas District. He returned to Europe in 1906 but agreed to serve a fifth term in the Congo as commissioner for administrative reforms. In 1909 he was back in Europe. The following year, however, he was again called to make a tour of inspection, from 1910 to 1911, and the year after that was made permanent inspector of the Kasai and Kwango Districts. He returned to Belgium on May 7, 1914, and at the outbreak of the war was placed in command of the 1st Light Infantry Regiment. He was killed in action at Impde. See *Biographie Coloniale Belge, 1,* 396–401.

8. Lotar, *Chronique du Bomu,* pp. 84–89.

The Fiévez Expedition

In September 1892 emissaries from Ḥamad Mūsā, son of 'Abbās Mūsā chief of the Feroge, and Andal, chief of the Njangulgule, arrived at Zemio's to inquire if they might retreat southward into Congolese territory if attacked by the Mahdists.[1] This request was not surprising. The Feroge, in the days of the first Mahdist invasion, had fought the forces of Karam Allāh for three years until obliged to retire to the south.[2] On the other hand, the Njangulgule under their great chief Yanqu of the clan Maduke had been one of the first to rise against the Egyptian Administration and support Karam Allāh; but after Yanqu's death, the Maduke clan lost its ascendency to the Maruwa led by Chief Dahia, who was inclined to be hostile to the Mahdists.[3] This hostility compelled Dahia to move further south from the Baḥr al-'Arab near the land of the anti-Mahdist Feroge. In fact Dahia placed himself under the nominal suzerainty of the Feroge chief 'Abbās Mūsā after the Njangulgule had been badly beaten by Zemio's Azande in 1890, and there is reason to believe that Dahia's son and successor, Andal, did the same.[4] It is true that the Njangulgule had no reason to make peace with Zemio, whose Azande had twice invaded their territory; but the Njangulgule could not maintain themselves against both the Azande and the Mahdists, and so consequently made their peace with Zemio, particularly since their nominal overlords, the Feroge, had no desire to pay allegiance to the Khalīfa.[5]

The Mahdists had for some time contented themselves with patrolling the north bank of the Baḥr al-'Arab when, in 1892, the news spread south that Hājj Zubayr wad al-Faḍl was preparing to

1. Lotar writes that Fiévez corresponded with Faki Ahmed and Adjer, whom Father Santandrea has correctly identified as Ḥamad Mūsā and Andal respectively. Ḥamad Mūsā referred to himself as the son of Yūsuf, Sultan of Wadā'i, "in an effort to enhance his authority." Santandrea, "The Belgians in the Western Bahr el-Ghazal," p. 140. Abel, p. 1385.

2. Santandrea, "A Preliminary Account of the Indri, Togoyo, Feroge, Mangaya, and Woro," p. 243.

3. Ibid., p. 245.

4. Ibid., p. 244.

5. Above, p. 138.

march into the Baḥr al-Ghazāl. Although the Mahdist expedition did not cross the Baḥr al-'Arab until the winter of 1892–93, the news of an impending expedition was sufficient for the Feroge and the Njangulgule to send agents to Zemio's in September 1892. The Congolese commandant at Zemio's, Fiévez, seized this opportunity and wrote "to these two chiefs that they should enter into direct negotiations with me and in case of an attack they should be allies of the whites." [6] Then, carried away by his superficial success, he continued: "By this stroke, I extended the relations of the State to 8° 30′ north." [7]

The Feroge and the Njangulgule did not, however, have to retreat to the south that year. The Mahdist expedition under wad al-Faḍl was forced by disease and desertion to withdraw to Shakkā without encountering any of the tribes of the western Baḥr al-Ghazāl, and it was not until the autumn of 1893 that the Feroge and the Njangulgule were again threatened by the Mahdists. In August a band of Mahdists led by al-Khatīm wad Mūsā invaded the western Baḥr al-Ghazāl, but their advance was momentarily checked by the Banda, who, in an engagement with the Anṣār, captured twenty-five guns and killed four Mahdists. In spite of this defeat, however, the Mahdists, reinforced by their allies the Dongo —who had made a raid into the territory of Rāfa'i in July—continued to march further into the Baḥr al-Ghazāl, invading the territory of Ḥamad Mūsā, son of 'Abbās Mūsā chief of the Feroge.[8]

6. Quoted in Lotar, *Chronique du Bomu,* p. 92. Achille Fiévez was born at Willeman on May 15, 1860. A lieutenant of the 3rd Light Infantry, he joined the service of the Free State and left for the Congo on February 11, 1892, arriving at Zemio's on August 5, 1892. Promoted to Inspector on July 4, 1893, he was the political officer at the residence of Rāfa'i and Sasa, and in September 1893 he made the first contact between the Free State and Ndoruma, Mbio, and Tambura. On March 8, 1894, with Walhousen and Donckier, he left the Bomu for Daym az-Zubayr. On April 2, however, most of the column had to be recalled to fight against the Mahdists at Dungu. He returned to Zemio's on April 26 and remained there until September, when he led an expedition to Bakari. On January 12, 1895, he left Bakari for the Uele, Boma, and Europe, where he arrived in June 1895. He died at Tournai on March 15, 1904. See *Biographie Coloniale Belge, I,* 374–75.

7. Quoted in Lotar, *Chronique du Bomu,* p. 92.

8. 'Abbās Mūsā to Masingo, Ṣafar 10, 1311 (August 13, 1893). Rāfa'i to Zemio, 1311 (1893), Abel, pp. 1391–92 and 1390–91, respectively. Both letters refer to Dār Bān and the Bān, who are undoubtedly the Banda situated south of Ḥufrat an-Naḥās and at the same time west of the Feroge.

'Abbās Mūsā immediately dispatched appeals for aid to Zemio and Rāfa'i, but in the meantime Ḥamad Mūsā was driven from his territory, and the Mahdists advanced into that of his father.[9] On October 20, 1893, the forces of 'Abbās Mūsā engaged the Anṣār, who, after a hard-fought battle lasting from dawn to midday, were compelled to retire, losing six guns and many swords. Although victorious, 'Abbās Mūsā, in a letter to Zemio dated October 28, intimated that he would be unable to halt the Mahdists again.[10] By the first of the year, 1894, 'Abbās Mūsā was dead and both the Feroge, now led by his son, Ḥamad Mūsā, and the Njangulgule were in full retreat southward.

On February 15, 1894, the news of this retreat reached Zemio's, and Fiévez immediately prepared to march northward under the following orders which had been dispatched to him from Leopoldville the preceding month:

1. To enter into commercial relations with the Arabs of the north and establish a post in the country of the Sultan Faki Ahmed [Ḥamad Mūsā], in communication with the Resident since September 1892.
2. To put a stop to the slave merchants [the Mahdists] who were pushing their incursions south of the Boro.
3. To trade with the Dinkas, pastoral people who own many cattle.
4. After the establishing [of a post] on the Boro, to reach Daym az-Zubayr and install oneself there either in the old residence of Lupton or in the immediate vicinity.[11]

On March 8, 1894, Fiévez, accompanied by Walhousen, Donckier de Donceel, and Zemio, left the home of the latter and marched northward by easy stages.[12] On the 16th they learned that Ḥamad

9. 'Abbās Mūsā to Zemio, Rabī' al-Thānī 3, 1311 (October 15, 1893), Abel, pp. 1405–06.

10. Ibid., Rabī' al-Thānī 18, 1311 (October 28, 1893), Abel, pp. 1405–06.

11. Quoted in Lotar, *Chronique du Bomu,* p. 93.

12. Xavier Donckier de Donceel was born at Ledeberg on July 18, 1871. A sergeant in the 2nd Lancers, he joined the service of the Free State and left Europe for the Congo on September 6, 1893. He arrived at Zemio's on January 20, 1894, and took part in the Fiévez expedition to the Baḥr al-Ghazāl. When Fiévez and Walhousen had to retire to the Bomu, he was left alone in the Baḥr al-Ghazāl until November 1894, at which time the Congolese forces were withdrawn. He

Mūsā was coming in to make a formal alliance with the Free State, and two weeks later a Feroge guide arrived to lead them to Ḥamad Mūsā's camp.[13] On April 2, 1894, they marched to Ombanga, where they were informed by a special messenger of the massacre on March 2, of the Bonvalet-Devos column, and of the defeat of Wtterwulghe on the Akka.[14] Baert ordered Zemio and 200 of his men to leave the Fiévez expedition and return to their home on the Bomu. Without sufficient support all the Europeans could not continue the march. Therefore, Fiévez ordered Donckier and fifty-six men forward to the Biri River and Daym az-Zubayr while he and Walhousen returned with Zemio.[15]

The news of the Congolese advance had spread rapidly northward into the Baḥr al-G͟hazāl, where al-K͟hatīm wad Mūsā, who was unaware that most of the Congolese force had been compelled to withdraw, became alarmed and immediately retired to S͟hakkā in Dār Fūr. The K͟halīfa, upon learning of the Congolese expeditions, was equally perturbed and ordered Maḥmūd Aḥmad, the Mahdist governor and commander-in-chief of Dār Fūr, Kurdufān, and the Baḥr al-G͟hazāl, to prepare an army consisting of 1,800 riflemen and 2,000 spearmen under the command of al-K͟hatīm wad Mūsā to march against the Congolese.[16]

After Fiévez and Walhousen had left Ombanga for the south,

returned to Zemio's on February 10, 1895, and on August 5 was assigned to the post at Bima. He returned to Belgium in September 1896. He went out again to the Congo in 1897 and was assigned to the Henry expedition, which was hunting down the mutineers of the Dhanis expedition. On July 5, 1898, he was wounded in an accident in camp and died on July 26, 1898. See *Biographie Coloniale Belge, I,* 338–20.

François Walhousen was born at Namur on June 16, 1865. A second lieutenant in the 3rd Infantry, he left for the Congo on July 25, 1893. Arriving at Zemio's on December 6, 1893, he took part in the Fiévez expedition to the Baḥr al-G͟hazāl. After the Congolese withdrawal to the Bomu, he left Zemio's on February 8, 1895, for the post of Amadis on the Uele. On February 23, 1896, he was made *chef de poste* of Dungu. He left for Europe in July 1896. He returned for a second term of service with the Free State in the Lado Enclave, where he was killed in an engagement against the Mahdists on May 21, 1898. See *Biographie Coloniale Belge, I,* 946–48.

13. Lotar, *Chronique du Bomu,* p. 94.

14. Above, pp. 110, 126–27.

15. Lotar, *Chronique du Bomu,* pp. 94–95.

16. "Statements Made by Slatin on Equatoria and the Bahr el-Ghazal," Intelligence Report, Egypt, No. 36, March 1895, Part VIII.

Donckier marched northwestward to the village of Bandassi.[17] Here, on April 8, orders arrived from Zemio commanding Bandassi and his followers to march also to the Bomu in order to reinforce the men of Zemio at that time preparing to aid the Congolese at Dungu.[18] Without the aid of Bandassi, Donckier judged that his escort alone was insufficient to proceed as instructed to Daym az-Zubayr, so he decided to retire to a Bakoumba village called Mimmiboie. Here Donckier awaited the arrival of Ḥamad Mūsā, whose whereabouts no one seemed to know. Finally, on April 28, a messenger arrived at Mimmiboie with a letter from Ḥamad Mūsā addressed to the governor of the Bomu. But the letter was written in Arabic, and since Donckier had no one able to translate it, he had no choice but to forward the letter to Zemio's for translation.[19] A few days later news reached Mimmiboie that Ḥamad Mūsā had abandoned his village on the Boro and fled northward to the River Gama. His flight was precipitated by the Congolese troops who had been left by the Nilis–de la Kéthulle expedition at Fort Adda under the command of Lieutenant Gerard. They had been sent on foraging expeditions to nearby Katuaka and beyond to Ḥufrat an-Naḥās and Dongo, where they had seized supplies and had done considerable damage to the villages. Consequently, he wrote to the governor of the Bomu the above-mentioned letter in which he professed his loyalty to the Free State but demanded that the Congolese troops be withdrawn from his domain before receiving the representatives of the Free State or discussing any commercial treaty.[20] He then burned his village and fled, as much in fear of the Congolese as the Mahdists.[21]

17. Bandassi is often referred to as Bodué.

18. Lotar, *Chronique du Bomu,* pp. 95–96.

19. Ibid., pp. 96–97.

20. Ḥamad Mūsā to the governor of the Bomu, Dhū al-Qa'da 5, 1311 (May 9, 1894), Abel, pp. 1403–05.

21. Lotar wrote (*Chronique du Bomu,* pp. 97–98) a radically different interpretation of these events: "Faki [Ḥamad Mūsā] had hoisted the flag of the State and had really prepared to receive and establish in his home the Fiévez column; but he came to learn, to his surprise, of the retreat of Bodué's people, and then of Zemio, to the south. He thus deduced that the Fiévez column had given up the intention of establishing a camp at the Borou [Boro]. After this there would be no aid for Faki or protection for his villages from the Mahdist incursions. He fled." The letter of Ḥamad Mūsā certainly does not give credence to this interpretation. In addition, if the Congolese were situated at Katuaka, Ḥufrat

Although Donckier, having sent the letter untranslated to Zemio's, was unaware of the demands of Ḥamad Mūsā, he persisted in establishing communications with the Feroge chief. On May 20 he sent another messenger in search of Ḥamad Mūsā, and within a fortnight the emissary discovered his zarība on the Gama. Ḥamad Mūsā not only appeared satisfied with Donckier's message, but dispatched in return a friendly greeting and two men bearing gifts of goats, chickens, and ostrich plumes. Encouraged by these signs of friendship, Donckier left Mimmiboie and marched northeastward to effect a meeting with the Feroge chief.[22] He crossed the Biri River on June 14, 1894, and turned northward, crossing the Sopo and arriving at Liffi south of the Raga River on June 25. On the way he had met emissaries from Ḥamad Mūsā "bearing gifts and a chestnut horse, and they announced that Faki [Ḥamad Mūsā] had already begun to build the post on the Borou [Boro] and the plantations intended for revictualling." [23] Donckier remained at Liffi from June 25 to July 6, during which time he began the construction of a zarība. He then made a reconnaissance to the village of Modanga southwest of Liffi but returned on July 14 after news had been brought to him that Andal, the Njangulgule chief, had died and had been succeeded by his son, Nasr, whose representatives had arrived at Liffi with peace offerings and gifts.[24] Donckier accepted these gifts and then on July 16 left for the zarība of Ḥamad Mūsā situated on the River Gama. During the march he learned that the Congolese had established themselves near Katuaka at Fort Adda and that the garrison, commanded by Lieutenant Gerard, had been reinforced by 140 soldiers and a cannon under the command of Le Marinel.[25]

---

an-Naḥās, and Dongo, Ḥamad Mūsā would most certainly not regard the retreat of the Fiévez column as an abandonment of the Baḥr al-Ghazāl by the Congolese. Moreover, Donckier was still at Mimmiboie. Furthermore, Ḥamad Mūsā retired toward the north to the River Gama—a strange move for one supposedly fearing a Mahdist invasion. There is a discrepancy between the date of Ḥamad Mūsā's letter (May 9) and the date given by Lotar for its arrival at Mimmiboie (April 28), though the misdating may be inadvertent. There is little doubt that Ḥamad Mūsā's letter dated May 9 is the one referred to by Lotar as arriving at Mimmiboie on April 28.

22. Lotar, *Chronique du Bomu,* p. 99.

23. Ibid.

24. Ibid., p. 100.

25. Georges Le Marinel was born in the United States of America on June 29,

Donckier reached the village of Ḥamad Mūsā on July 25, 1894, and was courteously received by the Feroge chief. After the preliminary greetings Donckier and Ḥamad Mūsā discussed their mutual grievances, which were apparently settled satisfactorily, and then they signed a commercial treaty in which the Feroge "accepted the protection of the Congo Free State, and that Sheikh Hamad [Ḥamad Mūsā] would be the medium of trade between the Congo Free State and all the country up to the frontiers of Darfur, in return for which concession the Congo Free State guaranteed to protect Hamad and his tribe and to establish fortified posts in his country." [26] Ḥamad also provided Donckier with 200 men to reinforce Liffi and agreed to come to Liffi to resolve all disputes. Donckier, in turn, agreed to build a station on the Boro, the construction of which actually began on August 6. The discussions terminated in the utmost good will.[27]

This treaty was most significant because of its potentiality for further action and because of the claims to Congolese rights in the Baḥr al-Ghazāl which it established. Donckier had not only opened up the possibility of trade between the Free State and the tribes of the Baḥr al-Ghazāl but had secured a protectorate well within the Nile watershed and far north of the Equatorial regions. Although European diplomacy was to rob the treaty of operative power and was to force the Congolese to desert Ḥamad and leave him to the Mahdists, there is no doubt that the Free State would have made the greatest efforts, if permitted, to consolidate the rights to the Baḥr al-Ghazāl established by the treaty.

After concluding his discussions with Ḥamad, Donckier left his

---

1860. An officer in the engineers of the Belgian army, he embarked for the Congo on August 5, 1884. He did service in the lower Congo and on the upper Ubangi. On September 6, 1893, he was named state inspector and led an expedition to Fort Adda in the Baḥr al-Ghazāl in July 1894. At the end of 1894 he was in charge of the evacuation of the territories ceded to France. He embarked for Europe on February 25, 1895. Thereafter he was very active in Congolese affairs and in 1908 was named director to the Minister of the Colonies. In 1914, he sought refuge in England, where he died. See *Biographie Coloniale Belge, I*, 659–64.

26. "Statements Made by Slatin on Equatoria and the Bahr-el-Ghazal," Intelligence Report, Egypt, No. 36, March 1895, Part VIII.

27. Lotar, *Chronique du Bomu*, p. 101.

zarība and marched eastward in search of supplies. He returned to the Boro on August 6, with cattle, goats, and other supplies and began to construct a post. On August 21 he received the news that Walhousen was marching from Zemio's to the village of Morjane to take command of the expedition and then push on to Liffi and Daym az-Zubayr. Four days later, on August 25, Nasr, the chief of the Njangulgule, came himself in to Post Boro to offer his submission to the Free State. On September 10, 1894, Donckier left Post Boro to meet Walhousen. On the 15th he reached Liffi and ten days later received a message from Walhousen requesting Donckier to join him immediately at Morjane to discuss plans for concerted action north of the Boro. Donckier departed for Morjane and arrived a few days later. The outcome of the talks was for Donckier to remain at Liffi in support of Walhousen, who was to push on to Daym Idrīs and Wau to the east. Therefore, Donckier returned to Liffi, where, upon arrival, he found the station in open revolt. The irregulars of Ḥamad Mūsā had mutinied and had attempted to seize the ammunition and stores but had been frustrated by the loyal Congolese regulars who were defending the station. Walhousen, being immediately informed of the situation, sent reinforcements which were sufficient to put down the insurrection after killing over thirty-three Feroge irregulars.[28]

On October 24 a messenger came in to Liffi from Ḥamad Mūsā's zarība to inform Donckier that the Mahdists had returned in force and were at that time near the River Gama. During the summer of 1894 al-K̲h̲atīm wad Mūsā had been assembling his forces in preparation to invade the Baḥr al-G̲h̲azāl at the end of the rainy season. In the meantime he had written letters to the tribes of the western Baḥr al-G̲h̲azāl reminding them that the Azande had returned (with the Congolese) to make them their subjects, but that the Mahdists had collected a great army which was preparing to march to their aid, drive out the Azande, and establish peace.[29] An example

28. Ibid., pp. 102–05.

29. K̲h̲ātim wad Mūsā to Ibn Zaqal, Muḥarram 7, 1312 (July 11, 1894), Abel, pp. 1401–03. After the Mahdists had withdrawn from the Baḥr al-G̲h̲azāl in 1885, the Azande invaded the province, inflicting serious damage and defeats on the native tribes. In 1890 they again invaded the Baḥr al-G̲h̲azāl but, as before, retired with their plunder (p. 138). Consequently, when the Congolese and their

of this propaganda was the letter to one Ibn Zaqal in which al-Khatīm wad Mūsā wrote:

> We have made known to you that the Niam Niam [Azande] wish to extend their power to your country and make you submit to their authority, in order that you will be their subjects.
>
> When we learned that—may God despise their action—and because you were our friend and our neighbor, we warned all those who are with us in any way because that has greatly annoyed us.
>
> We have thus assembled a great number of soldiers, Muslims, and vassals of Muslims. The number of men surpasses twenty thousand, collected because of the interest we take in you, and to deliver you. Immediately, we left in the direction of the enemy, with resolution, hastening to you to help you against your enemies, and we have been able to free you from this peril. We have wanted to extend our guarantee to you along with the guarantee of God, His Prophet, and his Mahdī, His Lieutenant—long life to them—with the guarantee of our Lord: Maḥmūd Aḥmad [the Mahdist governor in the West]. And this guarantee extends to your goods, your children, so that you have absolutely nothing to fear.
>
> When this letter arrives in your hands, you should be tranquil, resolute, confident; you and your families in your homes.
>
> Now, let nobody take it upon himself to ask you to move anywhere else. But remain there where you are and do not emigrate. I warn you that should this not be done we will not be able to continue what was arranged for you against the Niam Niam [Azande]. Neither can we come to you because of the years that weigh upon us. Never from this side [of the Baḥr al-'Arab] has anyone else gone to you, only we who in this situation have brought our intervention, for on us, following the tradition of Muḥammad, falls the duty of redressing injustice. The salvation of God and the prayers to him who delegated to us the good works to our vassals.

Azande allies marched into the Baḥr al-Ghazāl in 1894, Khātim purposely drew no distinction between the Congolese expeditions and the preceding Azande invasions in order to utilize fear of the Azande to drive the western tribes of the Baḥr al-Ghazāl into the Mahdist camp.

And now, we have sent on our part orders to Sultan Ḥamad Mūsā, and we have asked him to come to meet us at Kufundura.[30]

Ḥamad Mūsā, as the above letter indicates, received a similar summons to join the Mahdists; but apparently he refused, for after the news reached his zarība that the Mahdists had crossed the Baḥr al-'Arab with 3,800 men he proposed to Walhousen and Donckier that they should leave Liffi, cross the Raga, and rendezvous with him on the Boro to march together against the Mahdists. But it was impossible to carry out such a plan. The Congolese were extremely short of supplies. Donckier had only four days' supply of salt and fifty rounds of ammunition per man, hardly sufficient for a campaign against the Mahdists. Consequently, Donckier and Walhousen could do nothing but retire to Morjane.[31] This retreat convinced Ḥamad of the futility of dealing with the Congolese. He surrendered to the Mahdists, handed over the treaties made with the Congolese, and became the representative of Mahdist interests in the northwestern Baḥr al-Ghazāl. In November 1894 Donckier made a reconnaissance from Morjane across the Raga, where he expected to encounter the Mahdists; but no sign of them was to be found.[32]

Meanwhile, in the west at Katuaka, the local chief, angered by the Congolese demands for supplies and emboldened by Mahdist propaganda, secretly arranged an alliance with the Mahdists and plotted with them to attack Fort Adda. Gerard, the Congolese commandant, had no more than 200 troops, including the reinforcements of Le Marinel, with which to hold this very exposed station. Consequently, Nilis with Lieutenants Lannoy and Libois made a forced march from the Bomu to reinforce Fort Adda.[33] Arriving

30. Khātim wad Mūsā to Ibn Zaqal, Muḥarram 7, 1312 (July 11, 1894), Abel, pp. 1401–03. Ibn Zaqal was a chief of the Binga, a small Arabicized tribe situated east of the River Adda. The zarība of Ibn Zaqal was located on the Shallaikha River thirty miles west of the Adda at approximately 9° 40′ of longitude.

31. Lotar, *Chronique du Bomu,* pp. 105–06.

32. Ibid., p. 106.

33. Leon Lannoy was born at Nivelles on November 30, 1860. A lieutenant in the 1st Cavalry, he joined the service of the Free State and left Europe for the Congo on December 21, 1893. He participated in the Nilis–de la Kéthulle expedition and arrived at Fort Adda in August 1894. He returned to Yakoma in

at the fort, they were informed by Gerard "that an attack on the fort on the Adda by more than a thousand Mahdists was imminent." [34] The Congolese officers, deciding that resistance was impossible, abandoned Fort Adda on the following day and retired to the south. "The retreat was disastrous, for many of the men succumbed to the fatigue, the forced marches, and the privations." [35] It was not until the remnants reached Bandassi that the Congolese were safely beyond the reach of the Anṣār.

In spite of the abandonment of Fort Adda and the withdrawal of Congolese forces, Lieutenant Colmant was ordered to march north into the Baḥr al-G͟hazāl and to try to hold the country for the Congolese as well as attempt to re-open communications with Ḥamad Mūsā.[36] Colmant and his force immediately set off for the north, but their progress was slow because of the lack of supplies along the route of march and the great brush fires which after the rains swept over the undulating plains of the Baḥr al-G͟hazāl. Finally, on December 9, 1894, Colmant arrived at Morjane, where his men, added to those of Donckier and Walhousen, raised the number of Congolese troops to 220.[37] Feeling that this number was sufficient to march further north, Colmant, Walhousen, and most of the troops left Morjane for Liffi and Telgauna, where they hoped to

November 1894 and embarked for Europe on November 12, 1896, dying at Vilvarde on August 12, 1913. See *Biographie Coloniale Belge,* 2, 586–87.

Jean Libois was born at Bruges on April 10, 1869. A lieutenant in the riflemen, he left Europe for the Congo on September 6, 1893. In April 1894 he replaced Lieutenant Gonze, who had died on the Nilis–de la Kéthulle expedition, and marched with Nilis to Fort Adda to reinforce Gerard. When Fort Adda was abandoned, he retired to Zemio's but, taken ill, left the Congo on September 7, 1895, for Europe. He died at Brussels on June 22, 1839. See *Biographie Coloniale Belge,* 2, 623–25.

34. Gerard to Nilis, quoted in Lotar, *Chronique du Bomu,* p. 110.

35. Notes of Libois, quoted in Lotar, *Chronique du Bomu,* p. 111.

36. Letter of Delanghe, Lotar, *Chronique du Bomu,* pp. 112–13. Florent Colmant was born at Jemappes on November 22, 1861. A lieutenant in the 8th Infantry, he left Europe for the Congo on November 6, 1893. Arriving at Zemio's on October 10, 1894, he was ordered to join Walhousen and Donckier and then to march on to Daym az-Zubayr. The signing of the Franco-Congolese Treaty forced the recall of the Congolese forces in the Baḥr al-G͟hazāl, but not before Colmant made a rapid march to see Daym az-Zubayr. He went back to Zemio and served in the Uele Valley until his return to Europe in November 1896. See Lotar, *Chronique du Bomu,* pp. 140–41.

37. Lotar, *Chronique du Bomu,* p. 115.

re-establish relations with Nasr, while Donckier left Morjane with sixty troops for the Boro, where he hoped to find Ḥamad Mūsā. A few days after his departure from Morjane, Colmant received the following letter from Delanghe, dated November 30, 1894:

Dear Lieutenant:

I have the honor of informing you of the conclusion of a Franco-Congolese Treaty limiting the possessions of the State on the Bomu to their sources, and a line drawn from the Congo-Nile Divide to the 30° Meridian east of Greenwich.

All the troops which we have in the north will retire, and you will direct them, when they are gathered at Bili or at Rabeh to our Residence at Bakaraka [southwest of Zemio], with all the materials and merchandise.

You are not to communicate to any person the reason for our retreat; it is sufficient to say that it is I who have recalled you. The Sultan Zemio is informed.[38]

By February 1895 the Congolese had retired completely from the Baḥr al-Ghazāl.

Although the Congolese had been forced to withdraw from the Baḥr al-Ghazāl because of the vicissitudes of European diplomacy, the Mahdists were similarly compelled to retire—not, however, because of the fortunes of diplomacy but rather because of the heavy losses incurred from famine, disease, and desertion. When an insurrection broke out in Dār Fūr in 1895, the Khalīfa recalled al-Khatīm wad Mūsā from the Baḥr al-Ghazāl in order to assist Maḥmūd Aḥmad, the Mahdist commander in the West, in quelling the rebellion. Of the 3,800 men who had accompanied the expedition into the Baḥr al-Ghazāl, only 880 returned to Shakkā.[39] The Mahdists did not attempt to invade the Baḥr al-Ghazāl again. As before, the province returned to its natural state of anarchy and intertribal warfare until the coming of the Anglo-Egyptian forces in the first decade of the twentieth century.

38. Quoted in Lotar, *Chronique du Bomu,* pp. 115–16.

39. "Bahr el-Ghazal," Intelligence Report, Egypt, No. 39, June 1895.

CHAPTER 5

THE DEFEAT OF THE MAHDISTS

The Battle for Rajjāf

Throughout the years 1895 and 1896 the Congolese had been slowly consolidating their position in the Uele Valley in anticipation of marching at any moment to the Nile. On October 31, 1896, Commandant Chaltin received orders to advance and meet the main column of the Nile Expedition under Baron Dhanis which was marching from Stanleyville up the Aruwimi Valley to Lake Albert and the Nile.[1] In preparation for the march Chaltin immediately assembled his men and supplies and sent a mission to enlist the aid of the powerful Zande chief Renzi, through whose territory the column would have to march. Renzi, although long an enemy of the Free State and an open supporter of the Mahdists, was willing at last to desert the latter and join with the Congolese, who, after the flight of the Anṣār, were most certainly the strongest power in the Uele. Furthermore, Renzi grasped this opportunity

1. Lotar, *Chronique de l'Uele,* p. 235.

to bring the Congolese over to his side in the struggle between him and the successors of Ukwa.[2] He joined the forces of the Free State with alacrity, bringing the followers of Bafuka with him.[3]

On December 13, 1896, the column left Dungu for the Nile. There were 700 Congolese troops divided into eight platoons under the respective commands of Kops, Gehot, DeBacker, Sarolea, Cajot, Dupont, Laplume, Goebel, and a Dr. Rossignon, with one Krupps cannon. Ten days later at Surur they were joined by the 580 irregular troops and the 220 carriers of Renzi. The column was finally complete. In spite of the discouraging news that Baron Dhanis with the main body of the expedition would be unable to rendezvous at the appointed time and place, Chaltin nevertheless decided to continue the march alone. Consequently, on December 31, 1896, the whole column left Surur for Faradj, which they reached on January 10, 1897. On the 15th they continued, camping on January 23 at the foot of Mt. Adra, where two days later they received a message from Dhanis proposing that the Chaltin column wait for him and his men at Mt. Korobe. But Chaltin decided to push on. By February 1 the column was at Mt. Korobe, where they were informed that the Mahdists were strengthening Rajjāf. On February 10 the Chaltin column reached Mt. Bereka, only one day's march from the Nile. Here they learned that 'Arabī Dafa' Allāh, who had only just returned to Rajjāf from a foraging expedition, had fortified the station with three cannon and a strong zarība. On the 14th the column proceeded, and at 10 o'clock in the morning reached the Nile at Bedden, seventeen miles south of Rajjāf. During the day patrols were sent northward which encountered roving bands of Anṣār, who were put to flight. Yet Chaltin's position was far from secure. There was no news from Dhanis, and Goebel—who with 100 men had returned to Surur for supplies—had not yet come up to Bedden.[4]

2. Ukwa, a Zande chief, was the son of Wando; he established himself near the confluence of the Dungu and the Kibali rivers and carried on intermittent warfare against his brother and archenemy, Renzi. On his death, in 1895, his sons continued the struggle against Renzi—with, however, less success.

3. Lotar, *Chronique de l'Uele,* pp. 254–55. Bafuka, a Zande chief, was also a son of Wando.

4. Lotar, *Chronique de l'Uele,* pp. 255–58. It was indeed fortunate that Chaltin did not wait for Dhanis, whose column was soon disintegrated by mutiny and was unable to proceed to the Nile. Jules Goebel was born at Liége on

Meanwhile 'Arabī Dafa' Allāh had concentrated all of his men at Rajjāf. The garrisons at Shambe and Bor were withdrawn; and although this raised the strength of Rajjāf to nearly 1,400 men, the increase created a shortage of supplies throughout the autumn of 1896. To remedy the famine conditions at the station, 'Arabī carried out extensive foraging raids in the neighboring areas. When the surrounding countryside was exhausted, he decided to range further afield in the plentiful Azande country to the west. There is little doubt that he would not have so exposed his position if he had been aware that the Congolese were advancing against him, and he was extremely fortunate to have later regained Rajjāf before the forces of the Free State arrived. As the Mahdists moved to the west, Yambio, the great Zande chief, dispatched an emissary to the Anṣār with instructions to inform 'Arabī Dafa' Allāh to remain east of the River Wo. When the Zande emissary returned and reported that the Mahdists had only hostile intentions, Yambio withdrew from his village and ordered the Azande army to mobilize with all possible speed. On January 5, 1897, the Azande ambushed the Mahdists near the village of Yambio. A fierce battle ensued, in which the Azande were driven off, and the Anṣār, occupying the village, erected a strong zarība. For nearly a month thereafter sporadic fighting took place around the zarība until the Azande forces, growing continually in strength, pressed the attack for three full days. On the fourth day the Mahdists quietly retired under cover of darkness. When their flight was discovered, the Azande pursued the Anṣār as far as the River Yeta, at which time Yambio, having lost enough men, ordered the pursuit discontinued. Both sides claimed a victory. 'Arabī Dafa' Allāh lost 120 men, including many of his amīrs; the losses of Yambio were undoubtedly much larger. The Mahdists had procured supplies, but the Azande had successfully repulsed them.[5]

April 15, 1872. A sergeant in the 13th Infantry, he joined the service of the Free State and was ordered on November 1, 1896, to accompany the Nile Expedition. He participated in the taking of Rajjāf and resided at Loka throughout 1898. He returned to Europe in August 1898, but served a second and third term in the Uele from March 1899 to June 1909, and a fourth term as a military inspector at Lake Leopold. He died at Oshwe on August 9, 1910. See *Biographie Coloniale Belge*, 2, 420–22.

5. 'Arabī Dafa' Allāh to the Khalīfa, Rabī' al-'Awwal 12, 1316 (July 31, 1898), Intelligence Report, Egypt, No. 60, May 25 to December 31, 1898, Appendix 63,

Returning to Rajjāf in February 1897, ʿArabī arrested a large deputation carrying ten tusks of ivory from Kabarega, King of Unyoro, to the Khalīfa in Umm Durmān. Kabarega had been driven from his country to Dufile by the British and consequently had sent his emissaries down the Nile to enlist the support of the Mahdists. They never got beyond Rajjāf, however, for on February 14 a band of Anṣār encountered the patrols of the Free State, and from that moment ʿArabī was too preoccupied defending Rajjāf to concern himself with Kabarega. He merely impressed the representatives of the King of Unyoro into his army and sent Bishārī Muḥammad of the Taʿāʾisha to ascertain the position of the Congolese.[6] When Bishārī shortly returned to report that the forces of the Congo Free State were stationed at Bedden, ʿArabī wrote to the Khalīfa:

> I assembled the captains of the hundreds and men who should be consulted. I took counsel as to whether I should follow the Christians and slay them, and they agreed with me and so the council ended with that resolution. They all thought it best that I should stay in the markaz [station] and that they should go out with the army because of their fear that the enemy would come by another route seeking the markaz. So I stayed in the markaz with some men, a few tribal troops and jihādīya, and some of the Taʿāʾisha. The whole number did not exceed forty in the detachment itself.[7]

The rest of the Mahdist contingent, which probably numbered about 1,200 men, marched out of Rajjāf under the command of Muḥammad ʿAlī Bādī on February 16, 1897, to block the advance of the Congolese.

Meanwhile, after the Congolese patrols had established contact

---

No. 1, and Mahdīya, I/34/3. E. Evans-Pritchard, "A History of the Kingdom of Gbudwe," *Zaïre, 10* (October 1956), 819–22.

6. Sudan Intelligence Report No. 96, July 1902. One of Kabarega's emissaries, a Madi chief named Faragalla, actually reached Khartoum. After retiring to Bor with the Anṣār, he accompanied ʿArabī Dafaʿ Allāh when the amīr made his way west to Dār Kalaka upon the approach of an Anglo-Congolese force under Major Martyr. Faragalla later escaped from the Mahdists, and after many adventures and nearly five years since leaving Unyoro, he arrived in Khartoum from which he was subsequently repatriated to Uganda.

7. ʿArabī Dafaʿ Allāh to the Khalīfa, Rabīʿ al-ʾAwwal 12, 1316 (July 31, 1898), Intelligence Report, Egypt, No. 60, Appendix 63, No. 1, and Mahdīya, I/34/3.

with the Anṣār on February 14, Chaltin on the following day sent out reconnaissance parties, but they found no sign of the Mahdists. On the 16th the bulk of the Congolese remained stationed at Bedden, but 150 men were sent to assist Goebel and his patrol, who were coming up from Surur with supplies, and sentries were stationed at the base of a long ridge which formed the northern extremity of the Bedden Plain. At four o'clock Goebel, his platoon, and the 150 troops sent to hasten his march arrived. Shortly afterward the Mahdists suddenly appeared.[8] Chaltin wrote:

> At five thirty in the afternoon, our advance sentries retreated making frantic gestures. The men rushed to the stacked guns, and in less than five minutes, everyone was armed. I ordered combat formation. On the heights which were 1,500 meters from us we could distinquish groups of Dervishes [Mahdists] grouped around their flags. I ordered M. Cajot to fire two shells [from the cannon], which were aimed admirably and dispersed the enemy. The night passed without incident.[9]

The following day, February 17, the Free State column left Bedden at six o'clock in the morning. Gehot and Dupont with their platoons formed the advance guard; Chaltin followed with his escort and the cannon; then came the patrols of Laplume, Cajot, Kops, and Goebel and finally the rear guard, consisting of the patrols of Sarolea and DeBacker with the baggage. The 580 irregulars of Renzi were spread out as flankers on the left while the Baḥr al-Jabal protected the column on the right. They marched northward, traversed the plain of Bedden, and crossed a watercourse. At seven o'clock the advance guard signaled to Chaltin that the Mahdists were drawn up in battle formation about 400 yards ahead on the crest of a ridge running at right angles to the river. In the middle of the Mahdist line was a gap supported on either side by two huge rocks and through which passed the road to Rajjāf.[10] Laplume described the position: "The rocks which the Mahdists

8. Lotar, *Chronique de l'Uele*, pp. 259–60.

9. "Rapport de commissaire générale Chaltin, chef de l'expédition du Nil, et gouverneur général de l'État Independant du Congo," published in Léon Chomé, *Une Expédition Belge au Nil* (Brussels, 1898), p. 31.

10. Lotar, *Chronique de l'Uele*, pp. 261–62; "Rapport de commissaire générale Chaltin . . ." Chaltin wrote that the Mahdists numbered about 2,000, but this figure is obviously an overestimate.

occupied formed a very strong position, divided by several passages, notably the defile which branches off to the east. There is there a beautiful cirque surrounded by large stones . . . It is truly a natural fort." [11]

Chaltin drew up his forces in the following battle order: running from left to right were the platoons of Dupont, Gehot, Laplume, Kops, and Sarolea, whose platoon rested on the left bank of the Baḥr al-Jabal. The platoons of DeBacker, Goebel, and Cajot were held in reserve while the cannon was set up straddling the road. Behind the cannon were the irregulars of Renzi, divided into three groups headed by their chiefs, Bafuka, Tombe, and Basugbwa. The front stretched for a little over a mile and numbered about 1,280 men. After the Congolese had deployed and had begun to advance, the Mahdists opened a heavy fire that forced the troops to seek cover behind the many rocks strewn across the plain in front of the ridge. Cajot and his cannon returned the fire, but the troops were ordered not to do so.[12]

After a half hour Chaltin ordered the troops forward to a new position 200 yards from the enemy line; from here the Congolese could effectively return the incessant fire of the Mahdists. At this moment the right flank of the Mahdist line advanced against Dupont's platoon on the Congolese left with the intention of turning the flank and rolling up the Congolese line.[13] Chaltin, perceiving this maneuver, ordered the reserve platoons of Goebel and DeBacker to go to the left of Dupont to contain the Mahdists while the irregulars of Renzi were sent in a sweeping movement to attack the rear of the Mahdist right flank.

11. Quoted in Lotar, *Chronique de l'Uele,* p. 263.

12. Jean Cajot was born at Roclenge-sur-Geer on November 26, 1871. A sergeant in the 3rd Artillery, he joined the service of the Free State and was ordered to the Uele on February 6, 1896. He participated in the Chaltin expedition to the Nile and was wounded in the Battle of Rajjāf. He died from these wounds at Rajjāf on July 14, 1897. See *Biographie Coloniale Belge, 1,* 202–04.

13. Leon Dupont was born at Erquennes on November 25, 1867. He joined the service of the Free State and arrived at Dungu on February 4, 1893. He was wounded in the campaign against Ndoruma in 1896, but recovered and marched with the Chaltin expedition to the Nile. He participated in the taking of Rajjāf but returned to Europe on August 19, 1897. He served a second, third, fourth, and fifth term for the Free State at Lado, Kwango, and in the Uele from 1899 to February 1910. He died at Plancenoit on January 12, 1930. See *Biographie Coloniale Belge, 2,* 320–21.

It was now eight o'clock in the morning. The Anṣār had been making definite progress against the platoons of Dupont, DeBacker, and Goebel when suddenly the irregulars of Renzi burst forth upon the Mahdists, who were pushed back, then dislocated from the Mahdist line and finally forced to flee.[14] Meanwhile the platoons of Sarolea, Laplume, and Kops had assaulted the ridge, gained the summit, and put the Anṣār to flight after twenty minutes of the fiercest fighting.[15] The Mahdists, having suffered severe losses—including their commander, Muḥammad 'Ali Bādī—fled northward, pausing only occasionally to fire on the pursuing Congolese. Laplume, who had been leading the chase, finally halted on the Bedden-Rajjāf road between two watercourses. Here the remaining Congolese troops stopped, reformed, and rested for two hours. At 10:30 A.M. Chaltin again ordered the column to advance.[16]

At 1:30 in the afternoon the advance guard, commanded by Laplume, reached Mt. Rajjāf, where they found the Mahdists located on a ridge between the mountain and the river. The station of Rajjāf itself lay just beyond. Laplume therefore took up a position just below the ridge, with his right flank on the Baḥr al-Jabal, to await the appearance of the other platoons strung out along the Bedden-Rajjāf road. Almost immediately the Mahdists opened fire on Laplume's men, who again sought the shelter of rocks and boulders. The sound of firing made the other patrols hasten to the support of Laplume. Subsequently Gehot and Dupont arrived and were ordered by Chaltin to assault the center of the Mahdist line.[17] Then Goebel came up and immediately engaged

14. Henri DeBacker was born at Anvers on February 5, 1873. He joined the service of the Free State and was ordered to Dungu, which he reached on August 4, 1895. He took part in the Battle of Rajjāf and later was appointed *chef de poste* at Niangara on November 1, 1897. He returned to Europe in 1899 but served a second and third term at Kwango from 1910 to 1912. See Lotar, *Chronique de l'Uele,* pp. 299–300.

15. Henri Sarolea was born at Hasselt on September 26, 1872. A second lieutenant of artillery, he joined the service of the Free State in 1896 and took part in the Chaltin expedition to the Nile. He was killed in battle at Bedden on February 17, 1897. See *Biographie Coloniale Belge, I,* 813–16.

16. Lotar, *Chronique de l'Uele,* pp. 263–66; "Rapport de commissaire générale Chaltin . . ."

17. William Gehot was born at Alost on July 17, 1869. A second lieutenant of the 6th Infantry, he joined the service of the Free State and was ordered to the Uele on November 10, 1894. He was attached to Kabassidu Camp on March

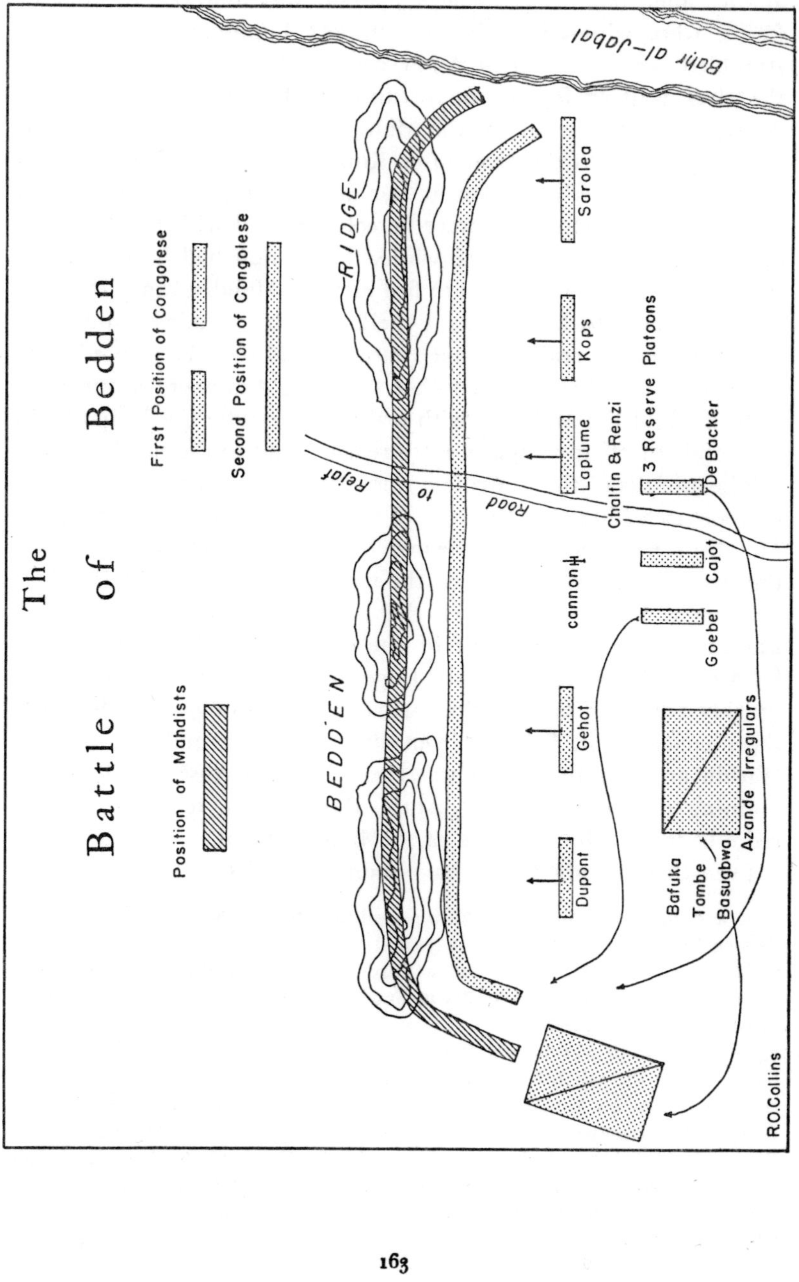
The Battle of Bedden
Position of Mahdists
First Position of Congolese
Second Position of Congolese
BEDD'EN RIDGE
Bahr al-Jabal
Rejaf to Road
Dupont
Gehot
cannon
Laplume
Kops
Sarolea
Goebel
Cajot
De Backer
Chaltin & Renzi
3 Reserve Platoons
Bafuka
Tambe
Basugbwa
Azande Irregulars
R.O.Collins

on the Congolese left flank a group of Mahdist sharpshooters hiding among some boulders. Goebel's platoon was followed by that of Cajot, who, while marching to support Laplume on the right, stumbled across a band of Anṣār concealed in the tall grass near the river waiting for the opportunity to fall on Laplume's rear. A savage battle ensued, but the Mahdists were finally driven out of the grass and into the river after Kop's platoon was brought into action.[18] DeBacker's platoon at last arrived and went into action beside Cajot's troops, who were fiercely engaged with the Mahdists on the Congolese right. Meanwhile, the cannon had been brought up and assembled and began to fire into the Mahdist ranks. A lucky shot happened to hit a box of shells, which exploded amidst the Anṣār.[19] Chaltin, realizing that victory would soon be assured, sent the Azande auxiliaries on another sweeping movement around the right flank of the Mahdists with orders to straddle the Rajjāf-Lado road and cut off any attempt to retreat by land to the north.

The assaults of the Congolese were completely successful. Gehot's platoon, smashing over the crest of the ridge, completely routed the Mahdist center. On the left the men of Goebel and Dupont occupied the two hillocks which formed the right flank of the Mahdist line. On the right near the river the men of Kops, DeBacker, and Laplume seized the summit of the ridge, with the cannon, and followed Gehot's men down the ridge toward Rajjāf. The Congolese quickly advanced against the zarība, broke through, and began a short engagement, fighting from street to street and hut to hut. Within an hour the zarība was cleared of the Anṣār; and the remaining defenders, led by 'Arabī Dafa' Allāh, retreated to the redoubt located by the bank of the Baḥr al-Jabal.

Even this redoubt would have soon fallen if Chaltin, content to

1895 and took part in the Chaltin expedition to the Nile. He returned to Europe in July 1897 but served a second term in the Congo as *chef de zone* at Makua from 1898 to 1900, and a third term at Mongalla and at Bangalas from 1904 to 1908. He died at Blaru, France, on July 17, 1932. See *Biographie Coloniale Belge,* 2, 402–04.

18. Joseph Kops was born at Bourg-Leopold on November 19, 1864. A second lieutenant in the 5th Infantry, he joined the service of the Free State and arrived at Dungu on January 30, 1895. He participated in the campaigns against Bafuka and accompanied the Chaltin expedition to the Nile. He returned to Europe in 1898 but served a second term in the Uele and the Nile, where he died at Dufile on July 29, 1900. See *Biographie Coloniale Belge,* 2, 546–47.

19. Lotar, *Chronique de l'Uele,* pp. 267–70. "Rapport de commissaire générale Chaltin . . ."

take this last Mahdist position on the following day, had not ordered his men to cease firing at 5:30 P.M. The Congolese were later to regret Chaltin's order, for during the night 'Arabī Dafa' Allāh and his men escaped to Bor, whence they later harassed the forces of the Free State. 'Arabī knew well that it would have been impossible to withstand the onslaught that was to come on the following day. Therefore, he ordered the canoes and boats to be loaded and sent to Bor. This evacuation was carried out with the greatest confusion and disorder. Many were drowned or injured attempting to get a place in the boats, but by the next morning only camp followers and children were to be found in the redoubt.[20]

During the whole day of fighting, the Free State lost 100 men killed, including Sarolea, and 160 men wounded, including Cajot.[21] The Congolese captured large quantities of ivory and cattle as well as official papers, 700 guns, and two magazines filled with supplies. There were also many women, children, and a few old men who were unable to flee with the Mahdist to Bor.[22] On the other hand, the Mahdists lost, according to 'Arabī, ninety-nine men—or, according to Chaltin, several hundred.[23] An intermediate figure is probably more accurate. There were killed at Rajjāf not less than 100 Anṣār and not more than 250. Captain Gleichen of the Intelligence Department of the Egyptian army astutely estimated the number of Mahdist dead at 200.[24] Included in these losses were eight of 'Arabī Dafa' Allāh's leading amīrs, several of whom, such as 'Umar Ṣāliḥ, Ḥamdan Allāh, Muḥammad aṭ-Ṭarayfī, and Muḥammad K̲hair Bādī, were men whose fighting skill, leadership, and ability could not be easily replaced.[25]

'Arabī's position at Bor was far from enviable. Although the

20. 'Arabī Dafa' Allāh to the K̲halīfa, Rabī' al-'Awwal 12, 1316 (June 31, 1898), Intelligence Report, Egypt, No. 60, Appendix 63, No. 1, and Mahdīya, I/34/3. Lotar, *Chronique de l'Uele,* pp. 270–73. "Rapport de commissaire générale Chaltin . . ."

21. 'Arabī Dafa' Allāh to the K̲halīfa, ibid., No. 3. Lotar, *Chronique de l'Uele,* pp. 272–73.

22. Lotar, *Chronique de l'Uele,* p. 274.

23. 'Arabī Dafa' Allāh to the K̲halīfa, Rabī' al-'Awwal 12, 1316 (July 31, 1898), Intelligence Report, Egypt, No. 60, Appendix 63, No. 6. "Rapport de commissaire générale Chaltin . . ." Lotar wrote (*Chronique de l'Uele,* p. 273) that 2,000 Mahdists had fallen. This is a gross exaggeration.

24. Gleichen, *Handbook of the Sudan,* p. 206.

25. 'Arabī Dafa' Allāh to the K̲halīfa, Rabī' al-'Awwal 12, 1316 (July 31, 1898), Intelligence Report, Egypt, No. 60, Appendix 63, No. 6.

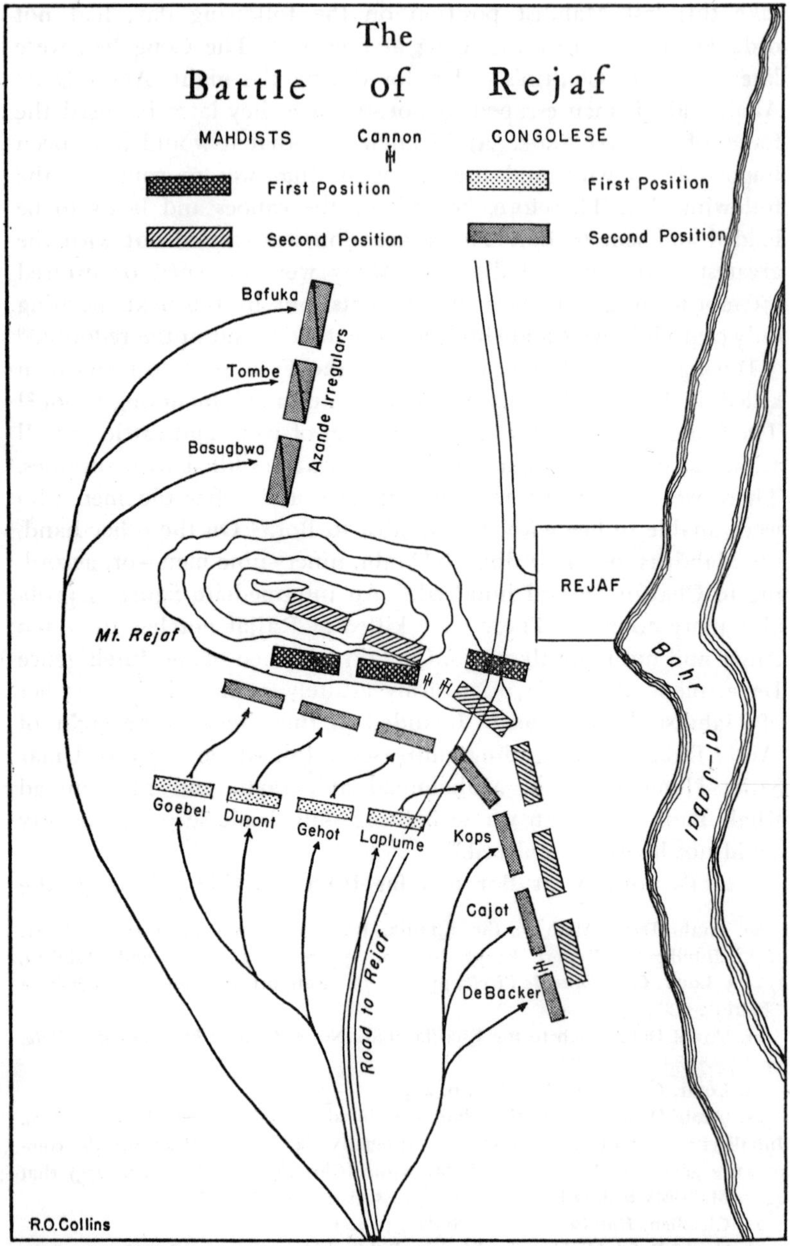
The Battle of Rejaf
MAHDISTS
Cannon
CONGOLESE
First Position
Second Position
First Position
Second Position
Bafuka
Tombe
Basugbwa
Azande Irregulars
Mt. Rejaf
REJAF
Bahr al-Jabal
Goebel
Dupont
Gehot
Laplume
Kops
Cajot
DeBacker
Road to Rejaf
R.O.Collins

Mahdist zarība at Bor was admirably situated for defense with a mud wall, containing at intervals loopholed watch towers, and an outer ditch, the Anṣār had lost 700 rifles and nearly one-quarter of their total number, while the remainder were demoralized and disheartened: an attitude not improved by the news that the Italians had re-taken Kasala.[26] But the most serious problem was the acute shortage of ammunition, which rendered the Mahdists almost defenseless. 'Arabī, to offset this weakness, bought, upon arrival at Bor, sufficient spears from the Dinkas to provide at least one for each man. With these spears the Anṣār were at least able to make foraging expeditions into the countryside (which was soon stripped of dura and cattle), carrying guns only to bluff and threaten the natives.[27] But there were many other vexatious problems. Several prisoners of the Mahdists escaped to Bor and fled to the Congolese, informing the latter of the weakened condition of the Anṣār. Among the fugitives was the famous Dunqulāwī amīr and former Mahdist commander in Equatoria, al-Ḥājj Muḥammad abū Qarja.[28] He had been imprisoned on the island of Rajjāf, sent north to Bor to work in the sadd, and probably had escaped during the confusion following the defeat at Rajjāf. But it was not only the exiles and prisoners who wished to escape and capitulate to the Congolese. Two men of the jihādīya plotted to assassinate 'Arabī, seize the steamer, and join the Congolese. The attempt failed, and the plotters were caught and summarily executed.[29] In addition to these internal dissensions, however, there were always external dangers. Endless skirmishes and even pitched battles with the neighboring Dinka tribes more often than not ended in defeat for the Mahdists. In one particular engagement a Mahdist force was ambushed by the Aliab Dinka west of Bor and nearly annihilated.[30]

26. Ibid., No. 1. 'Arabī's zarība was located about six miles upstream from the Dinka village and administrative headquarters of Bor. The mud walled enclosure was some 400 yards wide by 700 yards long protected by the river on two of its sides. The Italians, as part of their forward policy in Abyssinia, took Kasala from the Mahdists on July 17, 1894. So isolated, however, were the Anṣār in Equatoria that apparently the news of this Mahdist defeat did not reach them until several years later.

27. Ibid., No. 2.

28. Ibid., No. 3.

29. Ibid., No. 7. Lotar, *Chronique de l'Uele,* p. 280.

30. Telegram No. 042, Brock to Civil Secretary, December 16, 1919, Intelligence, II/30/249.

Furthermore, Dinka chiefs often came voluntarily to Rajjāf to report the movements of the Anṣār to the Congolese.[31] Indeed, it is a wonder that 'Arabī was able to maintain himself at Bor, let alone contemplate the recapture of Rajjāf.

In 1898, the river, which had been blocked by the sadd for nearly three years, suddenly and mysteriously opened a new channel to the north.[32] It is doubtful that the Mahdists had anything to do with this phenomenon, for although they had expended a great deal of effort attempting to cut a passage through the sadd, little progress seems to have been made. But the new channel was opened too late. In the summer of 1898 the Khalīfa had been massing his forces at Umm Durmān for the expected climactic battle with the advancing Anglo-Egyptian army. Scarcely a month after 'Arabī had sent the news northward that the river was clear, the Mahdists were decisively defeated at the Battle of Kararī.[33] During the year and a half between the Mahdist defeat at Rajjāf and the downfall of Mahdist power at Kararī, 'Arabī had managed not only to maintain himself at Bor but even to take the offensive against the Congolese and the nearby Dinka tribes. Threatened with treason from within and defeat from without, 'Arabī, although short of ammunition and supplies, held Bor with amazing skill and confidence. His devotion to Mahdism combined with his ability as a military commander, even in the face of certain defeat, has earned him a place in the ranks of the Khalīfa's most famous amīrs.

The weeks and months following the capture of Rajjāf were equally trying for the Congolese. The natives, who had been exploited by each successive invader, were naturally reluctant to have anything to do with the latest conquerors. They fled into the bush upon the approach of Congolese foraging parties; one exaggerated report even claims that the nearest inhabited village was ten days'

31. Lotar, *Chronique de l'Uele,* p. 280.

32. 'Arabī Dafa' Allāh to the Khalīfa, Rabī' al-'Awwal 12, 1316 (July 31, 1898), Intelligence Report, Egypt, No. 60, Appendix 63, No. 5, and Mahdīya, I/34/21. The Dinka at Shambe showed the new channel to 'Arabī after being provided with many cattle. Owing to damage done to its engines the steamer *Muhammad Ali* could not proceed northward. Consequently 'Arabī sent the news of the open channel overland to Umm Durmān. His first request of the Khalīfa was for writing paper.

33. The news of the opening of the sadd was entrusted to a Dinka who was captured by J. G. Maxwell on the Sūbāt River in December 1898.

march from Rajjāf.[34] Supplies were quickly exhausted and famine threatened, and even the shooting of fourteen elephants did little to alleviate the situation. As in the Mahdist camp at Bor demoralization spread through the ranks and was increased by frequent earthquakes, which terrorized the men—particularly the Azande, who thought that the weird rumblings and the flames shooting from fissures in the earth had been sent by the Mahdists to destroy them. But in spite of these difficulties the zarība of Rajjāf was rebuilt with a palisade, on which were mounted five Krupp and two Nordenfeld cannon, and beneath which was a ditch three yards deep and five yards wide. Later a steamer was brought to Rajjāf in pieces and assembled, as well as eight whaleboats equipped with machine guns. The strengthening of Rajjāf made it possible to reduce the garrison with comparative safety. Consequently the Azande irregulars, who were only too pleased to depart, left on March 23, followed by the regulars of Gehot and DeBacker on April 6.[35] This loss of manpower was more than compensated, however, by the improvement in the supply situation.

On August 12, 1897, news reached Chaltin at Rajjāf that the Mahdists were preparing to assault the station with a force of 200 men. Laplume was immediately sent to reconnoiter. He learned that 'Arabī had indeed advanced toward Rajjāf, crossed the river, and camped two hours' march downstream from Mt. Lado. But from Lado he had again retired to Bor. On August 20 the sentries stationed on Mt. Rajjāf captured an Anṣār who said that the amīr Baḥārī and twenty-four men had made a reconnaissance southwest of Rajjāf.

In late September another attempt was made by 'Arabī to approach the Congolese station. He came up river in a steamer, but after observing that Rajjāf was stoutly defended he retired for the third time to Bor.[36] Here he stayed throughout the remaining months of 1897. But 'Arabī had no intention of allowing the Congolese to go about their business unmolested. Mahdist raiding parties frequently marched south from Bor to the vicinity of Rajjāf to harry Congolese foraging parties, capture stragglers, and destroy isolated outposts. On May 21, 1898, one such raiding party am-

34. Lotar, *Chronique de l'Uele,* p. 283.
35. Ibid., pp. 275–78.
36. Ibid., pp. 279–80.

bushed and nearly annihilated a Congolese force, killing the Congolese officers Walhousen, Coppejans, Dieupart, and Bienaime.[37]

On June 4, 1898, at one o'clock in the morning the Mahdists silently advanced toward Rajjāf and suddenly attacked the station. The Congolese were caught unawares. Holding the station were only 550 men led by fourteen European officers, for 300 troops commanded by three Europeans had left Rajjāf some time before on an extended reconnaissance expedition. The Mahdists quickly dispatched the sentries and broke into the zarība on the south side. Once inside the station the fighting became chaotic and disorganized. Anṣār and Congolese fought individually or in small groups from hut to hut and street to street. Finally, many of the Congolese managed to rally around the hut of the commandant, Hanolet, or the munitions magazines. From these focal points the Congolese, assured of a constant supply of ammunition, gradually drove back the invaders to the palisade. Near the north enclosure the Mahdists put up a strong resistance which lasted for over an hour, but by dawn the whole station was again in the hands of the Free State forces while the Anṣār had vanished into the bush and retreated to Bor. The Congolese lost two officers killed and seven wounded, while over one-half of the Congolese troops were killed, wounded, or missing. The Mahdist casualties were considerably less. There were sixty-two dead inside the station and an equal number outside. The total Mahdist losses were probably not more than 150 men. Two weeks later Henry arrived from the Uele with 600 troops to reinforce Rajjāf. But the fears of another Mahdist attack were unfounded, for three months later, on September 2, 1898, the army of the Khalīfa was disastrously defeated at Kararī by an Anglo-Egyptian army under General Kitchener.

After receiving the authorization of the British Government to continue the advance from Dunqulā, Kitchener had begun the slow and laborious task of penetrating into the heart of the Sudan. At first it was thought necessary to follow the River Nile, but Kitchener soon abandoned this approach for the more direct but equally more hazardous route across the Nubian Desert. Taking the Mahdists by surprise and utilizing the technical superiority of his forces, Kitchener ordered a railway constructed from Wādī Ḥalfā across the desert to Abū Ḥamad. Although the Khalīfa had not anticipated this

37. Ibid., p. 283.

brilliant maneuver, it did not force a radical change of his plans for the defense of the Sudan. From the beginning he had determined to overcome the invaders by permitting them to advance deep into the country and then destroy them in one climactic battle before Umm Durmān. In preparation for Armageddon the K͟halīfa had concentrated all possible troops at Umm Durmān, including Maḥmūd Aḥmad and his great army of the West. Unfortunately a revolt of the Ja'liyīn tribe situated along the Nile north of Umm Durmān required the K͟halīfa to modify his original plan and send Maḥmūd Aḥmad and his army northward to crush the rebellion. Once at al-Matamma Maḥmūd Aḥmad remained; and in spite of the K͟halīfa's recommendation to withdraw, Maḥmūd's fear of large-scale desertions if he retreated advised against his retirement.

Bowing to the judgment of his amīr the K͟halīfa sanctioned Maḥmūd's plan to move against the Anglo-Egyptian forces under General Kitchener which had taken Barbar and were moving southward toward the 'Aṭbarā River. Advancing to the 'Aṭbarā and crossing the river, the Mahdists constructed a strong zarība at Umm Dabī' and awaited the attack of the Anglo-Egyptian forces. Here, on April 8, 1898, Kitchener ordered his troops forward to assault the Mahdist positions. Advancing against a concentrated fire from the Anṣār, the British, Egyptian, and Sudanese troops broke through the zarība and put the Anṣār to flight. The Mahdists lost over 7,000 killed and wounded; the Anglo-Egyptian casualties were much lighter, numbering only 560. The way to Umm Durmān was now open, and the final advance of the Anglo-Egyptian forces to the city was unopposed.

Following his victory at the 'Aṭbarā River, Kitchener spent the next four months organizing the final march to Umm Durmān. Additional troops, new gunboats, and large quantities of supplies were brought up the Nile until nearly 26,000 men were concentrated in summer quarters along the river. The K͟halīfa on his part was equally busy. A huge army was assembled before Umm Durmān, the river banks and the gorge of as-Sabalūqa were fortified, and all available supplies were brought in from as far away as the Shilluk country. Unfortunately the K͟halīfa did not utilize the natural resources at his command. He withdrew his troops from as-Sabalūqa, thereby abandoning the one natural line of defense and allowing Kitchener's troops to advance unopposed. On September 1, 1898, the Anglo-Egyptian forces landed at 'Iqayqa, situated about six miles north of Umm Durmān near the Kararī Hills. Rejecting a night attack, which would have offset the great advantage of fire-power in the hands of the Anglo-Egyptian troops, the Khalīfa launched his attack on the morning of September 2. Although the Mahdists pressed the assault with uncompromising valor and heroic courage, their antiquated firearms and broad-bladed spears were no match for the machine guns and repeating rifles of the Anglo-Egyptian forces. By noon the battle was over, the Khalīfa had fled (only to be hunted down over a year later), and nearly 11,000 Anṣār lay dead and another 16,000 were wounded on the plains of Kararī. The Mahdist State in the Sudan was no more.

Seven days after the victory at Kararī news reached Umm Durmān that a European force was stationed at Fashoda. Kitchener immediately sailed for the Upper Nile with a strong contingent of troops. Upon arriving at Fashoda, he found the Europeans to be a French expedition under Captain Marchand. Not only did Kitchener dispute Marchand's claim to the Upper Nile, but he stationed troops at Fashoda to watch the French and sent a steamer under the command of Major Peake Bey to investigate the Upper Nile and its tributaries. After several months Peake Bey returned to report that all three of the river routes to the Southern Sudan—the Baḥr al-Jabal, the Baḥr al-Ghazāl, and the Baḥr az-Zarāf—were thoroughly blocked to navigation by the sadd.

Epilogue

'Arabī Dafa' Allāh, unaware of the collapse of the Mahdist State, continued to remain at Bor throughout the autumn of 1898, patiently awaiting reinforcements, supplies, and instructions to come from the north. Unable to advance northward down the Nile because of the large sadd obstructions and not possessing sufficient men to march south and attack Rajjāf, 'Arabī had no recourse but to remain. But even at Bor the Mahdists were not secure from the advancing forces of the European invaders of the Southern Sudan. In November 1898 'Arabī learned of the approach of a combined Anglo-Congolese force under the command of Major Martyr.[1] Upon learning of this advance from the south, 'Arabī Dafa' Allāh, blocked

1. Cyril Godfrey Martyr (1860–1936) joined the British army in 1880 and rose to the rank of lieutenant-colonel. He served in the Nile campaign of 1884–85,

on the north and east by sadd and swamp, had to choose whether to fight, surrender, or flee to the west. Since his men wished neither to fight nor to surrender, 'Arabī burned his steamer, the *Muhammad Ali,* and all his boats and marched northwestward from Bor.[2] His route to the west skirted between the great swamps of the Baḥr al-G͟hazāl and the line of stations from Wau to Rumbek and Bor, for in February 1899 he camped near Lang and, marching parallel to the government stations, passed Kuk͟hūk 'Alī in March.[3] On the way he learned of the K͟halīfa's defeat at Kararī but pushed on across the Pongo, Lol, and Baḥr al-'Arab Rivers to Dār Kalaka, where he built a strong zarība. Here he rejected the demand of 'Alī Dīnār, Sultan of Dār Fūr, to surrender and instead established contact with S͟hayk͟h Mūsā Madībbū of the Rizayqāt.[4] Joining

fighting at Abū Ṭulaiḥ (Abu Klea), and was later seconded to the Egyptian army and took part in the battles of Jummaiza, Tūs͟hkī (Toski), and the reoccupation of Tokar. After serving in the Dunqulā campaign of 1896 as assistant adjutant-general, he returned to the British army and was sent to Uganda to help quell the mutiny of Sudanese troops. In November 1898 he reached Rajjāf at the head of a small column of Ugandan troops and then, with Congolese support, pushed on to Bor from which the Mahdists rapidly retired. Prevented by sadd obstructions in the Baḥr al-Jabal from continuing downstream to Khartoum, Martyr and his men returned to Uganda, establishing posts at Fort Berkeley, Afuddo, and Wadelai. He later served with the British army in South Africa and in the First World War. Hill, *A Biographical Dictionary of the Anglo-Egyptian Sudan,* p. 233. Gleichen, p. 270.

2. "Equatoria," Sudan Intelligence Report, No. 62, February 16–April 30, 1899.

3. A. de Tonquedec, *Au Pays Des Rivières* (Paris, 1931), pp. 57–58.

4. 'Alī Dīnār Zakarīyā Muḥammad al-Faḍl (1865–1916), was the sultan of Dār Fūr and the grandson of Sultan Muḥammad al-Faḍl, who reigned from 1779 to 1839. He succeeded Abū K͟hairāt, the son of Sultan Ibrāhīm, in 1899 at the end of the years of Mahdist supremacy in Dār Fūr. At first he held aloof from the Mahdists, and it was said that he meditated an insurrection against the Mahdist amīr of Dār Fūr—namely, Maḥmūd Aḥmad—who, suspecting his loyalty, sent him to the K͟halīfa at Umm Durmān in 1897. The K͟halīfa reproved him and gave him lowly employment in the Mahdist capital. He assisted in a Mahdist attack on the King of Taqalī in the Nūba Mountains in 1898, when, hearing of the Anglo-Egyptian victory at Umm Durmān, he deserted the Mahdist cause and, collecting followers and arms, made for Dār Fūr. There he captured al-Fās͟har from the Mahdist garrison, defeated Ibrāhīm 'Alī, another member of the Fūr royal house and the sirdār's dilatory candidate for the sultanate, and seized the throne. In 1900 he was officially recognized by the Sudan Government and paid a nominal tribute. He organized his sultanate in a fairly efficient, if barbarous, manner, crushing all opposition and ensuring the Fūr supremacy by a series of punitive raids against the dissident tribes in his dominions and on their borders. In 1907 on one of these raids he killed Sanīn Ḥusayn of Kabkabīya.

Shaykh Madībbū at Shakkā, the Mahdists and the Rizayqāt were confronted by the forces of 'Alī Dīnār, which after a hard-fought battle were driven off with considerable loss.[5] In spite of this victory, however, friction arose between the Mahdists and the Rizayqāt, and the hostility of the latter forced 'Arabī and his men to retreat from Shakkā to the old Mahdist encampment of Mandua in Dār Ta'ā'isha. Madībbū, on the other hand, made his peace with 'Alī Dīnār and then accompanied, on an expedition against 'Arabī Dafa' Allāh, 'Abd ar-Raḥīm Bey Sālim abū Daqal, who had been commissioned by the Sirdār to pursue stray Mahdist columns of Ta'ā'isha tribesmen.[6]

Upon the arrival of abū Daqal and Shaykh Madībbū at Mandua

His armies were not always successful, however, and twice were defeated by the Rizayqāt. The First World War was his undoing. Persuaded by Turkish and Sanūsī intrigue, he renounced his allegiance to the Anglo-Egyptian power in 1916 and prepared for war, forcing on his people a primitive, home-made currency to raise money. After a short campaign his main army was totally defeated at Birinjiya near al-Fāshar by an Anglo-Egyptian force commanded by al-Liwā' (Brigadier) P. J. V. Kelly Pasha, and fled only to be killed at Kulme, south of Zalingei, by a chance bullet during the pursuit. See Hill, pp. 45–46.

5. "Equatoria," Sudan Intelligence Report, No. 64, July 16–August 31, 1899; 'Arabī Dafa' Allāh to the Sirdār, January 1900, and Hassān Warrak to the Director of Military Intelligence, February 3, 1900, Sudan Intelligence Report, No. 67, January 1–March 8, 1900, Appendix E, Sections F and D respectively. Mūsā Madībbū (d. 1920), head shaykh of the Rizayqāt tribe of southern Dār Fūr, succeeded his father Madībbū Bey 'Alī, who was killed by the amīr an-Nūr Bey Muḥammad 'Angara during the Mahdist rule. He was summoned to Umm Durmān by the Khalīfa 'Abd Allāhi who, when R. C. von Slatin Bey escaped to Egypt in 1895, imprisoned him as an old friend of Slatin's and a suspected accessory to his escape. He was not present at the Battle of Kararī in 1898, having fled that day with his family. While they were returning to their lands, they were caught by the Missīrīya but were released after about a year. On his return to Dār Rizayqāt in 1899, he, with the aid of 'Arabī Dafa' Allāh, defeated the forces of 'Alī Dīnār sent against him. Falling out with 'Arabī, he made his peace with 'Alī Dīnār and pursued the retreating forces of 'Arabī to Mandua in Dār Ta'ā'isha. Returning to Dār Rizayqāt, without having defeated 'Arabī, he henceforth ignored demands for tribute from 'Alī Dīnār; and when the sultan sent an army under general Tīrāb Sulaymān against the Rizayqāt, he fled with his people to the Baḥr al-'Arab. He returned at the end of 1901, and hostile and intermittent war continued with 'Alī Dīnār until the latter's fall in 1916. He was succeeded on his death in 1920 by his son Ibrāhīm Mūsā Madībbū. See Hill, p. 285.

6. Madībbū to the Sirdār, January 28, 1900, Sudan Intelligence Report, No. 67, Appendix E, Section G.

on December 26, 1899, 'Arabī sent a letter to them rendering "his submission on certain terms which abū Daqal refused to accept as he was desirous of loot." [7] Abū Daqal claimed that whether 'Arabī surrendered or not he and his men would be regarded as booty. 'Arabī would have none of this. He had been resupplied with powder and ammunition by Makk abū Rishā and had no intention of surrendering if it meant the looting of his men and the loss of his own life.[8] Hassān Warrak, the Sudan Government Intelligence Officer accompanying abū Daqal's expedition, attempted to persuade the latter to give up his idea of looting and even went to have an interview with 'Arabī Dafa' Allāh. During the interview, however, abū Daqal rode up to the Mahdist camp and opened fire, and it was only through the efforts of Hassān Warrak that the shooting was stopped. After further negotiations, 'Arabī agreed to submit and to give half his arms and men to Hassān Warrak as a sign of good faith.[9] Hassān then returned to the camp of abū Daqal, who refused to accept these conditions and ordered 'Arabī's emissary to go back to the Mahdist camp and inform 'Arabī that abū Daqal would come and loot him. 'Arabī then attacked the camp of abū Daqal. The fighting continued in a desultory manner for several days until abū Daqal was forced to retreat because of lack of supplies and ammunition.[10] He retired to Turmana, where for his failure to bring about the surrender of 'Arabī, he was relieved of his command by Mukhtār 'Awad Ḥamīd. 'Arabī retreated to Kāra situated northwest of Ḥufrat an-Naḥās in what was regarded as French territory.

In January 1900 'Arabī sent a letter to the Sirdār offering his submission and suggesting that he either take over and administer

7. For the letters of 'Arabī Dafa' Allāh to abū Daqal and Hassān Warrak, see Sudan Intelligence Report, No. 67, Appendix E, Section C-3.

8. O'Connell to Staff Officer, Intelligence, February 20, 1900, Sudan Intelligence Report, No. 67, Appendix E, Section A. Abū Daqal is reported to have said: "Arabi Dafalla's property is to be confiscated whether he surrenders or not, none of his property is to be handed over to the Government except the head after it has been decapitated."

9. Hassān Warrak to the Director of Military Intelligence, January 25, 1900, Sudan Intelligence Report, No. 67, Appendix E, Section C.

10. "Report Made by Hassān Effendi Warrak on His Return to Omdurman from His Mission to the Western Sudan, April 15, 1900," Sudan Intelligence Report, No. 69, April 10–May 9, 1900, Appendix C.

the Baḥr al-Ghazāl for the Government or to remain at Kāra and pay tribute.[11] This letter reached al-Ubaiyaḍ on February 20, 1900, and was transmitted to Khartoum. The Sirdār decided to accept 'Arabī's terms, and a reply dated March 17 was entrusted to 'Arabī's brother. At the same time orders were sent to Captain O'Connell at al-Ubaiyaḍ to do everything in his power to facilitate 'Arabī's submission, while 'Alī Dīnār was warned in no way to interefere.[12] These efforts appear to have been in vain, for 'Arabī did not come in to submit. In fact he increased his belligerent activities along the frontiers of the Baḥr al-Ghazāl. On September 30, 1900, Nasr, the Njangulgule chief, reported that the Mahdists had raided, on the 20th of the month, Abū Dukum north of Ḥufrat an-Naḥās, killing many men and women.[13] These raids probably prompted the next attempt by the Sudan Government to obtain the surrender of 'Arabī. Slatin on December 17, 1900, dispatched a letter offering terms of surrender, but this effort like the others was unsuccessful.[14] There seems to be little doubt that 'Arabī was genuinely anxious to surrender, but his great fear of treachery caused him to be justifiably cautious. Throughout 1901 and the first half of 1902 'Arabī continued to reside at Kāra, whence he made frequent raids against abū Rishā and 'Alī Dīnār and into the Baḥr al-Ghazāl.[15] But all was not well in the Mahdist camp. For reasons unknown, 'Arabī's army mutinied in the summer of 1902. With only fifty loyal followers he fled from Kāra to the River Ibra, while the mutineers, numbering 650, marched to Melam. 'Alī Dīnār, wishing to preclude any possibility of either the mutineers or 'Arabī allying themselves with his old enemy, Sanīn Ḥusayn of Kabkabīya, surrounded 'Arabī on the Ibra and forced him to surrender while at the same time accepting the capitulation of the mutineers at Melam.[16] The latter were subsequently distributed among the different contingents of the Fūr army, while 'Arabī Dafa' Allāh himself was allowed to wander about al-Fāshar as a "common man." [17]

11. Sudan Intelligence Report, No. 67, Appendix E, Section F.

12. Newall to 'Arabī Dafa' Allāh, March 17, 1900, Sudan Intelligence Report, No. 68, March 9–April 9, 1900, Appendix C.

13. Nasr to Sirdār, September 30, 1900, Sudan Intelligence Report, No. 76, November 9–December 8, 1900, Appendix B, No. 2.

14. Sudan Intelligence Report, No. 77, December 9, 1900–January 8, 1901.

15. Ibid., No. 94, May 1902.

16. Ibid., No. 97, August 1902.

17. Ibid., No. 101, December 1902.

'Arabī remained in al-Fāshar in this condition until 1916, when he was put to death by 'Alī Dīnār "upon suspicion of attempting to treat with the Sudan Government"—a most unfitting end for one of the ablest and most courageous of the Khalīfa's lieutenants.[18]

Conclusion

The conclusions which one can draw from the Mahdist invasions of the Southern Sudan are neither numerous nor profound. In fact one must regard the Mahdist invasions as extended raids which upset the traditional pattern of tribal life and left nothing behind but anarchy and fear. Many of the tribal leaders were killed or carried off with their tribesmen to captivity. The villages were plundered for ivory and supplies, the crops destroyed, and Mahdism forced upon the inhabitants. Well armed with Remington repeating rifles and the courage and zeal of Mahdism, the Anṣār, although small in number, had little difficulty in defeating the Negroid tribesmen. But it was precisely their small numbers which perpetuated this anarchy and fear. Strong enough to defeat the Negroids but never sufficiently strong to establish their hegemony over them, the Mahdists were compelled to raid again and again not only to maintain their own position but also to secure even the most essential supplies. And the only lasting result of these continual raids was the Southerner's hatred and fear of the Northern Sudanese.

In 1955, a serious revolt of the Equatorial Battalions of the Sudan Defense Force broke out in the Equatoria Province. Although the causes of the revolt were many, one of the underlying factors made clear in the official government report on the Southern Sudan Disturbances was "that for historical reasons the Southerners regard the Northern Sudanese as their traditional enemies." [1] Although the beginnings of this traditional hostility toward the North undoubtedly arose during the Turkīya or even before, the Mahdist invasions intensified and magnified this hostility. In fact there is little doubt that the great problem facing the Republic of the Sudan today is this suspicion and enmity for the North so deeply rooted in the South during the Mahdīya.

18. H. A. MacMichael, *The Anglo-Egyptian Sudan* (London, 1934), p. 216.

1. *Southern Sudan Disturbances, August 1955: The Report of the Commission of Enquiry, October 1956* (Khartoum), p. 81.

The era of the Mahdīya in the Southern Sudan must therefore be regarded as the culmination of a long series of misfortunes which in the latter half of the nineteenth century had fallen upon that wild land. Before the coming of the slave traders and the Egyptian Administration the tribes of the Southern Sudan were chiefly concerned with survival—finding enough to eat and maintaining their freedom of action against the designs of neighboring tribes. Although virtually nothing is known about the Southern Sudan in the centuries before 1850, there is little doubt that the Baḥr al-G͟hazāl and Equatoria basked in a pristine anarchy clouded only by constant and continual intertribal wars, which were, however, free of any outside influences. Naturally, the strongest and most belligerent tribes prevailed against the weaker. For example the Azande people during the nineteenth century had been pressing northward across the Congo-Nile Divide until halted by the establishment of Egyptian Administration in the Baḥr al-G͟hazāl. The small weak tribes, like the Bongo, the Kreisch, the Shatt, and others could not withstand the Azande, who, under their autocratic Avungura sultans, formed a cohesive fighting machine, efficient in war and stable in peace. Or there were the Dinka tribes, who appear to have been also expanding at the expense of their weaker neighbors. Less cohesive than the Azande and unwilling to acknowledge a supreme ruler, the Dinka confederation was slowly pushing westward from the swamps of the Nile and, by sheer weight of numbers, driving the weaker tribes before them.

In the latter half of the nineteeth century the fluid, anarchical society of the Southern Sudan was disrupted by the arrival of three waves of invaders—the slave traders, the Egyptian Army, and the Mahdists. Each of these three in turn not only disrupted tribal life in the Southern Sudan but in many cases caused the breakdown of tribal society. The slave traders, playing on tribal jealousies and animosities, raided and plundered the tribes for slaves who were sent northward to fill the harems and the armies of Egypt and the Arab world. The advent of Egyptian Administration brought an end to wide-scale slave-raiding, particularly in the Baḥr al-G͟hazāl under Gessi Pasha and in Equatoria under Gordon, but the Egyptian Government was never able to persuade the tribes of the Baḥr al-G͟hazāl and Equatoria to accept the administration. Tribes like the Dinka or the Nuer or even the Feroge or the Njangulgule were as loath to be the subjects of a nominally stable Government as the objects of a slave trader. To maintain their rule in the Southern Sudan, the Egyptian Government found it necessary to coerce the tribes to accept the administration and to suppress tribal rebellions with punitive expeditions. The repressive measures of the Egyptian Government caused a further breakdown of tribal society. Chiefs were shot, their peoples killed, the cattle seized, and the crops taken. The hereditary rulers of the tribes were lost; the traditional way of life disrupted. The measures required by Lupton Bey to suppress the revolt of the tribes in the Baḥr al-G̲h̲azāl were by no means unusual or extreme. The third wave of invaders, the Mahdists, was the culmination of the other two. Fanatically inspired by the cause of the Mahdī and sure of their divine mission to scourge the earth of the infidel, the Mahdists carried the jihād into the Southern Sudan. The purpose of the jihād was to destroy the Egyptian Administration and to win the peoples of the Baḥr al-G̲h̲azāl and Equatoria to Mahdism. Although the tribes of the Southern Sudan were anxious to rid themselves of Egyptian rule, they did not wish simply to exchange the oppressive rule of the Egyptians for that of the Mahdists. Profoundly jealous of their new-found freedom from government and disinterested in the religion of the Mahdists, the tribes resisted attempts by the new invaders to force Mahdist rule and religion upon them. As before, fire and sword were spread throughout the Southern Sudan to force the tribes to submit. The Mahdists, like the Egyptian Administration before them, crushed the tribes, smashing what remained of their former traditional way of life and causing in turn a further breakdown of tribal society. Although the Mahdists did not remain in the Baḥr al-G̲h̲azāl and, in Equatoria, were confined largely to the riverain area, the fanaticism of their rule and the uncompromising nature of their religion disrupted tribal life in the Southern Sudan as much as if not more than did the longer periods of control by the slave traders and the Egyptian Government.

When Mahdist rule in the Southern Sudan was brought to an end by the appearance of yet a fourth wave of invaders, the Europeans, tribal society in the Baḥr al-G̲h̲azāl and Equatoria was badly weakened and in some areas totally disintegrated and unable to resist. With but a few exceptions the Anglo-Egyptian occupation of the Southern Sudan was accepted peacefully. Years of oppression had made the tribes suspicious of any new invader, but the dearth of capable leaders, the loss of the ablest tribesmen, and the apathy which had accompanied the decimation of the tribes left them little choice but reluctantly to accept Anglo-Egyptian occupation. After nearly half a century of chaos and instability the Southern Sudan needed peace.

The Mahdist invasions had another result of historical importance. In the last decade of the nineteenth century the Southern Sudan was coveted by Britain, France, and the Congo Free State. There is little doubt that the Congolese would have secured the Southern Sudan for the Free State in 1893 and 1894 if the Mahdists had not thwarted them; and if the Congolese had been successful, the repercussions in Europe would have been momentous. Furthermore, the presence of the Mahdists not only prevented the area from falling under the dominion of Leopold II and the Congo Free State but directly affected the plans of conquest and occupation of the Baḥr al-Ghazāl and Equatoria by Britain and France. Anglo-French colonial rivalry was not a new phenomenon in 1898. In the South Pacific, the Far East, and even in North America, Anglo-French relations were seriously strained by the conflicting colonial claims of each power, but it was in Africa that these relations reached the breaking point. Beginning in Egypt in the 1880's and continuing in West Africa and the Nile in the 1890's, this colonial rivalry culminated in 1898 at the Shilluk village of Fashoda. The French, on the one hand, were anxious to acquire the Southern Sudan as the final link in their trans-African possessions stretching from the Atlantic to the Indian Oceans. The British, on the other hand, were equally anxious to prevent any European Power from acquiring the Southern Sudan. Sentimentally, the Southern Sudan was another step in the Cape-to-Cairo route, but realistically Britain could not tolerate the control of the waters of the Upper Nile by any other nation, for whoever controlled the waters of the Nile controlled Egypt. In spite of warnings from the British Government, the French dispatched an expedition into the Southern Sudan under the leadership of Captain Marchand. The British Cabinet, not to be outflanked, ordered Kitchener to reconquer the Sudan from the Mahdists and secure the Nile watershed for Britain and Egypt. Kitchener and Marchand met at Fashoda, and under threat of war France capitulated, recalled Marchand, and sought reconciliation with England.

Fashoda was essentially a European question, but the events which took place in the Southern Sudan during the 1890's not only conditioned the crisis but formed a background for it. Until the Mahdists were defeated in the South, they were more than capable of repelling all but the most powerful and well-equipped French expeditions. Britain, confident in the knowledge of the capabilities of the Mahdists, was content to leave the Southern Sudan alone, and until this confidence was shaken the Mahdists controlled events in the Southern Sudan. The Mahdist defeat at Rajjāf signified the end of Mahdist influence in the South, just as the defeat of the K͟halīfa's army at Kararī a year and a half later meant the end of Mahdist influence in the North. With the defeat at Rajjāf the fate of the Baḥr al-G͟hazāl and Equatoria passed from Africa to the chancelleries of Europe, but it had been the Mahdists who had created the background for the diplomatic conflict among Britain, France, and the Congo Free State for control of the Southern Sudan and had irrevocably conditioned the result.

APPENDICES

A. Translation of the Arabic text of the letter sent by Lieutenant Milz to Faḍl al-Mūlā on September 15, 1892, from Camp Kibbi. Mahdīya, Class I, Box 34, Folder 3, No. 92, Sudan Government Archives, Khartoum.

River Kibbi Camp, September 15, 1892

From the Representative of the Independent Congo State to
the Commandant of Equatoria and His Respected Officers.
Greetings to you all:

I beg to bring to your notice that I have written to you before, explaining why I could not meet your excellency. I am not sure if that letter has ever reached you. I sent it with a Persian who spoke some Arabic to inform you that I am now near the River Kibali in your old station and zarība not far from the village of the chief who is called Lahmin. I send with this letter the present which I had promised; and I will always try to be of service to you in all matters, and I hope that friendly relations may always exist between us.

Now I shall proceed to explain to you the intentions of my government. You know nothing, I believe, about the Congress that assembled in Berlin which included the Representatives of all the Powers. This Congress has corresponded with the King of the Belgians, who is our Chief and King and Governor of all the Congo State and its surroundings, and issued an order authorizing Our King to take possession of all the above-mentioned country; he has brought order into it and has put stations of the government in all its parts and has extended his rule throughout all its limits and is permitted to stretch it further. I am ordered now, by His Majesty King Leopold, to take possession of all the northern and northeastern territories which connect our government with the Congo River. I have come from the Uele River where there are stations all along its banks until you reach the confluence of the Dungu River. I intended to bring you some goods which I was carrying with me; but the people of this country deceived me and misled me, so that I did not know how to reach you. I was obliged, therefore, to leave these goods in [the territory of] Wando. These were sent to you by the Congo Government, for they read what Mr. Stanley has written about you in his book saying that you are bare and have nothing to wear. I shall not fail to send men to bring these goods to you. They amount to 800 parcels of clothing, which contain what you would expect, and at the same time I am carrying to you now some necessary goods of which you are in need.

I would now inform you about your present condition.

It is not unknown to you that the Egyptian Government has left the Sudan and Equatoria and has consequently abandoned you. Do not think that the Egyptian Government will ever return to the equator and never expect any help from them; and although you are in Equatoria, it is of no advantage to you, for no power would ever take you under its protection.

His Majesty, Our King, was very sorry and wondered why Stanley wrote badly of you in his book and why you treated him badly. He (Our King) is willing to act with you in a friendly spirit and treat you very kindly. I have a letter from His Majesty the King asking you to obey him and be like one of the employees of the government.

My soldiers being many, amounting to 800, and not feeling well myself, I cannot have the honor of meeting you at Wadelai. I pray that you will send me any two of your officers or any two persons, so that I may discuss all matters with them and tell them about the intentions of Our King. Then I will go with them to have the honor of meeting you and this will give me great pleasure and joy.

I pray God lengthen your years, to keep you safe, and to give me the opportunity of meeting you, for this is my intention and wish.

Written by your faithful friend,

Commandant of All the Principality of the Equator,

[signed] Milz

B. Translation of the Arabic text of the Alliance made between Faḍl al-Mūlā Bey and the Representatives of the Congo Free State. Mahdīya, Class I, Box 34, Folder 3, No. 79, Sudan Government Archives, Khartoum.

Mr. Milz, the Commandant of the Equator Ma'mūrīyāt [District] and a Representative of the Congo Free State, has made an Alliance with the following persons: Faḍl al-Mūlā Bey, Ahmad Aghā 'Alī, Muḥammad Effendī al-'Ugaymī, Muḥammad Aghā aṣ-Ṣādiq, Faraj

Aghā Aḥmad, Muḥammad Effendī Ṣabrī, Isḥāq Effendī Muḥammad, aṣ-Ṣādiq Effendī Sa'īd, who were formerly employees of the Egyptian Government, who, on being assembled at Bora on the Baḥr al-Jabal, ratified the following Alliance with the following conditions:

Those above-mentioned persons, formerly employees of the Egyptian Government, together with all their followers, civil and military, have willingly and heartily consented to join the Congo Free State and to appropriate lands in the name of the Free State. They have agreed, also, to raise the flag of the Free State and to obey its laws and precepts and to serve it in a pure heart under all circumstances and in all services and to submit willingly to the above-mentioned Government.

[signed] Milz [and the seals of the above-mentioned persons]

Bora, October 19, 1892

C. Translation from the Arabic text of the Contract made between Faḍl al-Mūlā Bey and the Representatives of the Congo Free State. Mahdīya, Class I, Box 34, Folder 3, No. 89, Sudan Government Archives, Khartoum.

The following Contract has been passed and agreed upon by Commandant Milz and the personages, Faḍl al-Mūlā Bey, Aḥmad Aghā 'Alī, Muḥammad Effendī al-'Ugaymī, Muḥammad Aghā aṣ-Ṣādiq, Faraj Aghā Aḥmad, Muḥammad Effendī Ṣabrī, Isḥāq Effendī Muḥammad, aṣ-Ṣādiq Effendī Sa'īd. who were employees of the Egyptian Government and are now representatives of the people whom they govern.

The above-mentioned persons, witness, say, and acknowledge that they have willingly, heartily, and freely consented to join the Congo Free State in all its services for the sum of two thousand Egyptian pounds yearly, which sum is [to be] paid in two installments. The first installment, which embraces six months, is one-half the total sum and is paid in money. The other half is paid in kind during the next six months.

Article I: All employees in the Congo Free State, whether civil or military, must serve the above-mentioned Government faithfully, heartily, and willingly. They must daily raise the flag of the said State and obey its laws.

Article II: All employees must submit to the Government orders and must stay in the places assigned to them by the Government.

Article III: They must collect, if possible, only ivory, rubber, and ostrich feathers and send them to the said Government.

Article IV: A store containing different kinds of goods shall be placed under the charge of a station officer. These goods will be especially sent to the chiefs who send products for the benefit of the Government.

Article V: All employees must receive any officer of the Congo Government. The said officer may be in any station and the employees must give him and his followers all he requires. The officer's business is to execute the Commandant's orders as regards the benefit of the State.

Article VI: All officers of stations must send, if at hand, all illegitimate children who will be sent to Bora for the benefit of the Government.

Article VII: The Congo Government is obliged to give and equip them [the Equatorials] with all necessary stores of arms and the like.

Article VIII: This Contract may be changed when the Government sees that all employees are diligently engaged in their work. The Contract will be in force for one year, beginning on November 1, 1892, and ending on October 31, 1893, and it may be changed after every year.

[signed] Milz [and the seals of the above-mentioned persons]

Bora, October 19, 1892

D. Translation of the Arabic text of Faḍl al-Mūlā's Instructions to his followers with an accompanying letter. Mahdīya, Class I, Box 34, Folder 2, Nos. 35 and 25 respectively, Sudan Government Archives, Khartoum.

To the Wakīl of the Mudīrīya and Muḥāfaẓa of Baḥr Kibbi:

I have drawn up these twenty-one articles which I wish all officials to follow, and I send them to you to read to all officials, jihādīya, and others and to make them understand their contents. After this date anyone who dares to disobey any of these orders should blame [no one] but himself. You should keep this copy with you for reference.

[signed] Faḍl al-Mūlā
Mudīr of Khaṭṭ al-Istiwā'
[Governor of Equatoria]

29 Rabī' al-'Awwal, 1310
[October 21, 1892]

INSTRUCTIONS TO BE FOLLOWED AT THE PRESENT TIME AND IN THE FUTURE

I. Now that we have become the followers of the Independent State of the Congo, and its Government has become responsible for all our expenses, every official is expected to perform his duties in the most upright and worthy manner. He has to exert all of his energies, day and night, and to direct his whole attention and care towards the carrying out of the work demanded of him, so that he may deserve by so doing the pay and credit from the State.

II. As this Government is yet newly organized, its utmost desire and wish is the civilizing of the natives, their peaceful living, and their settlement. Therefore, above everything else, attention must be drawn to the companies now at work. Should any sign of rebellion appear amongst the people of a place, so that they refrain from paying tribute to the Government, the Wakīl or Ma'mūr of that station must present the case to the Mudīrīya immediately. He should ask permission to punish them; and must carry out the orders fully, but without excess.

Taxes, whether they be sheep or cattle, ivory or sesame, should be stored in the magazines prepared for them, and returns of them forwarded to the Mudīrīya.

III. In every office and in every station, a storekeeper and a director of flocks is necessary. They should be officers worthy to occupy such positions.

IV. Ma'mūrs and Wakīls of the different stations of the country are expected to use all means in their power to gain the favor of the chiefs and the natives. They should draw the hearts of the people towards them by gentle conduct and tender policy, for that will be to the highest and the greatest benefit to the Government.

V. No one is permitted to be extravagant or to squander any ammunition or percussion caps and should only use them in time of need. As for example in quelling an uprising or driving back an enemy, and even under these circumstances they cannot obtain the necessary amount until the written request presented by the commissioned officer is signed by their commander.

VI. All officials are required from this date to be quite submissive and obedient to the Government and to superior officers, and they are required to be diligent and energetic in their work. Should any of them show the slightest disobedience or neglect or even lack of vigor, whatever the cause may be, he is to be tried and punished according to the importance of his crime.

VII. Ma'mūrs of districts and Wakīls of stations in the different parts of the country have to build Government magazines for storing taxes usually gathered from the people. They have to make lists of the different kinds received and to give accurate accounts of the amount of each kind. The whole is to be delivered up to the Mudīrīya.
Military officers and other officials may get their payment from this.

VIII. All events that may take place in the headquarters of a battalion are to be reported to the Mudīrīya. The Mudīrīya then will consider the matter and issue orders according to the rules and constitution of the country.

IX. All cattle and sheep taken from rebellious people are by right the property of the Government. When taken, they are to be divided in the following manner: Sheep should be divided into two divisions, viz: good and bad. Cattle into three divisions, viz: good, fair, and bad. After that, all should be stamped with the seal of the Government which is to be obtained soon. These then are to be delivered to the director general of flocks with the necessary lists showing the number and kind of flocks delivered.

X. These flocks are to be dealt with in the following manner: Sheep may be given to the different officials as pay, after getting permission from the Mudīrīya, but in regard to cattle the Mudīrīya has to see whether they are numerous or not. If numerous, it is then the work of the Mudīrīya to dispense with them in the most suitable way. If, on the other hand, they are few, they are to be slain, and the beef given to the military and other officials as pay. The necessary receipts should be given.

XI. Officers of the State in the different parts of the country are required to keep a sharp look out and gather news of any enemies. Let this cost them whatever it may in gifts and in presents to the loyal natives; they have to accomplish it. The Mudīrīya should be informed immediately of every event, so that it may be always conversant with present and future events.

XII. Every Ma'mūr and Wakīl of stations in the different parts of the country is to build strong fortifications able to withstand the attacks of the enemy. If any one neglects his duties or shows the least laziness in the matter he will be held responsible for all consequences.

XIII. Every three or four months a report of all receipts, deeds, and witnesses and accounts of incomes and expenditures should be presented to the Mudīrīya so that the Bāshkātib [Chief Clerk] there might have a full knowledge and accurate account of all income and expenditure, lest any increase should appear afterward in the pay of the officials, with nothing left to make it up.

XIV. All officers, noncommissioned officers, and men have to stop the custom of wearing turbans and carrying canes. They ought to follow the example of their peers [the Congolese] in strictly following all military rules.

XV. In case of any increase of the necessary military organization, information should be presented to the Mudīrīya. The Mudīrīya has then to formulate the regulations and issue orders to the battalions showing the service to be required of them.

XVI. Ma'mūrs and Wakīls in all parts of the country have to do their best in causing the revenues of ivory, rubber, and ostrich feathers to increase as much as possible. A report of the amount is to be presented every month.

XVII. It is the duty of every director of a station to use all the means within his power to win the favor of the native chiefs so that the station will be supplied with all the necessaries of living.

XVIII. All officers, noncommissioned officers, and men are hereby notified that they are not allowed to come here, or to the Bimbāshī except by a special permission granted to those who offer petitions asking for it.

Officers with grievances who come to have their cases tried, are excluded.

XIX. Notices, warnings, and strict orders are to be always given for Public Security. Officers have to fulfill all orders given to them with great speed. Guards and patrols have to be in complete order at all times. Arms should be kept always clean—preservation of the honor and dignity of military rule is expected to increase day by day.

XX. Every official and every officer, noncommissioned officer, and man who disobeys any of the above-mentioned instructions shall be very severely punished without any regard to his position. The blame will be on himself.

XXI. All officials must know that this Contract upon which we have agreed with the Congo State applies only for half pay annually. It is to be acted upon for a whole year, beginning November 1, 1892, and ending at the end of October 1893. We have the choice after that to renew and remain in service or annul it. It is to be understood at the same time that our pay shall be paid half in cash and the other half in kind.
It has been understood from the accounts made by Ṣādiq Effendī and Maḥmūd Effendī [Maḥmud Aghā], the Bimbāshī, that officers of the degree of Bāsh Shāwīsh [Sergeant] down to a soldier shall receive half pay, while officers of the degree of Mulāzim [lowest commissioned officer] to Mīrālai [Colonel] shall receive two-thirds pay. All officers are required to know the contents of these instructions.

E. Translations of the Arabic texts of two letters from Lieutenant Gustin to Faḍl al-Mūlā Bey, June 22 and 23, 1893. Mahdīya, Class I, Box 34, Folder 4, Nos. 103 and 105, respectively, Sudan Government Archives, Khartoum.

Sir:

In accordance with the order of the Commandant [Delanghe], you must stay now in the station of Alema, namely the station which I have made.

You may leave Ganda on the 25th instant so that you may reach here on the 27th instant. You should not delay in this matter.

On the 28th I want you to send my sixty soldiers via Korobe or send them directly to Ganda. You ought not to delay one day.

If your troops are now at Mt. Moya, you should not wait for them, for they will overtake you on the way or at Alema Station.

There is no danger on the way.

[signed] Gustin

June 22, 1893

Sir:

I enclose a special mail concerning that matter of the Commandant. Leave Ganda on the 24th instant and try to be here in the morning of the 25th instant or before daybreak, that is to say before the time when the Commandant will reach the station of Alema.

If the Kirri mail has already arrived, send it with my soldiers.

The bearer of this mail will reach you in the evening of the 23rd instant and on the same day give him the letter which will reach me on the 24th instant. The soldiers of Maḥmūd Effendī [Maḥmud Aghā] must come with my soldiers.

[signed] Gustin

Alema Station, June 23, 1893

F. Translation of the Arabic text of the Contract made between Faḍl al-Mūlā and E. Baert, January 1, 1894. Mahdīya, Class I, Box 34, Folder 2, No. 71, Sudan Government Archives, Khartoum.

This Contract has been agreed upon by Inspector-General, Major Baert Pasha and Faḍl al-Mūlā Bey, Chief Officer of the Jihādīya [Equatorials], who has been commissioned to settle the terms [of employment] of the Jihādīya [Equatorials] and employees who are under his authority.

Article I: The Congolese Officers will have nothing to do with the laws and operations of the Jihādīya [Equatorials]. This is their business.

Article II: The Congo Free State will not permit its employees to journey from one place to another as they have been accustomed to do. This is to attract people to the stations and make them like the stations more and more so as to prevent, by this, the delay of Government income and so that both the Government and the Jihādīya [Equatorials] may be protected.

Article III: If the aim of the Government is the submission of the natives in order to gain necessary revenue, then it has to provide the Jihādīya [Equatorials] with the necessary arms and ammunition so that we may increase the military order and strengthen the stations.

Article IV: It is recognized that the military force [of the Equatorials] will have to be increased. The number of men with sufficient arms and rate of pay is to be decided by Major Baert, the Representative of the Congo Free State. This necessary additional expenditure will not be included in the primary sum required in this Contract.

Article V: It is well known that ivory and ostrich feathers are of the necessary requirements [of the Congo Free State]. Therefore, the Inspector should bring a large amount of knives and clothes by which the attention of the natives is attracted so that they may bring to us the above-mentioned articles which will be given to the chef de poste.

Article VI: The articles necessary for the exchange of ivory must be brought to us, and we will give each chef de poste (who is to be appointed with our knowledge) the necessary amount.

Article VII: When we were united to the Congo Free State, we had in our possession a number of arms given to us by the Khedivial Government, the great majority of which are Remingtons with ammunition. Now the Congo State has to supply us with ammunition for the Remington rifles and 200 additional rifles, 100 of which are to be breech-loaders with bullets and the other 100 to be muzzle-loaders with powder and lead.

The above-mentioned 200 rifles are to be quite sound.

Article VIII: The Congolese Officer in each of the stations of the Jihādīya [Equatorials] is to be placed there in recognition of the Congo Free State, but he is not to interfere with the affairs of the natives or the government [of the station].

Article IX: The Congo Free State must pay monthly each of the officers and clerks of our companies.

Article X: The sum of money necessary for the increase of the army must be added to the E£2,000. This sum is to be paid to us once every six months; half in cash and half in trade goods.

Article XI: The Government intends to provide for one additional company, for which purpose E£400 over the E£2,000 above-mentioned are necessary.

Article XII: We are not held responsible if the Government does or does not sign this Contract, but we will be bound by it from this day.

[signed] Faḍl al-Mūlā, Mīrālai of the Jihādīya
E. Baert

January 1, 1894

BIBLIOGRAPHY

Bibliographical material on the Sudanese Mahdīya is, surprisingly, more numerous than one would imagine. A most comprehensive bibliography on the Sudan in general and the Mahdīya in particular is R. L. Hill, *A Bibliography of the Anglo-Egyptian Sudan from the Earliest Times to 1937* (London, Oxford University Press, 1939). Unfortunately, it does not contain the more recent scholarly contributions to the literature on the Sudan, but this deficiency is partly rectified by the reviews and bibliographies in *Sudan Notes and Records* (Khartoum). A more recent and critical study of the source material on the history of the Mahdīya in particular is contained in an excellent article by P. M. Holt, "The Source Materials of the Sudanese Mahdia," *St. Anthony's Papers: Middle Eastern Affairs,* No. 1 (London, 1958).

Manuscripts

ARCHIVES OF THE SUDAN GOVERNMENT, KHARTOUM

The Archives of the Republic of the Sudan are found in the Ministry of the Interior, Khartoum. The many manuscripts are catalogued by subject, one division of which, designated "Mahdīya," contains the official and unofficial correspondence and papers of the Mahdist State. Information on the Mahdist Archives may be found in two articles by P. M. Holt, former archivist for the Sudan Government: "The Archives of the Mahdia," *Sudan Notes and Records, 36* (1955), Pt. I, 71–80, and "Three Mahdist Letter-Books," *Bulletin of the School of Oriental and African Studies, 18* (1956), 227–38.

The manuscripts in the Mahdist Archives which pertain to the Southern Sudan are chiefly the correspondence of the Khalīfa 'Abd Allāhi, 'Umar Ṣāliḥ, 'Alī Mukhtār Bakrī, 'Arabī Dafa' Allāh, and Faḍl al-Mūlā Bey. These letters provide the essential facts and corroborative material without which it would have been impossible to piece together events in the Southern Sudan between 1883 and 1898. The archival catalogue number is used as the reference cited:

'Umar Ṣāliḥ to the Khalīfa, 1306–1313 (1888–95), Mahdīya, Class I, Box 33.

'Alī Mukhtār Bakrī to the Khalīfa, 1310 (1893), Mahdīya, Class I, Box 32.

'Arabī Dafa' Allāh to the Khalīfa, 1311–1316 (1893–98), Mahdīya, Class I, Box 32.

Faḍl al-Mūlā and the Congo Free State, Mahdīya, Class I, Box 34.

The Khalīfa 'Abd Allāhi, Miscellaneous letters, Mahdīya, Class I, Box 33.

In addition to the papers of the Mahdist State, valuable source material relevant to the Southern Sudan may also be found under the classification "Cairo Intelligence" (abbr. Cairint). These manuscripts are, for the most part, reports compiled by the Intelligence Department of the Egyptian army from statements of refugees:

"The Statement of Maḥmūd 'Abd Allāh al-Maḥallāwī Respecting the Fall of the Mudīrīya of the Baḥr al-Ghazāl, June 26, 1890," and "Report on the Fall of the Baḥr al-Ghazāl, 1894," Cairo Intelligence, Class III, Box 14, Pieces 235 and 240 respectively, are two reports by Maḥmūd 'Abd Allāh al-Maḥallāwī, the antislavery inspector of the Baḥr al-Ghazāl, which give the most coherent description of any source known to scholars of the futile efforts of the Egyptian Government to quell the Mahdist inspired rebellion in the province. Although both reports cover the same period, they are, in many ways, supplementary to one another.

"Report of Emin Pasha, 1885," Cairo Intelligence, Class III, Box 14, Piece 236, is a long, detailed, official report by the Governor of Equatoria, Emin Pasha, describing the events in his province until 1885, including the invasion of a Mahdist force under the amīr Karam Allāh.

"Events Which Led to the Fall of the Baḥr al-Ghazāl," a statement by Abū al-Khayrat Bahārī, Cairo Intelligence, Class III, Box 14, Piece 235, Conference Report No. 76, is a brief report on the capture of the Baḥr al-Ghazāl by the Mahdists and, most important, what took place immediately following the conquest.

"Statement Respecting the Equatorial Provinces, 1890," Cairo Intelligence, Class III, Box 14, Piece 237, is a valuable addition to the official report of Emin Pasha.

"Statement of 'Uthmān al-Ḥājj Ḥamad, Qāḍī of Equatoria," Cairo Intelligence, Class III, Box 14, Piece 239, is an interesting statement by a high provincial government official who deserted to the Mahdists. His report when not corroborated is to be highly suspected.

"Report on Equatoria, 1890," Cairo Intelligence, Class I, Box 11, Piece 56, is a semi-official account of the events which took place in Equatoria from 1885 to 1890.

"The Report on the Arrival in Cairo of Twenty-one Officers and Non-commissioned Officers with Their Families from Equatoria via Mombasa, June, 1892," Cairo Intelligence, Class I, Box 35, Piece 205, is an exceedingly valuable and informative manuscript which is one of the few sources, and certainly the most authoritative, describing events in Equatoria between the departure of Emin Pasha and the arrival of the Congolese.

The three letters of Lupton Bey to Emin Pasha, Cairo Intelligence, Class I, Box 5, Piece 30, describe the last days of the Egyptian Administration before the Baḥr al-Ghazāl was handed over to the Mahdists.

Occasional manuscripts referring to the Southern Sudan may also be found under the classifications of "Palace Papers" and "Intelligence." The "Palace Papers" are the manuscripts which were housed in the Governor-General's Palace, Khartoum, for his personal use. By chance several letters from the Mahdist amīrs 'Uthmān Diqna and 'Umar Ṣāliḥ are found in the Palace Papers, Class III, Box 10. The catalogue reference "Intelligence" refers to that collection of Intelligence Reports from the various districts and provinces of the Anglo-Egyptian Sudan. There are occasional references to conditions in the Sudan during the Mahdīya.

UNPUBLISHED CONFIDENTIAL REPORTS

These were reports prepared by the Egyptian Military Intelligence Department and sent to the War Office in London, where they were printed for confidential circulation. They constitute a complete summary of all activity in each province of the Sudan and frequently include important documents, letters, and papers. A set of these reports was kept in the Archives of the Civil Secretary, Khartoum, during the Anglo-Egyptian Condominium. When the Sudan received its independence, the reports were transferred to the Archives of the Sudan Government, where, however, they continued to carry the designation "Civil Secretary's Archives":

Intelligence Report, Egypt, Nos. 1–59, Civil Secretary's Archives, Khartoum.

Sudan Intelligence Reports, Nos. 60–101, Civil Secretary's Archives, Khartoum.

Mongalla Province Summary, is a series of reports and statistics compiled by L. F. Nalder, former Governor of Mongalla Province, for use of administrative officers in the province. It contains many historical references to the Mahdists in Equatoria.

ARCHIVES OF THE FOREIGN MINISTRY, BRUSSELS

File A.F.l. -40, Lado. Although this file contains few references to the Mahdists, it furnishes valuable information on Leopold's policy in the Upper Nile.

PUBLIC RECORD OFFICE, LONDON

File Foreign Office, 10, Belgium. This file, which contains the correspondence between the British Ambassador at Brussels and the Foreign Office, has much information and valuable documents pertaining to Anglo-Congolese relations. File Foreign Office, 83, Great Britain and General has a few miscellaneous items which pertain to the Upper Nile.

Printed Material

GENERAL WORKS

Chomé, Léon, *Une Expédition Belge au Nil* (Brussels, 1898). An interesting account of the Chaltin expedition to the Nile in 1896–97. This work is of particular value because it contains Captain Chaltin's official report of the expedition including his account of the Battle of Rajjāf.

Dietrich, E. L., see Shoucair.

Franck, L. R., *Le Congo Belge* (2 vols. Brussels, La Renaissance du Livre, 1930). This informative book on the Congo contains a chapter written by Chaltin entitled "Vers le Nil" about his march to the Nile and the taking of Rajjāf.

Gleichen, Captain Count, *Handbook of the Sudan* (printed at the War Office by Harrison and Son, London, 1898). Captain Gleichen succeeded Wingate as Director of Military Intelligence of the Egyptian army and consequently his handbook, compiled for the use of the early British administrators, contains valuable information which could only have been found in the files of the Egyptian Military Intelligence.

Gleichen, Lieut.-Colonel Count, *The Anglo-Egyptian Sudan* (2 vols. London, printed for His Majesty's Stationery Office by Harrison and Sons, 1905). This two volume work is a revised edition of Gleichen's *Handbook of the Sudan* which contains numerous and valuable references to the Mahdists not included in the 1898 edition.

Hill, Richard, *Egypt in the Sudan, 1820–1881* (London, Oxford University Press, 1959). An excellent short study of Egyptian Administration in the Sudan before the Mahdist rebellion.

Holt, P. M., *The Mahdist State in the Sudan* (Oxford, Clarendon Press, 1958). A brilliant history of the Mahdīya and the finest work on that subject. Although based largely on the documents in the Archives of the Sudan Government, this otherwise excellent work deals cursorily with the Southern Sudan.

Langer, W. L., *The Diplomacy of Imperialism* (New York, Knopf, 1956). The standard work on the diplomacy behind the partition of Africa. It provides the necessary background to the schemes of Leopold II and the Great Powers to acquire the Upper Nile Valley.

Lotar, R. P. L., *La Grande Chronique de l'Uele* (Brussels, Institut Royal Colonial Belge, 1946). Father Lotar, as a Dominican Missionary in the Uele for many years, gathered from eyewitnesses the story of the Congolese expeditions into the Uele and their collisions with the Mahdists. These tales, corroborated by letters and papers of the Belgian officers opening up the Uele, form a chronicle of Congolese activities in the Uele Valley. Not only has Father Lotar written an important work on a little known period of African exploration, but the publication of letters and papers of the Belgian officers furnishes the scholar with valuable source materials.

Lotar, R. P. L., *La Grand Chronique du Bomu* (Brussels, Institut Royal Colonial Belge, 1941). Father Lotar has written a chronicle of Congolese exploration in the valley of the Bomu, based on native sources and the papers of Belgian officers who participated in the expeditions.

MacMichael, H. A., *A History of the Arabs in the Sudan* (Cambridge, University Press, 1922). A magnificent work based largely on Arabic sources. It has been most useful as a guide to the Arab tribes of southern Dār Fūr and Kurdufān which border on the Baḥr al-G͟hazāl.

MacMichael, H. A., *The Anglo-Egyptian Sudan* (London, Faber and Faber, 1934). An informative, general work on the Anglo-Egyptian Sudan with some interesting remarks, however, regarding the Mahdists.

Shibeika, M., *British Policy in the Sudan, 1882–1902* (London, Oxford University Press, 1952). An outstanding work by a Sudanese historian; it provides excellent background study to the Mahdīya.

Shoucair, N. (Na'ūn Shuqayr), *Ta'rikh al-Sūdān al-qadīm wa-l-ḥadīth wa-Jughrafiyatuhu* (Cairo, 1903). The part of this work dealing with the Mahdī has been partly translated into the German by E. L. Dietrich, "Der Mahdi Mohammed Ahmad vom Sudan nach arabischen Quellen," *Der Islam, 14* (1925), 197–288. An interesting account of the Mahdīya, but unfortunately contains little on the Southern Sudan.

Theobald, A. B., *The Mahdīya* (London, Longmans, Green, 1955). An excellent, short general history of the Mahdīya.

Thomson, R. S., *Fondation de l'Etat Indépendant du Congo* (Brussels, J. Lebegue, 1933). One of the best scholarly works on the founding of the Congo Free State.

Trimingham, J. S., *Islam in the Sudan* (London, Oxford University Press, 1949). The best work in English on the religious life and institutions of the Sudanese.

Wingate, F. R., *Mahdiism and the Egyptian Sudan* (London, Macmillan, 1891). Sir Reginald Wingate's position as the Director of Military Intelligence of the Egyptian army afforded him the opportunity to use the accounts of refugees from the Sudan as well as official intelligence reports and captured Mahdist letters. His book is not free from errors, however, and its lasting value is chiefly in its publication of Mahdist documents. Wingate was assisted by his chief clerk Na'ūn Bey Shuqayr, who has published almost the same material in his book *Ta'rīkh al-Sūdān.*

BIOGRAPHIES, LETTERS, MEMOIRS, AND JOURNALS

Allen, B. M., *Gordon and the Sudan* (London, Macmillan, 1931). This is not only the best account of Gordon's life in the Sudan, but particularly valuable because of the many official papers and documents which are quoted in the text.

Biographie Coloniale Belge (3 vols. Brussels, Institut Royal Colonial Belge, 1948, 1951, 1952). An excellent source for the biographies of the Belgian explorers who opened up the river systems which take their rise on the Congo-Nile Divide.

Buchta, R., *Der Sudan unter ägyptischer Herrschaft* (Leipzig, F. A. Brockhaus, 1888). A most valuable source book for a study of the Southern Sudan, it contains many of the letters of Lupton Bey as well as of Emin Pasha.

Casati, G., *Ten Years in Equatoria,* trans. the Hon. Mrs. J. Randolph Clay (2 vols. London, Frederick Warne, 1891). Casati was only on the fringe of Mahdist activity in the Southern Sudan, and his book is more concerned with personal adventure than a clear description of events in the Southern Sudan.

De Tonquedec, A. de Quengo, *Au Pays Des Rivières* (Paris, J. Peyronnet, 1931). Colonel Tonquedec was in command of a detachment of Senegalese troops of the Marchand Expedition. He arrived in the Baḥr al-Ghazāl at Kukhūk 'Alī in February 1899 and later learned of the retreat of the Mahdists from the inhabitants of the neighboring countryside. In his memoirs of service on the Upper Nile as part of the Marchand Expedition, he has recorded this fact and many other observations on the condition of the Baḥr al-Ghazāl between the retreat of the Mahdists from Bor and his own departure from the Southern Sudan in October 1899.

Hill, R. L., *A Biographical Dictionary of the Anglo-Egyptian Sudan* (Oxford, Clarendon Press, 1951). This dictionary is an absolute necessity for a student of the Sudan. A magnificent work, but unfortunately not totally free from errors.

Jackson, H. C., *Osman Diqna* (London, Methuen, 1926). A particularly important biography of 'Uthmān Diqna which includes the statements of eyewitnesses.

Junker, W., *Travels in Africa, 1882–1886,* trans. A. H. Keane (London, Chapman and Hall, 1892). Not only is Dr. Junker's narrative of his travels absorbing reading, but the publication of the letters to him from Lupton Bey and Emin Pasha makes this book an essential source for a study of the Southern Sudan during the Mahdīya.

Mounteney-Jephson, A. J., *Emin Pasha and the Rebellion at the Equator* (London, Sampson Low, Marston, Searle, and Rivington, 1890). As one of Stanley's officers, Mounteney-Jephson was, for a time, in the midst of action in Equatoria. Although his personal narrative is not a contribution to scholarship, the publication of various letters and official papers of the Mahdists gives this adventure story particular significance.

Ohrwalder, Joseph, *Ten Years' Captivity in the Mahdi's Camp,* trans. Sir R. Wingate (London, Sampson Low, Marston, 1892). Father Ohrwalder was an Austrian missionary in the Nūba Mountains who was taken prisoner by the Mahdī. He remained in captivity for ten years, then escaped to Egypt, where he recorded his narrative—unfortunately from memory. It is nevertheless of considerable value, particularly when corroborated with other material.

Perham, M., *Lugard, The Years of Adventure, 1858–1898* (London, Collins, 1956). An outstanding biography which is essential reading for a student of Central Africa.

Rodd, J. R., *Social and Diplomatic Memories, 1884–1893* (London, Edward Arnold, 1922). This book contains some interesting personal observation on Leopold's policy in the Upper Nile.

Schnitzer, E., *Die Tagebücher von Dr. Emin Pascha,* ed. Franz Stuhlman (4 vols. Hamburg, Westermann, 1919, 1922, 1927). This is the diary of Emin Pasha kept during his stay in Central Africa. As a source book it is, of course, of primary importance to any study of the Southern Sudan during the period of his sojourn in Equatoria.

Schweinfurth, Ratzel, Felkin, and Hartlaub, eds., *Emin Pasha in Central Africa* (London, George Philip and Son, 1888). This is a fine collection of letters of Emin Pasha to his friends in Europe. These letters contain valuable information regarding the Mahdist penetration of the Southern Sudan.

Schweitzer, Georg, *Emin Pasha* (2 vols. London, Archibald Constable, 1898). The best biography of the enigmatic German scientist-doctor turned administrator, which fortunately contains many of Emin Pasha's letters and official papers.

Slatin, R. C., *Fire and Sword in the Sudan* (London, Edward Arnold, 1896). Slatin was the last governor of Dār Fūr under the Egyptian Administration. He surrendered to the Mahdists and was held captive by the Khalīfa until he made his escape. During this time his position as servant to the Khalīfa afforded him the opportunity to acquire valuable information. Unfortunately, however, his book has been written from memory and, therefore, his information needs to be corroborated.

Stanley, H. M., *In Darkest Africa* (2 vols. New York, Charles Scribner's Sons, 1891). Stanley's account of his rescue of Emin Pasha.

Wingate, R., *Wingate of the Sudan* (London, John Murray, 1955). Written from his father's papers, it contains conclusive evidence on many speculative points of Sudanese history, but little on the Southern Sudan.

Letters of Queen Victoria, Ser. 3, Vol. 2 (London, John Murray, 1931). In their letters to the Queen, her ministers and friends frequently had some pungent things to say about Leopold II's Nile policy.

Zaghi, C., *Gordon, Gessi e la Riconquista Del Sudan* (Florence, 1947). An informative work, which pays particular attention to Gessi's antislavery policy in the Baḥr al-Ghazāl.

TREATIES

Hertslet, E., *The Map of Africa by Treaty* (London, Harrison and Sons, 1909). A semi-official publication of all official treaties concerning Africa. An indispensable guide to the student of African history.

OFFICIAL PUBLICATIONS

Southern Sudan Disturbances, August, 1955: The Report of the Commission of Enquiry, October, 1956, McCorquedal, Khartoum.

NEWSPAPERS AND PERIODICALS

Blackwood's Magazine, London, 1894.
Bulletin Des Séances, Institut Royal Colonial Belge, Brussels, 1941, 1947, 1954.
Bulletin of the School of Oriental and African Studies, London, 1956.
Congo, 1924, 1932.
Deutsches Kolonialblatt, 1916.
English Historical Review, 1942, 1950.
Expansion Belge, 1931, 1933.
New York *Herald*, 1890.
Nineteenth Century, 1901.
Proceedings of the Royal Geographical Society, 1884.
Revue d'Histoire des Colonies, 1950.
Sudan Notes and Records, 1938, 1947, 1953, 1955.
Zaïre, 1956, 1958.

Index